Another Way

Another Way

Finding Faith, Then Finding It Again

∼

KEVIN BROWN

RESOURCE *Publications* • Eugene, Oregon

ANOTHER WAY
Finding Faith, Then Finding It Again

Copyright © 2012 Kevin Brown. All rights reserved. Except for brief quotations in critical publications or reviews, no part of this book may be reproduced in any manner without prior written permission from the publisher. Write: Permissions, Wipf and Stock Publishers, 199 W. 8th Ave., Suite 3, Eugene, OR 97401.

Resource Publications
An Imprint of Wipf and Stock Publishers
199 W. 8th Ave., Suite 3
Eugene, OR 97401

www.wipfandstock.com

ISBN 13: 978-1-61097-864-4

Manufactured in the U.S.A.

Scriptures taken from the Holy Bible, New International Version®, NIV®. Copyright © 1973, 1978, 1984, 2011 by Biblica, Inc.™ Used by permission of Zondervan. All rights reserved worldwide. www.zondervan.com.

The "NIV" and "New International Version" are trademarks registered in the United States Patent and Trademark Office by Biblica, Inc.™

Scripture taken from the Good News Translation in Today's English Version-Second Edition Copyright © 1992 by American Bible Society. Used by Permission.

For the teachers who taught me to ask questions

For my students who ask them of me

"... be patient toward all that is unsolved in your heart and [try] to love the *questions themselves* like locked rooms and like books that are written in a very foreign tongue. Do not now seek the answers, which cannot be given you because you would not be able to live them. And the point is, to live everything. *Live* the questions now. Perhaps you will gradually, without noticing it, live along some distant day into the answer."

— Rainer Maria Rilke, *Letters to a Young Poet*

"Another way. There's always another way."

— The Keymaker in *The Matrix: Reloaded*

Contents

Preface: One More Memoir / ix
Acknowledgments / xiii

1. The Beginnings of Faith / 1
2. Rock and Roll Saves Teenager / 19
3. How Far Is Too Far? / 36
4. Answers to Questions That Didn't Matter / 57
5. Finding the (Hot) Buttons to Push / 75
6. The Questions Come Quickly; The Answers Do Not / 82
7. Questions Not Allowed / 101
8. Sneaking Back into the Church / 127
9. Finding Faith, Again / 150
10. Facing the Past / 166
11. A Firm Foundation of Questions / 186
12. Conclusion: The Questions Always Continue / 202

Bibliography / 207

Preface

One More Memoir

It seems that almost everyone has a memoir these days, much like blogs just a couple of years ago (or even now). An article in *The New York Times*, in fact, bemoans this fact, as Neil Genzlinger writes, "There was a time when you had to earn the right to draft a memoir, by accomplishing something noteworthy or having an extremely unusual experience or being such a brilliant writer that you could turn relatively ordinary occurrences into a snapshot of a broader historical moment. Anyone who didn't fit one of those categories was obliged to keep quiet. Unremarkable lives went unremarked upon, the way God intended."[1] He's right, of course. The publishing world is similar to other media, as imitation quickly follows success. The question that should be raised when thinking about reading (or writing) another memoir is what makes this particular story worthwhile. I'll readily admit I'm not royalty, nor have I served in any type of elected or appointed office. I have not struggled with a serious disease, whether mental or physical, nor have I helped conquer one. As the clueless and myopic father in *Orange County* asks his son, who wants to be a writer, "What do you have to write about? You're not oppressed. You're not gay."[2] As the reader, you have every right to ask what I have to write about and why, so let me try to answer those questions.

I began this book for one reason, but I ended up addressing two different audiences as the writing progressed. First, I was motivated to write it because of my job as an English professor at a Christian college, one that takes its mission as a Christian college quite seriously. I see

---

1. Genzlinger, "The Problem With Memoirs," para. 2.
2. *Orange County*, 2003.

students begin their college careers as devout believers, mostly teenagers who were raised in the church and think they know what they believe. As often happens in college, though, they are exposed to different ways of thinking, not just about religion, but about a wide array of subjects, not just in the classroom, but through their interactions with people from other regions of the country or the world. Even at a Christian college, they encounter Muslims and Hindus, even atheists who come for our academics and financial aid.

As also often happens in college, whether Christian or not, these students begin to question their faith, doubt it, sometimes even lose it. They realize that they never truly owned their faith to begin with, that it was something someone—parents, a pastor, perhaps—gave them or that they possessed simply because they were surrounded by it at home. However, because they have only known one kind of faith, one way to believe, when they begin to doubt what they have been taught, they often discard all types of Christianity, even all types of faith, in general. I watch this happen every year, and I often wonder what I can do to prevent them from throwing everything they believe away. I was like them when I was in college, though I found my way to my particular type of faith, as no one led me to it, really. When I questioned it, I found it lacking, so I set it aside and left the church. I have often wondered what my Christian college professors could have done to keep me from giving up that faith. Perhaps they could have done nothing, and perhaps I can also do nothing to help these students. Perhaps their losing their faith is a positive step to ultimately discovering what they do believe. Perhaps.

However, I do not believe students need to go to the extremes I went to in order to end up with an honest faith, one they can truly own. Instead, I believe they can find a different way of believing if they are exposed to other ways of being Christian, if they can see faith modeled in ways it has not been modeled for them before. I realized that what I have to give students, more than anything else, is my story. Unfortunately, covering material and grading papers does not leave much time to sit down with students for hours and tell them where I came from, why I left, and why I still believe. Thus, I wrote a book for all such students and for those who work with them.

In writing, though, I realized that such a story is not limited to students, whether they attend a Christian college or not. Instead, it applies to all of us who are engaged in the pursuit of God, no matter what age we might be. As Mother Teresa's letters illustrate, all of us doubt from time to time, and we all need to be reminded of why to believe and of ways to believe. It is my journey back to the church that has taught me much more than the reasons I left the church in the first place, all of which happened in my twenties and thirties. Anyone interested in the state of religion today must be aware of the deep divide that permeates American culture when it comes to faith. The New Atheists stake out one extreme, arguing that religion is irrational, nothing more than a construct the brain creates to make us all feel better about our inevitable death. On the other extreme, fundamentalist Christians argue that their way of reading the Bible, their way of viewing God, is the only way of doing so. They wish to dictate how all of us should live, whom we should or should not marry, what laws should be passed or not.

Most of us are not in either of these extremes; most of us live somewhere in the middle, interacting with faith in an attempt to understand it, not dominate it. Even if we fall on the more rational end of the spectrum, we admit that there are parts of life and the universe we cannot explain, even if we are uncomfortable calling any of those parts God. If we fall on the more spiritual side, we recognize the importance of knowledge and rationality, even of skepticism that asks questions of our faith, knowing that such questions ultimately make faith stronger, not weaker.

I wanted to tell how I moved from one of those extremes to the other, then to a place where I could live in the tension between the two, still with my questions, but also with a faith strengthened by the heavy lifting I ask of it. There are other ways of being Christian, of struggling with faith, of talking about faith, and those of us who live in that area in-between must speak. Otherwise, the extremes continue to dominate the conversation of faith, forcing others to flee from the discussion. This story is not one that dominates the headlines; it is not a voice that is often heard, but it does convey a struggle so many of us have in our lives. For that reason, it needs to be written, and it needs to be read.

Acknowledgments

When I wrote my first book and sent the acknowledgments I had written to DJ, one of my best friends, he commented that it sounded like I was trying to thank everyone who had ever helped me in any way, as if I were worried I would never get another chance to do so. I pointed out that I never believed I would write one book, not to mention multiple books, so I wanted to take the opportunity to thank as many people as I could while I had the chance. I won't do that here, as one interesting fact about writing a memoir is that most of the people I want to thank are in this book, as the book itself is a certain type of expression of thanks for people who have helped me get to this point in life. That said, I would like to highlight a few people.

First, my professors from Milligan College play a prominent role in this book and in my life. Terry Dibble, more than any other, not only changed my major, he changed the way I saw the world, which changed the way I live. Other professors, such as Charlene Kiser, Lee Magness, and R. David Roberts, also helped me more than they will know. The students during my time at Milligan also pushed me to become a better thinker through their commitment to questioning, none more than Scott, my roommate my sophomore year.

My family does not play a large role in this book, which is odd in a memoir, but it's mainly because they provided me with a stable and solid upbringing. While so many of my friends' families had turmoil and tragedies, mine did not. Instead, my parents simply worked hard to give us the best life they could and supported us in the best way they knew how. Growing up, I did not appreciate how important such stability was; now that I'm an adult, I know it gave me a foundation to accomplish much of what I did and to become the person I am today. I do not take the benefits of my childhood for granted any longer.

My colleagues at Lee University have been extremely supportive of my writing, and they encourage me both professionally and spiritually on a regular basis. They continue to push me to be a better professor and a better Christian. Rachel Reneslacis gave me valuable advice when I began this project and asked me several questions at the outset that helped me focus where I was going; she also used a portion of this manuscript in one of her classes, which gave me the opportunity to tell my story to several students and get their feedback. Our department chair, Jean Eledge, provides opportunities for me to pursue my writing interests, while also helping me and my colleagues better teach our students. I could list various other members of the department and list ways in which they help me, but the list would grow too long too quickly. I would be remiss, though, if I did not thank the administration. At a time when many faculty are not able to pursue such interests, our administrators have continued to support faculty through extremely generous funding. President Conn and Carolyn Dirksen have both helped me in a variety of ways, through financial support, but also through simple encouragement.

My students make getting up and going to work every morning a joy. Our students are not only bright and inquisitive; they are also genuinely kind, giving people. I enjoy spending time with them inside and outside the classroom, and I am always saddened when graduation day comes, and we lose a few more to the rest of their lives. Their questions were the motivation for this book, and I wish I could sit with every one of them and talk for days about who they are and who they want to be. I look forward to the time we can carve out of our busy lives to have such conversations. I cannot imagine doing the work I do without them in my life.

There are a select group of friends, as well, who have helped me along the way. Though we do not see each other often, Kate has been more of a support through the years than she will know. There were numerous times when she said exactly what I needed to hear, sometimes encouragement, but sometimes chastisement I needed. Mark shows up prominently in the book, so I will simply say that I grew more spiritually when he was my minister than at almost any other time in my life, not because of his sermons (which were and are amazing), but because of the life he leads. DJ and Steve have been my two closest friends for almost two decades now. DJ and I have talked about faith for most of that time, and he continues to challenge me to think in different ways. Steve and I have not talked much about faith, so he does not show up as often as he should to represent his importance in my life. We have, though, talked about teaching and writing and art and life, conversations that have shaped my ideas in so many ways. His constant faith is one I admire.

Last, I must thank Courtney, my wife. Her love and support undergird all I do; knowing she is beside me makes so much more possible. She also does not make much of an appearance, as most of my journey took place before we met, but her coming into my life marks a distinct change in itself. Her kindness, her generosity, her hospitality, and so much more than I could list, have made me into a better person than I would be without her in my life. There are not thanks enough for that.

1

The Beginnings of Faith

When I was eighteen years old, I was called to be a minister. I knew such a call might be in my future, which is one reason I chose to attend the local Christian college rather than the state university where both of my parents worked (yet another reason for not attending it). The call was clearly conveyed to me through two events that happened that fall, both of them relating to church.

The first came from Mr. Busch, a patriarch of our church and of the faith, in general. He was in his late seventies then, so his body was beginning to break down after a rough life, but his soul and mind were still clear. In our monthly men's meetings, he often sided with the youth when it came to new ideas for the congregation, as he was always looking toward the future, never the past. He had come to Tennessee from California, driving across the country in a Model T Ford with no heat; as he came that winter, his car was packed with straw in an attempt to keep him warm. He was coming to Johnson Bible College in Knoxville, Tennessee, as he, too, had been called to be a minister, and answering that call took him a long way from home. Along the way, he had his legs shattered in a car accident, but he learned how to take vehicles apart and put them back together by drawing them as he pulled off one piece after another. He used the same approach with people, learning how to take them apart and help put them back together.

One Sunday morning, I was coming up the stairs to our church, and Mr. Busch was standing at the top, helping to welcome people. Given the small size of the congregation, seldom more than one hundred on a Sunday morning, he knew everyone who was not a visitor, and we all knew him. I had been attending the church for two years by that time, and I was good friends with his grandson, Mike, so I knew him well. When I came up to shake his hand, he met mine firmly and said simply, "Morning, Preacher." He smiled, leaving me to wonder what he knew that I did not, as I knew his words were not to be taken lightly.

Later that year, no more than two months after that event, I was attending a church lock-in, where the youth stayed up all night, mainly playing games and watching movies, but also including some sort of Bible study. We did not have a youth minister at the time, so our full-time minister, Mark, was running the youth for the time being. Despite the name of the event, he took us out of the fellowship hall and loaded us all into the van and cars. We drove to Laura's house, one of our younger members who only lived five minutes from the church, and unloaded. Rather than going into her house, though, we went past it, into the woods behind where she lived. We finally settled on some rocks that surrounded a small entrance to a cave, as Mark asked us to spread out among the rocks. He talked about the early disciples and how they were persecuted by the Romans, how they had to meet in secret, in caves, much like the one we were outside of. He talked about the catacombs and the variety of methods they used to communicate, their perseverance in continuing to meet, despite the harsh conditions. He did not really say anything I did not already know. I was in my first year at a Christian college, and I had read a good deal about Christianity as a teenager, so I knew how difficult the beginnings of the faith were. However, something about that night was different. There is no way to describe how one feels in such a spiritual experience, but I felt quite clearly then that God was calling me to be a minister, specifically a youth minister.

I had begun college as a math major, as I planned on being a high school math teacher. The next week, I met with my Old Testament professor, Dr. Roberts, and talked about changing to a Bible major. I then had to tell my advisor, my calculus professor, Mrs. Huang, who took the news rather well, as I'm sure she was used to hearing about students who became Bible majors, teaching in a Christian college, as she did. She encouraged me to keep taking math classes, but I did not listen. I was too focused on taking classes that would help me fulfill my calling.

Two years later, I was an English major. Two years after that, I was on my way out of the church, not exactly the path I thought a calling to ministry would take. I found my way back to belief, found the faith I did not have when I believed my call was to be a minister. While the path I took is not the path for everyone, it was what I needed to help make my faith my own. I needed another way to be a Christian from the way I had known, and people pointed me on that path through small steps, but I had to take every one of them on my own. Along the way, I found that faith and the true calling I had missed somewhere along the way.

I have often wondered what it is that causes people to become religious. There are people who grow up in the church and never leave, but, more often, people wander in and out of religious institutions throughout their lives, sometimes for reasons we might expect, sometimes for ones we could never imagine. Evolutionary biologists and psychologists have spent time studying religion, wondering what makes people lean that way or not, and science has even begun applying its method to the effectiveness of religion, especially prayer. In fact, while I was working on the first draft of this memoir, a book called *Principles of Neurotheology* by Dr. Andrew Newberg was released, in which he reveals studies of people's brains during meditation or prayer and the effects those practices may have, physically and mentally, as well as spiritually. In my case, I have not only wondered why I turned to religion when I did, but also in the way that I did, with the extreme devotion that I did, as nothing in my background would have led people to believe I would become the fanatic I was as a teenager or how I would get to where I am now. If people from various times of my life could have seen me just five years later, they would have wondered if I were the same person, my religious trajectory following the path of a patient's heartbeat under extreme duress.

 I did attend church when I was younger; my family was almost always at church, as it was one of our main social outlets. There is a picture of me in a three-piece suit, holding my *Children's Illustrated Bible*—as I had read a passage of scripture that morning during the service, and, though the picture is not dated, I cannot be more than seven years old—and there are several pictures of me with my older brother and sister, Garland and Jan, on Easter Sundays before we went to church. I preached my first official sermon when I was twelve, though I had been informally preaching to the neighborhood kids for many years before that. Outside of the minister's daughter, I was the most regular Sunday school attendee for years, memorizing verses and learning the stories over years of repetition. However, I also fell asleep in church whenever I could, tried to lay down on the pew and put my head on my mother's lap, though she would often not allow me to do so. When our minister had a catechism class on Sunday afternoons when I was in middle school, I attended one session, then somehow talked my way out of others, as I wanted to play basketball with my friends. Even when I preached my one sermon, I did not prepare, had only five notes on a note card, thinking I could talk for four or five minutes on each point, and it was on friendship, not a particularly notable theological topic.

I sound like almost any other kid who grew up in the South in the 1970s and 80s, spending vast amounts of time surrounded by religion, but avoiding it all the same. It's not clear, then, what led me to behave as I did when it came to religion, standing out from all of the kids in my neighborhood, including the one everyone would have guessed would end up as a preacher. It starts when I'm young, though, so I'll start there, as well, then work my way up to apathy, fanaticism, feigned disinterest, then back to belief, I hope. That's what religion is about, after all: hope.

Many of my earliest memories take place in church or are in some way related to church. While I cannot remember the reading I did the day or evening the picture of me in the three-piece suit was taken, I can remember one Christmas when I was supposed to be a reader for some special event. I was not an actual actor in whatever Christmas pageant we were doing that year, as I was too young to memorize lines, but I was reading some part of the production, a role I seemed destined for from then on, as I seldom was an actor in anything, always getting the part of narrator. However, this Christmas I was quite sick, as I struggled with ear infections almost every year around Christmas, including one year where I thought I would not be able to go downstairs and open presents. I was sitting at the kitchen table, trying to read over my lines, to familiarize myself with them and make sure there were no words I would struggle with, while wondering if I would be able to do it at all. My voice was weak and scratchy, and ear infections are notoriously painful. My mother was there with me, telling me not to be disappointed if I was not able to participate that year, that there would be other years, but I could not imagine not being able to do my reading. I saw my role as a vital one in the production, probably imagined importance, and I felt I should live up to my obligation, a theme that would reoccur throughout my life.

I was well enough on the day of the event to read, and I made it through the service without any trouble. Reading at church was always nice, as everyone there was encouraging and effusive in their praise, as if they had never seen a six- or seven-year-old read before. To me, though, it was more than that. I felt a distinct kinship with our minister, Stan, and I wondered what it would be like to be a minister. Being able to dress up, walk to the front of the church, and read as he did made me feel as if I had taken a step on that path. There were no ministers in my family, nor was I ever encouraged to pursue that path, but it stayed with me throughout my life, even today, as I wonder from time to time if I should go to seminary.

I was in a few Christmas plays, though I do not remember most of them, only see myself in the background of pictures and wonder what part I played. When I was a bit older, though, I was the lead in one play, though I had few lines. My main job was to wander around the sanctuary while an older member of the congregation sang "Scarlet Ribbons (For Her Hair)." It tells the story of a young girl who wants those scarlet ribbons and her father who overhears her prayers for them, then wanders the town looking for some for her. I played the father who moped around, wondering what I was to do about the ribbons. When I returned and found her asleep, the ribbons had miraculously appeared beneath her pillow, making us both quite happy. I have no idea what theological meaning lay behind such a song/play at Christmas beyond the obvious miracle, but even that is an odd one. I'm sure there are plays/songs that better display the Christmas message than one about a young girl who receives ribbons in a supernatural fashion.

I wasn't bothered by that at the time; instead, I mainly remember one rehearsal in particular. At some point, we needed to turn the lights off; I believe it was when she was supposedly asleep. I was certainly no more than twelve, so the girl playing my daughter was younger than that, probably around eight. We had turned the lights off, but she was not yet in the makeshift bed on stage, which was up on a table so that people could see her. She went running toward the bed, as most young children would do, but she could not see where she was going. She ran into the table, which knocked the breath out of her. It was a bad hit for such a small girl, so we were all visibly worried, as one might expect.

She cried for some time, and I don't believe we actually finished rehearsing that night, saving it for another evening. The play might have been wonderful, but I still remember the sound of her hitting the table more than anything else about it.

Part of my involvement in church can certainly be explained by the fact that my father was an elder. His holding this position still strikes me as odd, as we never talked about religion outside of the church. I don't doubt he was a good elder, as he was respected in the congregation, and I later learned he did much more than I ever saw, but the disconnect between his role at church and the lack of religious influence at home was difficult for me to reconcile. There was one time, though, I saw him in a more formal role. I was a regular attendee of Sunday school, which was taught, for all of my childhood, by an elderly woman named Mrs. Lewis. I remember that she walked to church, cutting across a small field that separated our parking lot from the neighborhood where I always assumed she lived. She was not a lively woman, but she was dedicated and diligent, always showing up to teach us. When people now ask me where my biblical knowledge comes from, I always mention Mrs. Lewis in that narrative. When I think about all of the major biblical stories, from Adam and Eve to Moses to David and on to Jesus, I can remember sitting in the room with Mrs. Lewis and a few other kids, most of whom have faded from my memory, going over our lesson. I never recall her using anything beyond the book and her knowledge, never even venturing out to flannel graph, though she might have written information on the board, from time to time.

However, not everyone in the Sunday school class was as diligent as Mrs. Lewis, and not everyone had a father like mine who brought me to Sunday school every week. There were Sundays where I was the only person in my class. On some of those days, Mrs. Lewis would simply teach me, helping me to learn on a one-to-one basis. Given that I was one of the more vocal participants in the class anyway, the absence of the other kids didn't make that much difference, at least not to me. Sometimes, though, she must have thought I could learn more in a different setting, or perhaps she was simply tired of teaching that week. On those days, she and I would go into the adult class. I can remember where I would sit when we would join the adult class and how I struggled to stay awake there, not really able to follow what they were talking about. One Sunday, though, my father taught the lesson. He was not a riveting teacher, at least not to me at that age. He went through the book like the other teachers and like Mrs. Lewis did in our class, but it was strange for me to see him doing even that. Just the fact that he was leading a Sunday school class kept me a bit off balance. I had seen him do previous work as an elder, such as serve communion, and I had heard him pray, both in church on days where we did communion and at home on Thanksgiving and Christmas. Somehow, though, this role was different. I don't believe he ever taught the class again when I was there, but I always wondered if he did, wondered if I would one day be in his class, but I never was.

For the first decade or slightly more of my life, I attended a wide variety of events at the church, such as Vacation Bible School programs where Mrs. Lewis taught us to sew, as we were making puppets for the show we would do at the end of the week. I was sewing a tunic for Moses, and, to this day, I can at least sew buttons back onto shirts or pants, though I cannot do the seams I did then. My father taught us variations on games of tag one year, which we then played in the neighborhood, as I taught them to other kids. We went to fellowship dinners, where the older kids, including my sister and brother, tried to teach my mother to skateboard on a banana board, which she did better than I would have expected. I even attended the Boy Scout troop that met at the church before I decided I liked playing sports better.

What is most interesting about my religious interests during childhood, though, is not what happened at church, but what happened around the neighborhood. My neighborhood had a number of positives for a kid growing up: it was self-contained, so we could play in the streets without much concern about traffic, even using the street in front of my house for streetball games; there was a park we could use for football or baseball or anything else we could devise; we could join the neighborhood pool, if we wanted, which is where we spent most of our time in the summers; there were large numbers of other kids, so I often had ten to twenty children around my age to play with, varying as people moved in or out of the neighborhood. However, one positive my neighborhood definitely did not offer was religious diversity. Growing up in a small town in the South, I'm not sure I could have found this benefit anywhere in our area, but our neighborhood was notoriously homogenous. The largest group actually belonged to the number of people who did not go to church at all. Countless friends spent their Sunday mornings sleeping in or playing, while I got up, got dressed up, and went to church.

Even when I was younger and enjoyed it, I couldn't wait to get home to play with everyone who had already begun playing. The clearly devout family in the neighborhood, the Bracketts, attended church more often than we did. They were Baptist, to the best of my knowledge, and they were the ones who would invite all of the neighborhood kids to their church's Vacation Bible School program or other such events. They proselytized, but not in a way that offended any of our parents or us. There were two Catholic families, one of which we knew better than the other. The Paduchs were related to the person who had originally owned much of the land of the neighborhood, and I knew their son Frank from playing baseball with him. I remember his saying something about attending church on a Saturday night, amazing me with such an idea. The Stapletons were more involved in the neighborhood, so I knew their youngest son Thomas better than Frank. None of us understood Catholicism, though, evident in the nickname Thomas later acquired. He tended to pick up nicknames for some reason, even becoming known as Slop when he played baseball, supposedly because that was what he threw. He wasn't a great pitcher, but he somehow managed to get people out and become one of our most reliable pitchers. Because of his Catholicism, though, he somehow garnered the nickname Jew-Boy. This name sums up the level of religious understanding in our neighborhood, as we could not even develop an appropriate nickname for a clear religious minority in our midst.

When I was entering middle school, a Mormon family moved into the neighborhood. There was actually a Mormon church across the street from the Stapletons, where we played football on a regular basis, as it was one of the best pieces of flat land around. We would ask Mike, the oldest son of the Mormon family, questions about his religion, but the only information we ever seemed to get from him was that he couldn't have caffeine, which we deemed cruel and unusual punishment. We passed around stories about the secret services that took place in the Mormon church, which somehow involved holy underwear, among other odd ideas, but I have no idea where we even gathered such false information.

For a few weeks one year, a family that lived on the outskirts of the neighborhood became involved in our religious life. A woman decided she would have a Bible study for us kids, using cookies and Kool-Aid to draw us in. That ploy worked fairly well, and we would go to her house in the afternoon, eat and drink the snacks she provided, then listen to some sort of Bible story, often using flannel graphs. The room was crowded—not because large numbers of kids came, but because the room was small and cramped—and the stories were not interesting. Our normal neighborhood activities won out within a few meetings, and we gave up the snacks for the ability to play outside again.

Even with our limited discussions of religion, then, my family was clearly one of the most actively religious in the neighborhood. Perhaps the lack of interest other families demonstrated led to my desire to preach to the neighborhood kids. My parents tell of coming out to the back porch, only to see me standing before a handful of them, my *Children's Illustrated Bible* in my hands, holding forth on some particular story that I picked up from Sunday school or even the sermon. I never held any sort of altar call, never invited my friends to come to church, never tried to get them saved in any sense, but I stood in front of them and preached. I wonder if I liked the standing in front of them more than I did the stories and ideas I was trying to share with them. Regardless, I would do this routine until, as my mother says, they grew tired of it and went home.

I used that Bible in other ways in the neighborhood, as well. As a small, passive kid, I was used to getting beat up on a regular basis. My next door neighbor, Alan, seemed to see his attacks on me as a particular hobby, as I spent a good deal of time running around cars in people's driveways, trying to get away from him and back home. Joey, who lived at the far end of the neighborhood, took over for a while, but his family moved out of the neighborhood after only a year or so, leaving the job to Alan. I tried to use my Bible to defend myself. When there were times I was expecting a beating, as I could often tell when they were coming, I would carry my Bible with me out to play, believing they would not attack me if I had it with me. Later, I switched to a Gideon's New Testament, which was much easier to carry. If I saw one of them coming, I would pull it out of my pocket and show it to them, as if it were a cross to their vampiric attack. Oddly enough, this approach worked much more often than it should have, as even they had a superstitious fear of the Bible, believing that beating a boy who carried one somehow carried a greater weight than beating someone who was spiritually unarmed.

We did have a few religious conversations, and their content often makes me wonder where I developed the ideas I had. Once, two of us were riding our bikes in the street near my house, and the topic of suicide came up. I spoke like an authority, as I often did, and I said that people who committed suicide went directly to hell. What puzzles and bothers me about this assertion is where I could possibly have developed this theology. We attended a Presbyterian church that was fairly moderate, so I'm sure our minister would not have preached a sermon on the subject, nor would we have covered such an idea in Sunday school. My parents wouldn't have discussed such a subject with us, certainly not when I was no more than twelve, probably younger than ten. However, it was that type of religious ignorance that spread fairly easily in our neighborhood. Since the Bracketts were the only family other than ours who seemed to have any Protestant devotion, and the Catholic and Mormon families did not talk about their faith, which led us to misunderstand them both, our conversations were riddled with basic errors. However, until I was nearing my teen years, I continued to talk about religious matters, as I seemed obsessed with them when most kids simply wanted to play football.

Something changed, though, as I made my way through middle school. Part of it was age, as I wanted to be more involved with my neighborhood friends and what they were doing. I spent my free time playing basketball, baseball, or whatever sport was in season, as I grew up in a neighborhood where we rotated sports like farmers do crops. We would try anything we saw or heard about, even trying to play field hockey with bent tent poles. When our minister scheduled a catechism class for the handful of us kids who were still attending the church, I went to one meeting. It was as boring as one might imagine. First, I had no idea what a catechism was, and he didn't bother to explain that to me, or, if he did, it didn't register. Second, there was assigned reading, which I had lost interest in around the same time, and it was clearly not enjoyable reading, just lists of questions and answers. If there had been some story to it, I might have suffered through it, but even that is doubtful.

The worst problem, though, was that he scheduled it on Sunday afternoons at a time of the year where it was clearly warm enough to play outside. It must have been late fall, as we had moved on from playing football to basketball; college basketball must have already started, but it was still not cold enough to keep us inside. Given the weather in East Tennessee, that could have been December, but it was probably November. My friends and I met every Sunday afternoon at the Havolas' house. Oddly enough, none of the Havolas (there were four children, ranging from two years older than me to eight years younger than me) played basketball with us, but they let us use their driveway, as they had a basketball goal mounted to the side of their house. There was no backboard, as it was mounted directly on the brick side of the house, which we used for the backboard. The goal was only eight feet high, which is one reason we loved it; that fact, coupled with the location of the goal, which allowed us to run up the wall, enabled us to pretend that we were college or professional basketball players, able to play above or at the rim. We also used a smaller ball that we could either palm or come close to palming, which furthered the illusion.

It should be easy to see why a middle school boy would choose to spend his Sunday afternoons with this group instead of at a catechism class. My parents even understood, allowing me to stop going after the first class, though I'm still not sure what they told the minister, if anything. I do know he wasn't particularly happy with my choice, as he would ask me on a weekly basis if I would be there. Then, at the end of the class, he had the students who had completed the course (there were either two or three) come before the congregation, and he recognized their accomplishment. That wasn't enough, as he added a comment about "those who completed the course" versus "those who did not."

There were other changes, though. The group of children I had grown up with in the church had largely stopped attending church or no longer attended ours. I lost track of every one of them, and I only remember one of them by name. We went from a group of close to fifteen, according to a picture of one of our Easter egg hunts down to a group of three or four, one of whom was the minister's daughter, a mousy girl whom I did not enjoy spending time with. There were two other girls who had recently begun coming, driving thirty minutes from Kingsport for some reason, and I enjoyed spending time with them, but certainly not more than my friends in the neighborhood. Since I was so young, I didn't really notice as people slowly stopped coming, and I certainly was not aware of why they stopped coming. I've never been able to find out what happened. I know our minister, Stan, had left, so it could be related to that, as I've now been around enough churches to see people leave when ministers they are fond of do, as well. It could be that our church was a small church, certainly no more than forty or fifty people at its highest point, and this period of time was when megachurches were just beginning to become popular. While we still didn't have any of those around our town, we certainly had much larger churches that could offer better programs, especially for children. The trend today is for people to look for churches that offer such programs to their children, and this development could have played into people's leaving. I hate not knowing, as I always enjoyed the church, and I wonder why so many people seemed to leave at the same time, what the underlying reason (or reasons) was.

I remember when things were still going well, and there was a development that could have led to a decline, but I have no evidence to show that it actually did. We had a new minister, Bill, and we had a new couple who had begun attending our church. Vince was an assistant basketball coach who had recently been hired at East Tennessee State University, where both my father and mother worked, my mother actually working with Vince in the basketball office. Vince was black, and his wife was white. Given that this was the early 1980s in a small town in Northeast Tennessee, one can easily see how this mixed marriage would be a problem. Even though our church had gone with the Presbyterian Church (U.S.A.) in the recent split in that denomination, moving to the more progressive side of the denomination, we were probably more moderate than most who went that direction. However, as far as I could tell at the time and have been able to tell since, the presence of a mixed-race couple in our church did not lead anyone to leave. Instead, they became regular, active members of the church.

There are a few other events that give me a bit of a clue of what might have been going on, though. The first centers around our new minister. For some reason, my mother never got along with him, and stopped attending the church for quite some time, beginning after he had been there for a short time and continuing until a bit after he had left. She would often invoke his name as the reason for not attending and complain about him, but she was never specific in those complaints. I have no idea what he was doing or not doing that bothered her, but I know she was clearly bothered. I have to wonder, then, if he also alienated other members of the congregation, as the decline clearly occurred during his time there. I have seen such changes in other churches related to ministers coming or going, so it would make sense that his arrival had something to do with the changes at this time.

The only thing I really ever did know about him was that he was a former Baptist. I don't know if that connection led to any complications, as he seemed devoted to the Presbyterian denomination. Even though I was in middle school, he was already encouraging me to consider Montreat College, a Presbyterian college in Western North Carolina, which leans toward the conservative side of Presbyterianism. He also took me and a friend of mine to a youth retreat in Montreat (the city, not the college) and tried to get me more involved in the leadership aspect of the denomination. My encounters with him were only positive, though I still did not have the same amount of respect and admiration I had for Stan. That might simply be the effects of age, as I was much younger when Stan was there, or my mother's feelings about Bill. Regardless, I know I thought of him differently.

One other event continues to puzzle me, as it relates to the church tangentially, but hints of larger problems there. One evening, I was eating dinner with my parents at the Piccadilly Cafeteria, a buffet known throughout the Southeast U.S. We saw a young woman named Lyn who attended our church. She had grown up in the same group with my brother and sister, as had her two brothers, and we had visited their house at least a few times, once for a New Year's Eve celebration and several times for bonfires they hosted for the church, as they lived on a farm. They were one of the families we had been closer to for much of our time there, and my parents often spoke well of them. However, on this evening, my parents brought up the fact that Lyn was dating a man who was much older than she, not quite twice her age, but fairly close. She would have been in her early twenties or so, and he might have been forty. Not only did they bring the subject up in a negative light, but my father even went so far to say that he would vote to have her removed from the church because of her relationship. I'm puzzled, first, by the fact that her age would cause such a response, as there were other people in their lives who had fairly significant age differences, though, admittedly, those couples were much older than Lyn was. I'm also confused by the fact that they would make such a decision about a family they got along with quite well.

Within at least a year or two, her family stopped attending the church. Part of that could be attributed to the fact that their children were grown, and I've seen many families in different congregations stop going to church once they no longer have children who are involved.

However, I have to wonder if something happened between her family and the other members of the church, especially the Session, the group of elders who manage the affairs of the church. I'm not sure if someone simply said something to them about how they thought the relationship looked or if any type of official action was taken. Regardless, the connection between the comments at dinner and her family's eventual departure seems too strong to be attributed to coincidence. At the time, I did not make the connection, but, now, having worked behind the scenes at several churches, it is easy to see how there might have been clear disagreements that led to that family leaving, possibly even more. The decline at the church might have a perfectly logical explanation, but I simply do not know what it might be.

Even though I was becoming less involved in church and less interested in religion, it still was clearly a part of my life, though in more extreme ways. If I wonder why some people are drawn to religion and others are not, I wonder even more what moves one to extremes within religions, especially when nothing in a person's background should lead him or her down that path. Even though I grew up in a moderate household that attended a moderate church in a neighborhood with friends from all ranges of interest in religion, I somehow ended up veering toward the extremes.

For example, some friends and I had built a fort on the edge of the woods behind the neighborhood pool when we were moving from elementary to middle school, just about ten or eleven years old. We found the boards in the woods, as people abandoned all kinds of materials on a dirt path that ran behind our neighborhood, one that would ultimately be developed, but, for now, just gave people a place to rid themselves of unwanted items, and gave us a place to play. The fort stayed for a year or two, but we lost interest fairly soon after building it, especially as it was not a well-designed or well-built fort, only coming up to our waists, as we only were able to scavenge so much wood. When I was in middle school, for some reason, I decided I needed to build a cross in the woods where I could go and pray, as if I were Mrs. Greenleaf in Flannery O'Connor's short story, "Greenleaf." I had never read that story or even heard of O'Connor and wouldn't for almost a decade. I had never heard of anyone building a cross in the woods and going there to pray. I simply came up with this idea, then decided to follow through on it. I took the boards from the fort, selecting the best two for a cross, then nailed them together. I was not then, nor am I now, any type of carpenter, so the cross was certainly not stable, but it worked well enough for my purposes. I took the boards to a point farther in the woods, just at the top of a hill, certainly symbolic in itself, then built the cross. If I was a poor carpenter, I was a worse hole-digger, as I was weak and lazy; I dug down just far enough for the cross to stand up, if I propped it up with rocks, but even then, it fell on a regular basis.

When I would get home from school, I would sneak away from everyone else and go to the cross in the woods to pray. I have no idea what could have weighed me down so much I thought I needed a private place in the woods to pray, as my life was as stable as anyone's could be in middle school. True, I really did not have any friends at school, having spent the year before in a different track than my friends from fifth grade, so I was now in new classes with students I did not know well, and it was taking time to make new friends. I'm sure I prayed about that, but the very fact that I had a private place in the woods where I went to pray certainly hurt my already poor social life. My neighborhood friends found out about it, and, being middle school students, they mocked my practice whenever they had the chance. Looking back now, I'm not surprised that kids of that age would behave that way, nor was I particularly surprised then. What may have driven such behavior was the fact that I wanted to be some sort of outcast, and religion was simply one way to become that. As most kids know, negative attention is better than none at all. This trend toward garnering attention ran throughout middle school. Once, we were riding the bus to school on a winter morning, and one of its windows had been knocked out. No one would sit there, so, of course, I did. Not only did this alienate me from everyone on the bus, but, given how it made me look when I arrived at school, it did not encourage anyone to want to socialize with me there.

This alienation was complemented by my overdeveloped sense of guilt, which continued to plague me as I grew older. Since I was moving into puberty, as were my friends, girls became a much more dominant topic of conversation, though we didn't know enough to talk about sex. We simply knew we liked girls, especially certain parts of girls, but we had no idea why. However, my guilt complex kicked in even here, and I felt guilty for liking those certain parts of girls, though I did not know why I shouldn't like them or why I should feel guilty for liking them. Again, no one in my childhood talked to me about sex or girls or told me anything that was wrong about any aspect of sexuality, and no one at church discussed the subject at all. I somehow developed my own ideas about the subject, which almost always correlated to what was wrong. One of the ways we would talk about girls was to look at the annual *Sports Illustrated* swimsuit issue, as we grew up without the internet, and only one father in the neighborhood had a subscription to *Playboy*, as far as we knew. That was Alan's father, and, given how often Alan beat me up, I wasn't inclined to go there for any type of knowledge. However, I felt guilty for even looking at women in bikinis, so I took the latest issue that I had somehow gotten, along with several other magazines with similar pictures and took them to the woods. Somehow, I had gotten Russ, another boy from the neighborhood, to go along with me, convincing him that something was wrong, as well. We used more boards from the fort and gas from his father's gas can and started a fire in a clearing the woods. This was years before we heard of anyone burning records or books because of their evil nature, so somehow, I came up with this approach on my own again. However, some other friends found out what we were doing and came to the woods to try to stop us. They would take individual magazines out and haggle with us over them, trying to argue that *this one* is clearly not as bad as the others, and it should be saved. By doing so, they talked us out of almost every magazine, leaving only a few pictures to burn. Russ was more easily convinced than I was, but even I gave in to peer pressure after a while.

Since I was not as interested in the church, I looked outside of it for answers to questions I had or simply looked for any answers. For some reason, I kept feeling as if I was looking for something, and these actions were my attempts to try to find what it was I was looking for. What I cannot understand is why so many of my attempts moved toward the negative, toward trying to prevent myself from looking at things or doing things, rather than trying to find positive approaches to whatever I was lacking. I did not take things on; instead, I tried to give them up, a practice that still impacts who I am and how I live. The only exception to that might be a book I once ordered from television. TBS was a relatively new channel then, as we had slowly moved from a handful of channels to close to sixteen or so by now. Cable companies were just developing the box for the tops of televisions that enabled people to have premium channels for premium prices. However, we were slow to catch up to the revolution, so I was happy enough to have the basic cable channels that played sports or cartoons on a more regular rotation. For some reason, one advertisement that ran during the afternoons on TBS, a time devoted to programming aimed at the after-school crowd, was from the Arthur S. DeMoss Foundation, out of California. I had no idea they were a cult-like group (a 1999 *Time* article says that one journalist who called its offices in Florida received this message, "We're not a cult, but we can't say what we are")[1], as the ad sounded reasonable to me, even though I had never heard of the group. Since it sounded legitimate, I decided to give it a try. If I called a toll-free number, I would receive a book called *Power for Living*. I requested the book, and I actually read it. I'm sure I thought, given my middle school anxiety, that I needed any help I could get with the business of living, so I made sure to read the book when it came in. I don't remember any particular theology or self-help mentality they were pushing, but I remember the effects of the book.

One of my best friends in the neighborhood was Kenneth, the only son in the most religious family in the neighborhood, whom we called Ken-Boy, a name he gave up sometime in middle school and asked to be called by his given name. He and I were both interested in two girls in the neighborhood, Sheri and Beth, but we were not currently dating them ("dating" in the middle school sense of that term). He and I were out riding our bikes when they tried to get us to come to Beth's house, but I sensed something was up, so I bailed out, calling for him to come with me, but he went on to the house, later telling me he did not hear me. Not long after, he showed up at my door quite angry, as it seems Sheri and Beth had given him the middle school version of a beating; he, being the Christian boy, would not hit them back. He was not hurt badly, I could tell, but he was angry at me for leaving him alone with them, and he would hit a boy, so I knew there was a fight coming. I stood at our kitchen door and talked to him through the screen, tried to calm him down any way I could. I drew on *Power for Living*, told him I had been reading it and the effect it was having on my life. I talked about being more peaceful and less violent and that I didn't want to fight him. Kenneth and I had fought before, and we ended in a draw every time, as neither of us were good fighters, nor did we really have the heart for it. We were not mean children. However, he was angry, and I was not, so I knew I would be in trouble this time unless I talked him out of it. Sheri and Beth showed up and watched our discussion, then, ultimately,

---

1. van Biema, "Who Are These Guys?" para. 2.

my mother came home and asked me why I was standing inside. I had stalled long enough for him to calm down, using religion to talk my way out of a fight, just as I had done with the Bible several years before. That was my general approach to religion throughout my childhood. My interest in it would wax and wane as I felt I needed it with no real commitment to church or belief. When I took an interest, though, I would pick out extreme points or behaviors and focus only on them, ignoring any other aspect of it. Anyone who paid attention to such an approach should have seen what was coming when I went to high school.

2

Rock and Roll Saves Teenager

So how and why did I move from where most of my friends were, only passably interested in religion, though still clearly fascinated by it, to an extreme that concerned most of the people who knew me? I can still lay out the date the change occurred: March 12, 1985. However, some background knowledge would be helpful.

Like most teenagers, I spent a good deal of my time listening to music; however, growing up in rural Northeast Tennessee in the late 1970s and early 1980s, my musical knowledge was severely limited. We listened to top forty radio, enjoying performers and bands, such as Hall and Oates, Michael Jackson, and even early boy bands, such as New Edition. When Kenneth somehow produced U2's *Sunday Bloody Sunday*, all we could do was argue over whether or not the title track was about the crucifixion or not, knowing nothing of Irish history or even that the band was Irish. It will offend most music fans to know I did not learn of Bob Dylan until sometime in college (and I didn't like him then), and my only exposure to the Beatles was the movie *Sgt. Pepper's Lonely Hearts Club Band*, which starred Peter Frampton and the Bee Gees in a musical centered around songs from that album. The one bright spot, musically speaking, came from Delmar, the oldest son in the only African-American family in our neighborhood. He still had friends in New York, and they sent him tapes of DJs who were performing in clubs. Whenever he had his boom box with him on the bus, we would beg the bus driver to turn off the radio, so we could hear the latest tape. This influence, along with the rise of movies, such as *Krush Groove* and

Breakin' (and the awful sequel *Breakin' 2: Electric Boogaloo*, not that the first movie was cinematic genius), led to my love of late 1970s and early 1980s rap. However, I never invested in a tape by Run-DMC, the Sugar Hill Gang, or Grandmaster Flash, listening instead to "Freakazoid," a popularized (and much worse) version of rap by Midnight Star, which, unlike the other groups, was played on our local radio station.

When Kenneth and I were talking one day on my back porch, I was surprised when he brought up music. His question was simple: "Who is your favorite contemporary Christian band?" Given my lack of knowledge on the subject, it is not surprising I had never heard the term "contemporary Christian" connected to *music* or *band* or pretty much anything else. I fell back on the limited knowledge I did have and responded, "The Statler Brothers." My only defense for this answer is that I grew up listening to the contemporary Country music of the day, as that's the music my parents played in the car and around the house, so I could actually speak rather intelligently about Charlie Pride, Kenny Rogers, Dolly Parton, the Cash family, and, yes, even the Statler Brothers. One of my favorite songs was "Home Grown Tomatoes" by Guy Clark. Kenneth didn't seem too surprised by the absurdity of my answer, but that could have been because he was more focused on covert evangelism. It turns out that he wanted to invite me to a contemporary Christian concert his youth group was attending the next week. Given that I had no idea what the genre consisted of, but that I trusted Kenneth and liked hanging out with him, I agreed to go. I later found out my girlfriend's church group would also be there, so I could sit with her, which made the situation even better.

The concert was held on East Tennessee State University's campus, a public university. As I discovered later, almost every Christian concert that was too small to fit into our larger venues was held at Milligan, the local Christian college I would later attend. Over the next five or six years of my life, I attended hundreds of concerts in the area, and there was only one other performance I can recall taking place at ETSU. I knew the campus well, given that both of my parents worked there, and I had spent summers attending basketball and baseball camps there; we had season tickets to the football and basketball games, and I just generally spent time around campus with my parents. I had even spent a good deal of time in the D.P. Culp Center where the concert took place, as that's where the food court, bookstore, and game rooms were, which is where we tried to spend a good deal of our time when we attended the camps. However, I did not know they hosted concerts there, and I had never been in the auditorium where it took place, didn't even know it existed.

The performer was Steve Camp, a musician whose work I would come to know much better in the next few years before I moved on to very different styles, and I don't recall there being an opening act. Again, with my lack of musical knowledge, I could not have said if he was a particularly talented musician, but I seemed to enjoy the music, as his style could clearly be categorized as mainstream pop music. However, the content of his songs was different, as they all centered around Christian themes. The one song I have never forgotten from that concert was about a UFO (a cover of Larry Norman's song called simply "UFO," a song Camp never actually recorded). However, in the song, Camp was comparing Jesus to an unidentified flying object. For some reason, two lines of the work continue to stick in my head to this day, though I cannot remember any other songs he performed that night. In an upbeat pop beat, he sang, "He's an unidentified flying object / Coming back to take you home." Though this comparison sounds quite odd, even now, I realized later and perhaps even at the time that Camp was comparing Jesus to a UFO in an attempt to create a new metaphor about the rapture, the time at the end of the world when Jesus comes back down from heaven to take all the Christians to heaven. There are long-running theological debates about this event, as people argue over whether or not Jesus will come down before the awful events of that time happen or after they do or in the middle, trying to answer the question of whether or not Christians will have to endure the sufferings described in the book of Revelation. Not surprisingly, Camp's song did not attempt to deal with these concerns in less than four minutes with a four-four pop beat. I discovered Christian concerts are notoriously thin on complex theology, as many of the songs avoid any kind of complications that might occur in life. Instead, the focus is on what Evangelicals would argue is the core of the gospel. Christian musicians want people to believe Jesus is the Son of God, he is the Christ, we are all sinners, and we all need to accept Jesus as our Savior. The songs drove this point home over and over, and almost any preaching that occurs between songs focus on this point, as well. In this way, they resemble a Billy Graham crusade, as he never bothered to debate abstract points of theology, focusing instead on attempting to get people to see that central message.

Steve Camp centered his preaching around this point, as well, though he also added one idea, which is the one that caught my attention. I largely ignored all the talk about accepting Jesus, as I had done that years ago. Having grown up in church, of course I believed I was one of the saved. In looking around at my friends, I spent much more time in church, so it was clear I was a true Christian. I was even at a Christian concert, as Kenneth had asked me to come, not anyone else from the neighborhood, and my girlfriend, a Christian herself, was also there. There was no doubt I was a Christian. Then, though, Camp went on, asking people if they were truly living for Jesus. He wanted to know if those of us who said we were Christians truly lived out that lifestyle. If not, now was a good time to rededicate our lives. If anyone has grown up in an Evangelical church or spent any amount of time in one, such language will not be new to him or her, but, for me, having been raised in a mainline Presbyterian church, what he said was completely different. We didn't talk about back-sliding or rededication, though we also would not have professed the Baptist theology of "once saved, always saved."

To use the traditional Evangelical Christian language, I was convicted. I felt he was speaking directly to me, that he had found out exactly how I had been living and was calling me out. I had only been going to church, nothing more. I didn't read my Bible on a regular basis, and I certainly didn't pray outside of church. I didn't even know what contemporary Christian music was. I listened to rock and roll, only learning later that it was called secular music, music that was of the world. No, I was clearly not living as a Christian, no matter what I would have answered a couple of hours before the concert. When he gave people an opportunity to stand and either dedicate their life to Christ or, as in my case, rededicate it, I stood up. Kristin held my hand tightly and looked up at me beatifically. Truly, this moment was sacred, a religious experience of the like I had never felt before. We did not have altar calls in the Presbyterian church, believing that anyone who decided to join the church or get saved would do so quietly, talking to a minister in an office. This event, however, affected me emotionally, something my faith had never done before, and I definitely liked it. I'm sure we prayed some prayer, but I cannot recall what that might have been. Given the knowledge I have now, I'm sure it was short and simple, asking Jesus to come into my life in a real way, nothing more.

After the concert, Kristin hugged me, and Kenneth's youth minister, Rick, invited me to come to their youth group whenever I wanted. One criticism that is leveled at Christian concerts and religious crusades is the lack of follow-up on people afterwards. Some events have cards people fill out that local churches can then use to make sure people are not left out on their own. My only real connection was with Kenneth and his youth group, as no one else kept in touch with me. However, I did have the chance to go backstage and talk to Camp after the concert. He was signing autographs, but I did not buy one of his tapes, for some reason. My guess is that I did not have any money with me, as I'm sure I would have otherwise. I told him about my decision, and he was supportive, but there was not much more he could do. He signed a sheet of paper I had and wrote a verse on it, I Timothy 4:12, which states, "Don't let anyone look down on you because you are young, but set an example for the believers in speech, in conduct, in love, in faith and in purity."[1] I'm sure he put that verse on what he signed for most teenagers, but it certainly meant a good deal to me then. After all, everything changed for me that night, so it had to mean something.

What changed, most obviously, were my musical choices. Since I rededicated my life at a Christian music concert, music must have been the answer to my past religious apathy. I stopped listening to any secular music and only listened to Christian music. Given that I was unable to drive, I still had to endure the music on the bus to school, in the car with my parents, and while riding with older friends. But, given that Christians were told they would endure sufferings and persecution—Matthew 24:9 told me quite clearly, "Then you will be handed over to be persecuted and put to death, and you will be hated by all nations because of me"—such hardships simply reinforced the idea that I was making the right choice. Part of the problem, though, was that there were not many options for Christian music in a small town in Tennessee in the mid-1980s. We had one Christian bookstore in the mall, Gifts of Love, and its selection was about what one would expect from its name. The first tape I bought was by a band called The Imperials, a quartet who sang songs most people's parents or grandparents would have been familiar with.

---

1. All quotations from the Bible are from the New International Version, as that's the Bible I used at the time.

That first tape, *Sing the Classics*, had such songs as "We Shall Behold Him," "We Are the Reason," and "El Shaddai." The only reason I continued listening to such music was my belief in the rightness of it. That, and perhaps my lack of musical knowledge from before. If I would have listened to bands, such as the Beatles and the Rolling Stones, or a true artist like Bob Dylan, I would not have been able to tolerate the change in quality. However, going from top forty pop to essentially gospel music was not as drastic a change as one might imagine.

We also only had one Christian station, WPRQ, with their tagline, Power Radio for the Quad-Cities. Given that everyone else referred to our area as the Tri-Cities region (Johnson City, Kingsport, and Bristol), I had no idea what the fourth city in their slogan could have possibly been. Even now, I have trouble coming up with an answer that satisfies me. I have a feeling that they were either located in a city that was not one of the tri-cities, so they added their city to make it more important, or they had rights to those call letters and made up something to fit them. PRQ, as we called them, played the Christian equivalent of top forty pop music of the time. Most of the bands and performers were ones people who were passably familiar with Christian music of the time would have heard of: Petra, Amy Grant, Michael W. Smith, and, of course, the Imperials. It would take me close to a year to realize that the world of Christian music was much more diverse than the bubble gum pop and rock of PRQ, both in style of music and even in theology. Another problem was that PRQ didn't even play music all of the time, as they shut off at some point late in the evening, and they played a talk show during peak listening hours for a teenager, from four to six in the afternoons. They played the Bob Larson show, the religious equivalent of Rush Limbaugh, I now realize. I used to play his show from my small boom box while I was outside shooting basketball, while my friends made fun of him.

In the 1970s, Larson was best known for his books on the evils of rock and roll music, but, by the 1980s, as his talk show began, his emphasis shifted toward witchcraft and Satanism, which is what he spent a good part of each show talking about. People who were supposedly possessed by demons or who were witches and warlocks would regularly call in to argue with him, which gave him a chance to ask for people to donate money to keep his ministry going. It is difficult for me to write about the program and Larson now without sounding cynical about the endeavor. At the time, I believed everything I heard on the show, despite the fact I had grown up in a world where we never discussed such supernatural occurrences. Later, my feelings shifted somewhat; as I learned more about such programs and people, I became bothered by my gullibility and Larson's approach. I still believed, though, that he was probably quite sincere and believed what he said. I did not believe he created those scenarios, that he paid people to call in and pretend, but that he honestly believed such people existed and he was doing good through his show. However, like Limbaugh, what he created was a feeling of fear in people, as he encouraged people to see Christians as under attack, an idea still too prevalent in the Evangelical movement today.

Recently, though, I discovered that there were numerous questions about his show, his books, and everything he claimed. A 1993 article in *Cornerstone* magazine raised serious concerns about the way the show was run, whether or not he wrote the books he claimed to have written, and about the accuracy of his portrayal of his earlier life, before he turned to Christianity.[2] Given the downfall of so many Christian leaders from that time in my life, I should not be surprised by all of the information that has come out about Larson, but the fact that I encountered him so early in my newfound conversion made these revelations more painful than the others.

Whenever the music was on, though, I was taking in as much as I could. Having found myself in this new subculture, I wanted to own it, to know everything about it. Music became one of the key components of my life. Such a statement could be spoken by almost all American teenagers of the past sixty to seventy years, and the change in my interest in music could simply be attributed to the change that happens to most people at that age. However, it did not happen to me until the night of the Steve Camp concert, so I've always seen it more as a religious decision than a natural progression of growing up. I began subscribing to *CCM, Contemporary Christian Music*, the magazine that kept track of everything going on in the Christian music world, or at least so I believed at the time. Given that I was a teenager well before the internet, magazines were one of the only ways for me to keep up with new bands and albums, so I devoured every issue, poring over it, looking for the latest development: a possible tour of one of my favorite bands, trouble between band members, a new album, or even new genres of music that

---

2. Trott, "Bob Larson's Ministry Under Scrutiny."

were developing as the Christian music industry began expanding rapidly. As a 1995 *Forbes* article states, "Ten years ago there were fewer than 200 stations playing contemporary Christian music. Now there are over 500." By 1994, Christian music "probably grossed $1 billion," which was 10 percent of all music sales.[3]

I also started looking for concerts wherever I could find them. I hadn't been driving long, so I wasn't able to go outside of an hour and a half radius, but I looked everywhere I could within that area. I used whatever extra money I had to buy tickets for those concerts, always trying to get the best seats, usually front row, even if I knew nothing about the performer. Once, Michael Card was coming to Johnson City, and I had heard one of his songs, which I enjoyed well enough. A couple of friends and I went to Gifts of Love on the first day tickets were available, and we were thrilled to get front row tickets. We talked about how we would rush the stage and spend the entire evening rocking (yes, that's how we would talk). What we did not know was the song we were the most familiar with was his heaviest song, and it could hardly be said to inspire anyone to rush the stage. Card played acoustic guitar throughout his concert, which was as sedate as we imagined our grandparents' worship services to be. Front row turned out not to be that important to us on that night.

However, I was still at the point where I did not show any distinction between bands, as I would go see anyone who was a Christian artist, and many of them did rock for me, so I would go to great lengths to get those front row seats. Whenever the tickets were general admission, which happened fairly often, I and a few friends would get to the concert hours before the doors opened to make sure we got the best seats possible. If we got out of school just before three o'clock, we would be at the concert venue just after three, having taken whatever we needed to school. One person would go get food a bit later, while everyone else sat at the door, playing cards and talking, all to protect our place in line. Most of my friends did not share this obsession, though, so I had to rotate between friends based on the particular bands they liked, so I could have people to hang out with before concerts. Even some of my friends who were serious fans of Christian music thought my behavior was a bit odd. Three of them made fun of me once for getting to a White Heart concert so early when they arrived no more than thirty minutes

---

3. Gubernick and La Franco, "Rocking With God," paras. 3, 9.

before the doors opened, and they found great seats. However, I was on the front row, and, during one of the band's songs, they leaned the microphone down to me, and I got to sing out one of the choruses. Such events helped me to believe I was living the kind of life I should be living now, that I had truly changed my life and become a real Christian.

Brian, a friend from high school, and I became pseudo-groupies of a local band called Lex Rex ("the law is king" in Latin, which they interpreted as "God's law is king"). We would travel anywhere in the area to hear them perform, often hearing them multiple times in the same month. At one point, when we had been in the front row of three or four concerts in a row, all within a span of a few weeks, the lead singer actually pointed us out to the crowd. He said that they saw us at all their concerts, and he praised our dedication and our commitment. He clearly implied that such commitment was not just to the band, but to God, that we were acting out our faith by behaving in such a way. All along the way, I received positive reinforcement that helped me believe my obsession with Christian music made me a better Christian, may, in fact, have made me a better Christian than others, though I would have denied that.

My bedroom even began reflecting this obsession, as if I needed to document it for myself or for others. I bought sheets of poster board and painted posters of the concerts I had seen. I have no real artistic talent, so they were nothing more than block letters of the band, along with the date, location, and some information about the tour, either their catch phrase or album name or some word or phrase I associated with the show. The word for the Steve Camp concert was *rededication*. These posters were amateurish in the worst sense. Chad, a friend of mine who shared my enthusiasm for Christian music, once saw them and said, "You have this thing about straight lines. You never use any." I later began buying posters and imitation album covers that I used to surround my room, covering every blank place on the wall I could find. Later, when I went to college, I used the ceiling for extra space. I bought buttons at concerts and covered the front of my jean jacket (with the sleeves cut off, as it was the 1980s) with them. Again, I was indiscriminate in my purchases, as I would have buttons from Amy Grant and Sandi Patti, along with ones from Stryper and Jerusalem, two heavy metal Christian bands. I seemed to believe I could best illustrate the depth of my devotion by sheer numbers.

The same was true when it came to tapes I ended up owning. My friends and I somehow rationalized that copying tapes and sharing them was not only legal, but moral, as we were sharing music that praised God and that would help us in our spiritual walk and might even help someone to get saved, though I'm not sure who we thought would get saved, as everyone we hung out with were already Christians. We would go to any store we could find that sold Christian music and buy one tape each, making sure we knew who was going to buy what else we wanted so that we could tape it within the week. I had several tape suitcases that were popular (more or less) at that time, and I ended up with hundreds of tapes I would carry with me in my car or on trips. We discovered that ninety-minute tapes, which had just come out, could fit a complete tape on each side, if one were careful and did not waste precious time at the beginning or when flipping the tape. Given that dual cassette recorders had just become affordable, we would spend the night at each other's houses, recording tape after tape after tape. I would then spend evenings at home, sitting on my bed with large monkey ear headphones on so I could play the tapes as loudly as I wanted, with lyrics in my lap so I could better learn them. Once, when my best friend Wayne had spent the night, we were waiting for his parents to come and pick him up. My parents had gone somewhere, so we had a Steve Taylor tape playing loudly in the house, while we watched out the window to make sure we didn't miss his parents. We had the lyrics sitting in the window sill so we could see them and sing them out quite loudly. Neither Wayne nor I could sing well at all, but God didn't care about singing ability. As Brian and I always commented, "The Bible says to make a joyful noise, not necessarily a good one."

Since MTV certainly wasn't playing Christian music, we would try to discover any shows that aired late at night that would play Christian music. At that time, several channels, especially USA, had music video shows, and, from time to time, a show would start up playing only Christian music. We would pass around such information as if sharing information about parties, as most high school students did. We would set our VCRs and try to save as many of these videos as we could, which were of a quality even lower than the videos playing on MTV at that time. Once, Chad somehow got a copy of two hours' worth of videos we had not seen, spliced together one after the other with no information about where they came from. We could not yet afford VCRs that would copy tapes, and hooking up two VCRs to one TV was an undertaking we only did under special circumstances, so we spent hours at his house viewing and reviewing the tape until we had them memorized.

Christian music did not build the bridges with other Christians, though, that I hoped it would. For example, I did end up in the youth group at East Unaka Church of Christ, the one I attended the Steve Camp concert with, but, oddly enough, I never fit in with them. Part of it might have been socio-economic differences, as the church was certainly made up of people with more money than my family had. I recall visiting a young woman's house with a few friends, and I realized I had never been in a house as large as that one. One floor was probably as large as our entire house, and we lived in a three-floor, split-level house with three bedrooms. These were students who were popular at school, not relying on the youth group to be their sole social outlet, as I was trying to do. Another problem was the fact that my parents did not allow me to participate in some of the activities where deeper relationships were established. My neighborhood friends who attended were able to go on a trip to the beach with everyone else, while I stayed at home. When I went to the first meeting after that trip, the youth minister called out: "Do you want the title or the testimony?" I had no idea what that meant, so I began to call out "Title!" "Testimony" was the right answer, something they had learned at the beach. In another instance, the youth group participated in a thirty-hour fast, where they stayed at the church for the entire thirty hours, playing games, watching movies, doing some Bible study. My parents were worried about what might happen if I didn't eat for thirty hours, so I wasn't allowed to go. I met a group of my neighborhood friends afterwards, and they talked about how great an experience it had been, yet another one I missed out on.

However, there was one more reason I didn't fit in. Ironically, it was the issue of Christian music. Given that this group was the one I attended the Steve Camp concert with, the one that changed the way I thought about music and Christianity, I thought they would have been supportive of my newfound devotion to Christian music only. They were not. At almost every youth group meeting, I had to defend my choice not to listen to secular music. This problem was exacerbated when Mister Mister came out with their song "Kyrie." Members of the group would corner me and try to get me to admit that this song, if none other, was a beneficial song, was, in fact, a Christian song, despite the fact that it was not labeled as such, as they would remind me that the song contained the lyrics, "Kyrie Eleison," which means "Lord, have mercy" in Greek. The chorus contained lyrics, such as "Kyrie eleison, down the road that I must travel / Kyrie eleison, through the darkness of the night,"[4] which can certainly sound Christian. Such songs and groups come along from time to time and raise this issue again and again. The most famous is U2, whom Christians tried to co-opt in the late 1980s and early 1990s. U2 refused to profess any form of Christianity, however, leaving the Christians to interpret their lyrics in whatever ways they chose. When I tried to make this argument later, my friend Mike, who was much more familiar with their songs, pointed out that many of their songs clearly didn't match up with orthodox Christianity, using lyrics from "Ultraviolet (Light My Way)" as only one example: "And now we lie together / in whispers and moans."[5]

When the youth group members would harangue me about Mister Mister and other such groups, I would tell them that the song sounded great, and I was glad to know it existed, but I would not listen to it. I tried my best to convey that I was not saying anything about their faith because they chose to listen to such a song, but that I would not do so. I'm not sure that was true at the time, as I'm sure I was being self-righteous, even if I were not trying to do so. At times, I'm sure I was trying to be smug about my newfound faith. I'm sure I did both imply and even state that one was a better Christian if he or she only listened to Christian music, so they were right to question me on that. However, I'm amazed at how adamant they were that some secular music was not only fine, but actually Christian. I did not know then how fervently people will cling to their beliefs if they are challenged, no matter how much evidence is mustered against them. They desperately wanted to justify themselves and their actions in the same way I did mine. My extremism pushed them to an extremism to counteract it, rather than the moderation they were trying to live with before I joined the group.

Not surprisingly, my stance on music also affected my standing at my high school, but in very different ways. Growing up in the rural South, I never had to deal with people who were not at least familiar with Christianity, as many people attended church, at least nominally, and Jesus was simply part of the culture. As one of my students once

---

4. Mister Mister, "Kyrie."
5. U2, "Ultraviolet (Light My Way)."

described the South, "It's where Jesus is in the air and sugar is in the tea." It would seem that my focus on Christian music would not be that out of the ordinary, but my focus on it exclusively and my tendency to be vocal about such a focus certainly drew the attention of people who had never paid me any attention before.

Because of this newfound definition of myself, I was able to move between cliques and classes within the school, being both welcomed and questioned by all groups. Once, in a classroom where a few of us ate lunch to avoid walking to the main classroom building, three students heard the music I and my friends were playing: Christian music, of course. These three students were not popular, and, looking back now, part of it was because they were outside the norm, as well, questioning the idea of masculinity through their behavior and dress. I'm not sure if all three of them were homosexual or not; perhaps one or two were, but perhaps none of them were; they may have simply been effeminate in a culture that did not allow for such deviation. My friends and I were sitting behind a cubicle where the only two computers (Apple IIes) were located, simply talking and eating. The more vocal of the group, Roger, stood in the middle of the room and began a long discussion over the cubicle wall about why my focus on only Christian music was misguided. He was a Christian, he said, and he attended church, but he still listened to good, non-Christian music. I stood up and argued back, as I often did, that Christian music helped one grow in his or her relationship with Christ, which secular music could not do. I felt like I was at East Unaka again, though I expected such an argument at a public high school. The conversation became rather animated, as almost all conversations with Roger did, and he finally just left. Henry, one of his quieter friends, actually came around the cubicle to tell me that he didn't fully agree with me, but that he could see my point. In my misguided theology, I had just done what Jesus had wanted me to do; I was spreading the gospel, though it was clearly not the gospel as anyone else would have defined it.

Oddly enough, my extreme Christianity made me somehow more popular than I was before, as it certainly drew a good deal of attention my way. It helped that one of the most visible groups in our high school was one simply called the Prayer Club. It met every Friday during home room, and students would stand up and preach, more or less. I'm still unclear why it was not the Bible Club or some other name, as we did very little praying, but that had always been the name, so we never bothered to change it. Since I had changed my life, I had become much more active in this group, though I had attended before, so I attained some leadership in the group. The older leaders encouraged those of us who were coming behind, but they were also worried about my fanatical focus on Christian music. Robert, one of the key leaders, wrote in my yearbook, "If you learn how to put the love of Jesus before the Hate of Rock and Roll you'll go a lot further," something I certainly needed to hear, but could not yet allow in. By my senior year, I was one of the better known students on campus, even earning the Most Likely to Succeed superlative, though I wondered why anyone in my class would believe I would make a good deal of money or climb some career ladder. This notoriety led to a number of odd situations, as people from across the campus treated me as their friend, even if I did not know who they were. One day, at lunch, two students sat down across from me and Wayne and talked with us throughout the entire lunch period. As he and I were walking back to class, he turned and asked me who they were. I could only comment, "I thought you knew them." People were so desperate to be heard and accepted, it seemed, they would ultimately overlook my narrow view of music and simply talk to me, a situation I now wish I could go back and take full advantage of, actually care for people and accept them as they were.

School also helped me in another way, relating to faith. I had become good friends with Wayne, as we had ended up with all of our sophomore year classes together, though we had only known each other in passing during our freshman year. We both enjoyed Accounting, so we began working ahead in the book, finishing it well ahead of the rest of the class. In our junior year, we did an independent study of Accounting II with the teacher, which largely consisted of our reading chapters in a book, then doing projects that came along with it. The teacher, Mrs. Payne, would simply loan us the teacher's copy so we could check our work and see what we were doing right and wrong. One weekend, I had taken the book home to do some work, but Wayne called because he needed it. In trying to figure out a way to meet and exchange the book, he simply suggested I come to church with him that evening, and I could give it to him then. Wayne has never been a pushy person, but, on that day, he continued to insist that this plan was the best approach, answering all of my excuses with explanations of why this meeting would work best. There are few times in my life where I would ever argue that God was involved, as I simply don't view God's role in the world that way. However, if one were inclined to see God moving in my life, this phone conversation would be one of those times, as attending church that evening changed my life, though it took the next few years to do so. I knew a few other people in Wayne's youth group, which helped convince me to meet him there, and I enjoyed the study quite a good deal. Unlike at East Unaka, I felt completely comfortable, even speaking during the study time on the first evening, something I had never done before. Part of the lesson that evening involved contemporary Christian music, so I knew I had found a place that was right for me.

Music was a centerpiece of my time at Central Church of Christ, the church where I spent the next seven years of my life. Even if we were merely hanging out in the youth room, someone would always have a tape in the sound system, providing the background for our playing ping pong, nerf basketball, or just talking about mundane or important matters. In this way, as in several others, we behaved like any other group of teenagers. We went to a Michael W. Smith concert in Knoxville, and a group of us were sitting near the top of the arena, where there were rows of empty seats. We spent our time during the concert running up and down those rows, jumping seats, not in any Pentecostal fervor, but simply as teenagers with too much energy we found an outlet for in music. At a teen convention the next year, we heard Margaret Becker in concert, a musician not many people had heard of before that point, but whom I greatly enjoyed. Near the end of her performance, people began climbing up on the stage to dance, with my help, I should add. At some point, after I was able to get on stage, I found myself backstage with her, as she had left to take a break from the madness or, perhaps, she was even worried about her safety. We barely spoke, as it seemed more like a reverent moment than anything else, and I now realize she may have been leaving the stage to pray. These events were the ones we talked about in church vans when we weren't listening to a tape over the speakers or, individually, in our headphones.

I will say I was not so infatuated with the rightness of Christian music that I transferred that feeling onto the musicians themselves. I did not take the typical teenager slant of worshipping the people who performed, even if I did not always allow the music to direct my worship to God, either. At one other concert in Knoxville, a couple of members of our youth group were able to get front row seats to hear Petra, one of the best-known bands in Christian music, while the rest of us were much farther back. I had not yet become obsessed with concerts, as this performance was one of the earliest I attended, so I was content to sit closer to the back. After the show, one of the young women told us that she had been able to touch Greg X. Volz, the lead singer during one of the songs. However, her comment was, "I touched him," as if he were some divinity she had been able to approach and interact with, as if she were saying she had been able to touch Jesus on his way to the cross. Wayne, who was not known for witty rejoinders, simply looked at her and said, "No, *he* touched *you*," clearly pointing out Volz was just a guy on the stage who went around slapping people's hands during songs, showing that she had done nothing special at all, simply held up her hand for him to touch.

Not all of our moments with music were positive ones, and I was largely to blame for those. My antipathy toward non-Christian music led me to perform acts I am now not proud of, as I and a few of my friends burned records. After all, I had read Bob Larson's book on the evils of rock and roll, and I had read several after that, including *Backward Masking Unmasked* by Jacob Aranza, which, as one might guess, argues that there are hidden Satanic messages in a variety of songs, though his emphasis lies much more on the lyrics one can understand quite clearly played forwards, and *Why Knock Rock* by Dan and Steve Peters, who provided plenty of reasons to do so. I had encouraged Wayne and Jamie, the two members of our youth group who seemed most willing to go along with my ideas, to join me in burning our secular music collection. I contributed the KISS records that my brother and sister had left with me after they had left home, as it was clear that those Kids (or Knights) in Satan's Service, as fundamentalist Christians believed their name stood for, were opposed to Christianity. Unfortunately, as Wayne reminds me even now, he burned his *Born in the USA* album (not tape), which would be worth a good deal, and Wayne seldom threw music away, so I'm sure he would still have it.

Whenever I see passionate people do absurd things, I remember I was once one of those people. My friends tried to show me how wrong I was when it came to this issue, but I simply ignored them, found friends who would either encourage or permit my fanaticism I fed with the books I was reading, all of which did nothing more than encourage my fears and hatred. It would have been one thing if I would have added Christian music to my collection or even to have only listened to it, but I turned my newfound commitment against an enemy that did nothing to me, that had no desire to harm me, that did not particularly care about my existence. Non-Christian music only seemed to dominate my life because I was a teenager, and teenagers spend their time listening to music, but it was clearly not the active agent of evil I envisioned it to be. When I hear of book burnings, especially a church in Arizona that burned J.R.R. Tolkien's books, obviously not knowing he was a Christian, I remember who I was and what led me to burn those records. I remember that such actions do not spring from love, as much as I would have insisted to the contrary when I was seventeen years old. I remember that there were people trying and trying to show me the mistakes I was making, not just in action, but also in thought. And I remember that nothing they could say or do would dissuade me. But change was coming, though it would take several years to move me as far as I needed to be moved. And so I remember that such attempts to stop such actions might not succeed in the short term, but there is hope for long-term effects.

3

How Far Is Too Far?

THE CHURCH, ESPECIALLY WHEN I was growing up, has never been particularly adept at talking about dating relationships. Youth ministers and leaders never seem to go beyond "Don't have sex until marriage," leaving everything else to teenagers to try to figure out. They either ignore the subject or take an extreme approach to it, but they certainly don't want people talking about it. I had to deal with all of the struggles in this area on my own; even my friends and I didn't discuss it, and they had no idea what I was doing in most of my relationships most of the time. I'm not sure if discussing my behavior would have changed it, but it would have made me feel less alone, less guilty about what I was doing, but I chose to struggle alone, and the church didn't offer to help.

I had been dating Kristin since well before the Steve Camp concert, though I had somehow not known that she had any interest in Christian music, which is why I was surprised by her presence there. She and I had been friends in middle school, and I began consciously flirting with her, as well as a more-immature-than-usual eighth-grade boy can do anyway, near the end of our eighth-grade year. Nowhere was this behavior more apparent than our class trip to Nashville, where I spent a good deal of time with her and, especially, arranged to sit across the aisle from her on the bus ride back. I was listening to my headphones, but I asked her to take them off of me, if I happened to fall asleep, so my Walkman's batteries would not run down. I knew quite well I would not fall asleep, but I wanted something that would help keep her focus on me.

From time to time, then, I would pretend to fall asleep, only to have her begin to take them off, at which point, I would say something and scare her. Clearly, I was flirting as only a middle school boy could. However, summer came before I had a chance to make any kind of declaration to her, so I had to wait until our freshman year, when we began dating. She was one of the smartest students in our class, and I was near the top, but not as good of a student as she was, so we were in most of the same classes together. Her mother was an English teacher at the school, which made dating awkward, as one might imagine. However, that fact helped me considerably, as English was my worst subject. I would visit Kristin at her grandfather's house, and she and I would sit on his back porch, working our way through *Romeo and Juliet*, which I could barely understand. We would read a passage, and she would ask me what it meant, while I wanted only to find a way to sneak away from her family so that we might behave more like Romeo and Juliet. I was usually more successful at that than I was at interpreting Shakespeare.

Though Kristin and I began dating before my second conversion experience, religion impacted our relationship in clear ways. She was devoted to her church, often playing piano for them, and she seldom missed a service. Her parents were involved there and were clearly devout Christians. That influence was always present when we were planning times we could get together, but it also simply pervaded their household, as religion was omnipresent in a way it was not in ours. Religious language and ideas simply came up in conversation, as her parents would talk about "being blessed" or about praying for someone in ways my family never did. Also, not surprisingly, guilt played a major role in what Kristin and I would and would not do. However, even though she was clearly the more devout of the two of us, I was the one who was haunted by guilt at what we did, physically speaking. For some reason, I was overly concerned with what was acceptable and what was not, even before I began taking religion more seriously, while she was much more willing to experiment.

Given the culture the two of us grew up in, though, sex was definitely out of the question. In the same way that I simply believed matters when I was younger, such as suicide as a direct route to hell, I knew that sex before marriage was wrong, despite the fact that no one had ever taught me anything along those lines. My parents never had any kind of discussion about sex with me, and I was probably too ignorant to even know how to have sex at that point, so I was lucky she and I agreed on the subject. Beyond that, though, there was room for negotiation. The dating books I read later would try to give me clear lines that should not be crossed, but, for some reason, I seemed to already have mine. I had no problem dropping below her neck, but I never wanted to go below her waist, a distinction she often did not share. I spent so much time exploring her breasts she said she thought her mother was getting suspicious of the red places surrounding her nipples, so we had to watch that. Once, she convinced me to slide my hand down her pants, though outside of her panties, and without even unzipping her pants, which was terribly uncomfortable, at least for me. Either because the feeling was not at all what I expected or, more likely, because I felt severe guilt for such a behavior, I did not enjoy it and did not repeat it. She also liked to climb on top of me, straddle me, as if we were having sex. I eventually felt guilty about even this behavior and asked her to stop doing that. She argued that there was nothing at all wrong about it, that we weren't having sex in any way. However, my guilt overcame any argument she could muster to convince me that we were remaining innocent while having an enjoyable time, but the guilt certainly would not allow me to enjoy what we were doing, so there wasn't much of a contest for me.

After the conversion, our relationship seemed to change, but, in reality, not much did. We did start doing more overtly Christian things together, mainly because of her suggestions, not mine. For example, she decided that we should go through a workbook together—not one of those pre-marital Christian counseling workbooks, thankfully—just a basic Bible study. I had done one from Campus Crusade for Christ, so we did more of that one. It was fairly typical, asking us to look up verses and write out what we thought they were saying. Often it would remind us of our priorities in life with the acronym JOY (Jesus, Others, You), or some such technique. While she enjoyed this activity greatly, I did not and tried to get her to spend our time doing something else, pretty much anything else, actually. I've never been a fan of group work, and this study reminded me way too much of such an approach. I prefer to work alone, then come together to discuss ideas, not work together to find answers to fill-in-the-blank questions. Even now, it seems, I was already chafing at the simplistic answers I was finding in the particular Christian path I had chosen. Despite my focus on finding the right way to live, the right answers to the questions I wasn't really even asking, I really wanted to find some freedom within faith.

A simple complicating factor was the fact that I was a sixteen-year-old boy who didn't want to spend his free time sitting around filling out a workbook, especially when with his girlfriend. I wanted to be active, doing something, or finding places to hide from her parents and make out. My conversion had done little to change me, make me more studious and less focused on girls. Nothing really changed in our physical relationship, as I had already curtailed that because of my guilt. What I wanted to do, though, I really wanted to do, so that's where I kept the focus, not on workbooks and Bible study. Oddly enough, she thought I was too extreme, though, as my musical focus was much narrower than hers. She still enjoyed the pop music of our teenage years, listening to Madonna and Tears for Fears, while also enjoying Amy Grant and Michael W. Smith, and she could not understand why I could not find that balance. She believed one could be a devout Christian, spend time filling out Bible study workbooks, and still enjoy secular music, clearly illustrating a balance I could not find.

We did not stay together long, though we did date twice—once for nine months, the second time for six months. I would like to say that we broke up over these disagreements, that I had a good reason for causing her to cry when I said I thought we should break up, but, again, I was a teenage boy. I broke up with her simply because I got tired of dating her. I wasn't interested in any specific other girl, but I knew there were other girls around whom I could date, and they would be different. Almost any man knows this feeling—some of them, unfortunately, never outgrow it—that feeling that there is someone else better around the corner, even if dating before the current relationship had been bad or nonexistent. Men tend to seek this perfect relationship that does not exist, so we leave perfectly good girls and women wondering why we're moving on. We become extremely gifted at creating reasons, picking fights we know will lead to a split, all because we're not enough of a man to simply say that we're just not interested anymore, even though we have no particularly good reason. And note that no theology, no conversion experience I had, ever changed such behavior. Instead, I simply needed maturity, and it was a long time in coming.

That summer, I worked at the church where I had spent my childhood, the last summer I was at the church, actually. We had developed a summer program for children who lived in the housing projects relatively near our building. We would drive over in the morning, pick up the younger children and do a morning program for them; then, in the afternoon, we would go back over to pick up those who were closer to being teenagers and do an afternoon program with them. The morning was spent singing, having Bible stories and lessons, and playing games, such as four square. The children taught me how to do hand-clapping games, showing me a different culture than the very white upbringing I had experienced, while I tried to teach them about the Bible. One of my favorite memories from that time was when I asked a group of children if they knew what it meant to repent. One girl, who had obviously paid attention in school, said, "To pent again." Good for her.

The afternoons were fun in their own way, but they were significantly more challenging for me. I enjoyed playing volleyball or running an obstacle course with the older kids; I probably enjoyed it too much, as I was quite competitive, and I was always trying to win, not necessarily teach them any life lessons. The problem was that I was only a few years older than some of the kids, as I was fifteen, about to turn sixteen the next month. When I was working with eleven- and twelve-year-olds, they already didn't see me as an authority figure, and I did little to change that impression. Teaching them became especially difficult, as the older workers—three young women who were all college age—would leave me alone with them, trusting me to manage the class. The most difficult kid was Charlie, who would challenge my authority at every turn. I tried bringing a squirt gun to class to shoot him every time he acted out, as I had heard that could work, only to see him bring a larger squirt gun the next day, leaving us no choice but to ban them completely. At one point, I became so frustrated, I picked him up, while he was in his chair, and moved him to a different side of the classroom. Given that I was not a large, strong teenager, I'm still not sure what, besides frustration and anger, gave me the strength to move him as I did. I could easily criticize the church and the other workers for putting me, at that age, in that situation, but they honestly believed I was more mature than I was. They had heard me analyze the Bible in church and youth classes, and they were trying to develop my leadership skills by giving me such opportunities. However, they ignored any type of supervision and did not mentor me in any meaningful way. Thus, I made a serious mistake while working there that summer: I began dating Charlie's sister.

I am a bit ashamed to admit I do not remember her name, but I do know that she was twelve, and I was almost a full four years older than she. The age gap bothered a number of people, but never me, as I clearly was not as mature as most sixteen-year-old boys, which is a sad statement by itself. Kristin, my most recent ex-girlfriend, called me that summer to tell me that I could do better. I took this as evidence of her jealousy and desire to start dating again, but it was simple concern over my choice. What was more interesting to me was the class difference between the two of us, as she lived in a housing project that was out of sight of my middle-class neighborhood, but within a five minute walk. She went to a different school and lived a different life than I did, despite being in almost the same geographic area of the city. When I went to visit her one night, I remember being struck at the apartment they lived in, with one smallish living room and a hallway that led to a few bedrooms. It was no larger than most of the townhouses I would later live in as a single person when I was in graduate school or working my first few jobs, yet they had a family of five, the same size as my family when I was growing up.

Also, by dating her, I compromised my position at our summer program, as I began behaving as a friend to the kids she spent time with, even sitting with them during our movie night one weekend. It was that night that finally showed me what a poor decision I was making. She had two friends who were also dating, and we were spending a good deal of time with them that night. Finally, the girl of the other couple suggested that we switch partners for a while, something I had never heard of. Now, when she said switch partners, she was not suggesting some weird sexual behavior, as Charlie's sister and I had done nothing more than kiss, but she was clearly indicating that none of us had any strong attachments to the other, a concept I had never considered in my previous dating relationships. When my girlfriend seemed interested, I decided it was best that things end right there. Needless to say, the rest of the movie night was not enjoyable, and she stopped coming to the program. Thankfully, it was the last week of our time there, and we never saw each other again. I wondered what happened to her and, probably more so, to Charlie, as well as a few of the other kids from that program. The church never did anything like that summer again, and my life never intersected with them once it ended. I never even rode my bike down to the projects to see them, leaving them to their lives, while I went back to mine.

Oddly enough, that relationship may have allowed me to have another one the following month, one that was strikingly similar to the one with Charlie's sister. Betty was not the type of girl I would usually date. She was drastically different from anyone I had dated or anyone I would date. I was set up with her through Brent, one of my friends from our neighborhood, who was dating her best friend. Brent needed someone to go out with Betty to keep his girlfriend happy, so he suggested me. It was not Betty's appearance that sets her apart from other girls I dated, save for the fact that she was probably prettier than the girls I usually dated. She was certainly not the best looking girlfriend I ever had, but she was probably fairly close. No, it was both her socio-economic background and her outlook on the world and religion that were different.

Brent had met his girlfriend while working at the convenience store his father owned, which was located near a different set of housing projects. Given that we lived in a small Southern town, the housing projects were not the negative stereotype portrayed in movies where there are shootings and drug deals on a daily basis. However, the kids who lived there certainly had lives I could not imagine, despite the fact that I had played baseball with several boys who lived not far from Betty. When I was ten and eleven, though, I was not terribly aware of the class difference. Even at sixteen, I was not completely aware of that difference between me and Betty. I ascribed the fact that she often called me and asked me to come pick her up and just drive around town to the fact that I was old enough to drive, and she wasn't, not to the fact that she really just wanted to get out of the house and neighborhood. The fact that my mother's car, an Oldsmobile, was one of the nicest in the neighborhood did not occur to me at the time.

Betty was simply more experienced than I was in pretty much every sense of that word. On one of our early dates, Brent, his girlfriend, Betty, and I went riding in Brent's Suburban. We ended up at a local park, The Laurels, as Brent was not really interested in conversation with his girlfriend. Betty and I left the Suburban and walked around a bit in the dark, never far from the car, given that the area was quite secluded, and we didn't feel completely comfortable wandering into the woods. When she kissed me, I tasted Doritos and cigarettes, a combination that had never really crossed my mind before. Overlooking the fact that she smoked for just a minute, what really surprised me was how she described the kiss later. Brent told me she was disappointed in that first kiss, and, not surprisingly, I wanted to know why. She had expected me to give her a French kiss, to use some tongue, even on a first kiss. I had had plenty of girlfriends throughout middle and high school, so I had kissed a fair number of girls to that point. I do not ever remember giving a French kiss, though I'm sure I knew what one was. If pressed, I could have roughly described it, but I would not have understood why anyone would want to do it. There was also the fact that she smoked. Given my turn to conservative Christianity, it is rather surprising that I would date someone who smoked and, now that I think back on it, probably drank alcohol, as well, though I was not aware of that. My only explanation is the one so many people give when they find themselves dating or even married to someone who participates in something they do not approve of: I didn't like being without a girlfriend, so when the opportunity to date a pretty girl came up, I took it. It certainly shows I was not standing on principles that should have been rather easy to follow at that point in my life.

One could wonder, too, what Betty saw in me. Part of it, I'm sure, was simply my innocence. Throughout middle and high school, girls who were similar to Betty had been at least slightly attracted to me for that very reason. Two in particular come to mind from middle school, as they would easily embarrass me by calling me a teddy bear with braces. Betty and they thought I was harmless and cute, and they were amused by my innocence, nothing more. At one point, Betty, Brent's girlfriend, and I were on the escalator in the mall, and Brent's girlfriend noticed my Gideon's New Testament in my shirt pocket. She asked me about it, and I told her that I carried it so that I could always have God's Word with me, could always refer to it, if I needed to. She thought such a practice was cute, not revolutionary or radical, certainly not earth- or life-changing, just cute. Also, I'm sure Betty saw me as a possible break from the realities of her life. Having spent her life in the projects, Betty was always eager to get out whenever she could. She even went with me to a Christian concert where I tried to get her saved. There was a local coffeehouse owned by a church, located in the basement of that church, called The Melting Pot. They had concerts by local Christian musicians, which was just below the quality of music in any local coffee shop, as Christian music has notoriously been behind the curve on quality and trends, though I would never have described the music this way at the time, as Christian music was great then as long as it was upbeat rock and roll. The Melting Pot offered snacks and drinks, the quality of which was about on par with the music. Since I didn't drink coffee, I would get a Coke and some snack, such as fries or a candy bar.

Betty seemed to enjoy the music, as far as I could tell, but she may simply have been happy not to be at home for a night. The important part for me, though, came near the end of the concert. As with all good Christian concerts, the band took a few minutes to talk about Jesus and the possibility of salvation. It wasn't quite an altar call; they didn't ask for people to come forward and make any kind of commitment. However, they did ask everyone to close their eyes, then gave people the opportunity to raise their hands if they had not been living a Christian life. I was thrilled when I felt Betty's hand raise in the air. I might have even peeked to make sure. I knew that this night would be the turning point in her life, just as it had been in mine. As soon as the concert was over, I told Betty that we were going to go backstage to meet the band so that she could talk to them. I did not ask if she wanted to, did not wonder if she would feel awkward or embarrassed, as I was bent on making sure she followed through on her raised-hand commitment. However, I was disappointed by the lead singer's reaction. He simply said that he was glad that she had raised her hand, nothing more. He did not give her any words to live by, no type of sermon to help her get her life in order, nor did he pray with her. I'm not sure what I was expecting, exactly, but certainly something to help her completely come to Jesus. I could have done something, but I'm not sure I knew what to do. I talked with her about it, told her I was happy that she had raised her hand, but I did not go beyond that. I did not even invite her to church with me, which would have been the most obvious gesture I could have made. In fact, I never invited her to church with me. My guess is that I was embarrassed of who she was, subconsciously knew she would not fit in at a church, and so I never invited her to any events. I simply expected someone else to take care of her salvation, while I worried about my own.

Betty and I didn't last more than the few months of the summer. I don't recall any official breakup; she simply called less and less often, and my visits became more and more infrequent. I was slowly returning back to my world, and she to hers. When school started, she would go back to her friends at the city school, while I would return to the county school, both of us with a few interesting stories to tell. I never saw her again, have no idea what happened to her, though I often drove by her house, even saw her mother from time to time out walking. I never prayed for her, either.

That fall, I began attending Central Church of Christ, thanks to Wayne's insistence that I meet him there to return the Accounting book, and, like many teenage Christians, I took this move as a chance to see if I could find someone there to date. Since my relationship with Betty clearly had not worked out, I thought I would stand a better chance with someone from within the faith, someone who shared my beliefs, though, in all honesty, I simply wanted a girlfriend. Central did not provide me with as many opportunities as I had hoped, as it was a rather small youth group, and many of the girls were younger than I was. The two who were closer to my age—and who were both rather pretty—attended Elizabethton city school, the one that was much better than our county school. I'm not sure if it was that or that they simply weren't interested in the youth group, but they did not show much interest in meeting the new kid. Amy and Misty were probably both well beyond my dating class, but I didn't recognize that at the time. I made an effort to try to talk to them, to get to know them a bit, but they would barely speak to me. It took me several months to learn that they really were not friends with anyone in the youth group. Their parents made them come from time to time, and they were related to several people in the group, so they could mingle with them, but not really as friends, more as cousins who only got together every other year or so at family reunions.

However, there was one other girl who caught my attention. She was three years younger than me, thirteen to my sixteen, which would cause problems, and she was rather quiet and introverted, the opposite of my approach at the time. She and I never really had conversations as much as we had flirtations in the way that teenagers do: we picked on each other almost any time we were around. Whenever we broke out of the model and actually spoke to each other in a civil manner or even did something nice for one another, people in the group noticed it. People spent a good deal of the time watching one of us chase the other one around after some sort of poke or comment. To anyone who paid any attention, it was only a matter of time before we began dating. In the long-honored tradition of teenagers, I called a friend of hers in the group and asked her what she knew about Leeanna's feelings for me. Laura said that she wasn't sure, but she would find out, so she then called

Leeanna, got the truth out of her, then called me back. When I called Leeanna to ask her to "go with me," in the parlance of the times, I was assured of a positive answer.

The problem, however, was that her mother did not think we should be dating at all, that Leeanna was too young or I was too old or that the age group was too wide. She never told me what the problem was, as she never really spoke to me during the first month or two that Leeanna and I were together. She did tell Leeanna about her concerns and even told Leeanna that she and I could not date; however, we simply chose to ignore such a declaration, acting as if her mother did not exist. Since we spent so much time at the church with the youth group, we could be together a good deal without ever going out on our own. We saw each other a few times a week, talked on the phone, and generally carried on a fairly normal relationship until her mother simply stopped trying to fight against what seemed inevitable to us. That did not stop her, though, from putting up obstacles whenever she could. If I were hanging out at the fellowship hall, which she could see from her house, as I often did, Leeanna would try to find an excuse to come up there. Her mother quickly realized what she was up to, so she would at least tell her that she couldn't go anywhere whenever she saw the lights on. In honor of the Arnold Schwarzenegger movie out at the time, we nicknamed her mother "Commando." There was no real connection to the movie; the term simply summed up how we felt about her tactics. She must have heard that we used this term, as one Sunday, she used it herself. After church, Leeanna and I had walked to her house, just across a field from the church, before anyone else had gotten there. Her mother, upon leaving the church, said in the hearing of my friends, "I suppose I have to get home and use my commando tactics." I thought her use was actually fairly humorous, but Leeanna, who had to live with her, failed to see the humor.

As Leeanna was the first girl I dated within the same church after my newfound conversion, I was not quite sure how to behave, both in church and on church outings. On one of our first youth events after she and I started dating, a trip to the local bowling alley, she and I sat in the back of the van and spent the entire time kissing. I had behaved the same way with Kristin, so I didn't perceive a problem. I had been in the youth group for more than six months by then, so we were all comfortable with each other, I thought. The next week, the youth minister, Allan, said that he wanted to talk with us. He told us that our behavior was disruptive, that it could make others uncomfortable, though he didn't mention anyone by name, and that we should cool it, essentially, while at events. As we were demonstrating simply by dating one another, we didn't listen very well to adults who were trying to keep us in line. She and I both also played Bible Bowl, which, while it was made up of members of the youth group, we took to be separate from the youth group activities. When we went on the next Bible Bowl trip, we sat in the back of the van and spent the entire time kissing. We had our defense ready, as we knew that we were in the right, knew that we had found a loophole that we could exploit. Bob, the sponsor of the team, and Allan pulled us off to the side before the end of the trip and quickly closed the loophole. As an adult, I can now see that they handled the situation quite well, taking care of the issue firmly and quickly. As a teenager, I only saw people who were trying to prevent our love from blossoming. We did stop that behavior, though, as we did respect them and their position.

Like most teenagers, though, that did not stop us from trying to find other opportunities for such behaviors. Since my time with Kristin, though, I began to see I needed more guidance in how to behave as a Christian boy who was in a relationship. I turned to several, actually *many*, books on Christian dating and relationships. Though I clearly did not recognize it at the time, I was already on my way toward higher education, as I always seemed to look for answers in books, first, with music, now, with relationships. Sometimes the books' titles did not quite give away that they were Christian, even though I knew they were, as with *Dating: Picking (and Being) a Winner* by Barry St. Clair and Bill Jones, while others were not subtle at all, as with *Dating: Guidelines From the Bible* by Scott Kirby, as if the Bible had a good deal to say about dating, and I had just missed it. These books were not helpful, though, in the two ways I wanted them to be. First, they gave pointless advice, such as when St. Clair and Jones quoted an article that stated, "In the sixteenth century, a gentleman of Renaissance Italy was cautioned against using bad language in mixed company, wearing a toothpick around his neck, scratching himself in immodest places and looking in his handkerchief after blowing his nose as if pearls and rubies had fallen from his brain."[1] I knew better than to scratch myself in public, but I didn't even carry a handkerchief, so what good was that going to do me? I know they

---

1. St. Clair and Jones, *Dating*, 115.

were trying to teach me etiquette and manners, which may actually have worked, as I still open the door for my wife, but that's not what I wanted in such a book. No, what I wanted was guidance on what I could and could not do, physically speaking. As with the youth group/Bible Bowl situation, I was looking for a loophole, of sorts. For someone like me, someone who took the Bible literally, sex was out of the question. We had been told the Bible was clear that sex outside of marriage was wrong, as the "sexual immorality" of verses, such as 1 Corinthians 6:9–10, refers to such behavior. Honestly, my belief in the wrongness of sex before marriage squelched any desire for sex, so I was not looking for someone to tell me that doing so was acceptable, in any way. If I had been, Christian dating books would not have been the place to search, as they were all quite clear on that issue. Kirby's book says simply, "The Bible clearly teaches that it is wrong to 'go all the way.' . . . God's design is that sex is to be *only* for the marriage relationship. . . . Apart from the marriage relationship, however, sex destroys and kills."[2]

However, what I was looking for was a clear definition of what was acceptable before that point, as the Bible is notoriously unclear on this subject. I could look at verses, such as Matthew 5:28, that tells me not to lust in my heart, but I had no idea what that meant. As a teenage boy, I was fairly sure that I spent most of my time lusting, but I didn't know if it was in my heart or not, and I was unsure of whether or not something counted as lust if I simply thought a girl was pretty, but I didn't want to have sex with her. There was also Philippians 4:8 that told me to think on whatever is pure, but I had no idea whether or not my thoughts of kissing a girl were pure or not. It certainly felt pure to me at the time, but my over-riding sense of guilt that continued to nag at me left me unable to discern what was wrong or what I simply created from some odd sense of morality. The dating books, though, were of no help here, as they all effectively made the same points when it came to relationships. I should avoid temptation and not put myself and my girlfriend in a situation that might lead to sex. We should agree on limits ahead of time, which were clearly defined—the books suggested nothing below the neck and nothing above the knee—as that would prevent us from ultimately ending up naked in the back seat of a car, a thought that honestly never occurred to me until I read about it in a book. However, they would also say, as Kirby does, that different people have different limits: "This point

---

2. Kirby, *Dating*, 77.

[when hormones, not judgment, are in control] is different in different people. Some people have serious problems just holding hands. Almost all guys, however, have problems after prolonged kissing."[3] In case there was any doubt, though, on the next page, they say clearly, "Leviticus 20 teaches that uncovering the nakedness of another is sin. Any removal of clothes or caressing under the clothes is wrong."[4] I regularly ignored the below the neck restriction, as I was a teenage boy who was fascinated by girls' breasts. I took every opportunity I could to find out what was so fascinating about them. Once, when I was dating Kristin, we went to see *The Empire Strikes Back*, which we had both already seen. While sitting in the front row, I had my arm around her, and I was able to get my hand down the front of her shirt. I'm sure people around us must have seen what was going on, but no one said anything that we heard.

The problem, though, was that I continued to struggle with the guilt complex that told me I was doing something wrong. I would tell Leeanna that we shouldn't do such things. She would take me at my word and prevent me from trying to get my hand up her shirt the next time we were together, as my commitment was much more wavering than hers. After a week or two, though, she must have missed it as much as I did, so we would begin again until the cycle of guilt came back around, and we would have a week or two of only kissing. What amuses me now is that I would have had no idea really how to have sex at that point in my life. While I had taken my freshman biology class that was supposed to explain how two people had sex, I clearly did not understand how it worked. I remember believing that a man could simply bump into a woman, slide her shorts aside or lift her skirt or some such move, and quickly have sex with her. My parents had not told me; the church was effectively silent on the subject, telling us only not to have sex, if they told us anything at all; and sex education was unimaginable to us then. Any situation I would have put myself in would clearly not have led to sex. There were even two times where I had an experience that almost any teenage boy now would understand, but that confused me completely. Leeanna and I were on her front porch, sitting on the swing, where we often sat to kiss and grope until her mother turned on the light to let us know that it was time for me to go home. It was one of the times where I had my hand up her shirt, and she had her hand down my pants. From my perspective,

3. Ibid., 78.
4. Ibid., 79.

out of nowhere, I had an urge to go to the bathroom and even felt like I went a bit. I cut things short, told her I needed to go upstairs, then found myself unable to go when I was there. It's clear now what happened, but, even after having this experience happen those couple of times, I did not understand what had occurred. Even though she was three years younger, Leeanna clearly understood; she simply thought I didn't want that to happen, so she stopped making it happen. The church's teaching on sex often leads to such ignorance and such guilt, though my case was largely of my own devising, even though the books I read and the talks I did hear certainly did nothing to dissuade me of that guilt. Christian teenagers end up having sex without any kind of protection, end up pregnant because they believe myths they hear about sex, believe they can't get pregnant if they have sex while standing up or because it's their first time, and the church still says nothing beyond telling them not to have sex until they're married. Then, when they are married, they still struggle with the guilt over sex, having been told how bad and evil it is, as if they can somehow flip a switch when they get married that makes it acceptable now. I also have students tell me they can't wait to get married so they can have sex, as if that's the purpose of marriage, and I wonder how long until they are disappointed when marriage and sex both do not live up to all they imagined they could be.

Leeanna and I had other problems, though. Since she was so quiet, we didn't spend much of our time talking. When I would call her on the phone, I would have to ask her questions about her day in such specificity just to force her to talk. I would ask, "What happened in first period? What about second? What did you eat for lunch?" I wanted to know about her life, but she didn't want to tell me. I was far from perfect, as well, and as I had done before, I later broke up with her just because I was tired of dating her and wanted to date someone else. However, we kept trying to get back together, partly because of proximity, I'm sure, but also because we somehow really liked each other, despite the lack of real communication. Over a six-year span, we officially dated somewhere around nineteen times, though it was clearly difficult to keep track, and we had brief flings several more times. Sometimes we were together for a few weeks or a month, but sometimes we would be together for several months. Neither of us could make up our mind. It didn't help that, when we were broken up, one or the other of us would date someone else and, inevitably, bring that person to church. One of us then had to watch the other one holding hands with or kissing the other person, which would drive the other one crazy with jealousy. Such a situation did not help the cohesion of the youth group, but we managed it well enough that it never caused significant rifts. However, at the end of my time in college, when I was engaged to marry someone else, Leeanna actually wanted to talk to me. We couldn't find time to meet in person, so we talked on the phone. She never said I shouldn't get married to someone else or that she wanted to marry me, but she did say she always thought we would end up together. I reminded her of our last fling, a youth group outing at an amusement park where we ended up holding hands and spending the day together. The next day, when I came to church, she didn't sit with me, so I assumed she had no interest in a relationship and moved on to someone else. She told me she didn't want me to presume that everything would be easy, that it would just be one more time with Leeanna. And so we missed that last opportunity. Much later, after I was divorced, she told me she had been crying during that conversation, but I didn't notice. I was too wrapped up in my own happiness to hear her pain.

When I wasn't dating Leeanna, one of the only other significant high school relationships was with Angela. Our relationship did not last more than six months, but, given that I had several relationships with girls that lasted less than a week or two, this one qualifies as important, and it was yet another example of my naïveté when it came to physical relationships. Angela was actually very similar to Leeanna, in that both were introverted and quiet. If I had trouble getting Leeanna to talk, I had even more problems with Angela. The only reason we ended up together was a school trip I took with the Tennessee Office Education Club. Since Wayne and I were so interested in Accounting, we had ended up in this club, where we were two of very few boys; on the trip, we were the only two boys, a situation neither of us complained about. Somehow, on the final night there, at a dance, Wayne, who never spoke to girls, ended up dancing with a girl from another school who came over and asked him to join her. I spent the evening wandering around with Angela and a few other friends. She also sat in front of me on the bus ride home, so I spent a good deal of time talking to her then. The only other thing we really had in common was church, though we attended different places. She was rather involved in church and seemed to really enjoy the church she attended. She was the only girlfriend who ever enthusiastically invited me to come to church with her, which I did once. I really didn't want to skip a service at Central, as I enjoyed it greatly, but I wanted to spend the time with her, so I went, which seemed to make her happy.

As with my other girlfriends, our church attendance didn't really have much impact on the physical side of the relationship. The only real difference is that I never talked with her about the guilt that I felt, as she and I never had any conversation that meaningful. Instead, we sat on the couch of her living room, talking very little, until I could find an opportunity to get my hand up her shirt. Somehow we had enough freedom in her house, where her parents often were, that there were a few evenings where she ended up with her shirt and bra completely off. I have no idea how we were able to get to that state of undress, but I remember those evenings distinctly, as I had never really had that clear of a view of a naked girl before. However, Angela never reciprocated and did anything to (or for) me, which always frustrated me. Since we never discussed much of anything, I didn't know if she had a problem with doing anything to me, as that would have been too close to sex, or if she simply never thought about it, as I was her first substantial relationship. I wasn't even sure she enjoyed what we were doing, though her continued participation made me think she did. In the end, I should have at least guessed that it was something due to hesitancy about sex. There were several times where we would begin to get more involved than others, often those nights where she ended up more naked than others, when she would abruptly stop what we were doing. She never said anything was wrong, even when I asked, but there was always some sort of line I was not aware of that we could not cross.

What further complicated this problem was the fact that I absolutely loved her legs. I had never dated anyone whom I thought had great legs, but she did, and I was fascinated with them. I would tell her so on a regular basis, and I would often spend time trying to feel her legs. She was clearly uncomfortable by my attentions, but I could never understand why. I certainly wasn't talking about a clearly sexual part of her body, nor was I doing anything remotely related to sex. Later, though, I realized that when I talked about her legs, I was mainly talking about her thighs, and I would slide my hand up them, ending up rather close to the hem of her shorts, which were rather short, as it was the 1980s. I'm sure she thought I was using her legs as an excuse to get into her shorts, though I never tried to do so. Since we could not talk about the issue, though, we were never able to clarify where we stood on such matters, leaving us both guessing about the other's motivations. That lack of communication would continue to be a problem in relationships, and I've often wondered if there is a connection between this breakdown and my and the girls' faith. I do not know if we did not talk about the issue because they were simply quiet and shy or because Christians did not talk about such matters.

I did have one relationship where we actually did talk a good deal, not only about the physical aspect of our relationship, which was virtually non-existent, actually, but also about theology itself. I dated Tempa during my sophomore year of college and her senior year of high school. She was even more innocent than I was, and she was determined to keep it that way. The only physical contact we had was holding hands, hugging, and kissing. When I kissed her for the first time, she said simply, "Sweet sixteen, no more." I had no idea she had never kissed anyone, and her comment made me feel as if I had taken her virginity. I'm quite glad our relationship never progressed past that point, physically speaking. I would have felt even guiltier than I normally did after she and I broke up, as I would have encouraged her to go well beyond what she felt comfortable doing. When we talked about the physical aspect of the relationship, she was so naïve she didn't even understand why I might want to do more than just kiss. However, since the relationship's focus was not on the physical aspect, we were actually able to have conversations about a whole host of other subjects, taking on theological issues I could not have imagined discussing with my previous girlfriends. Part of the change was my growing maturity, but most of the credit belongs to Tempa. One night, we were discussing the role of women in the church, as we both were members of churches that did not allow women to be elders, deacons, or ministers. I had been reading some writing that questioned that, though, so I brought the subject up. After we had talked about it for a while, Tempa suggested we talk to her parents. Now, while this behavior does show her level of maturity and a healthy relationship with her parents, it also makes sense, as her father was a seminary professor. Oddly enough, he was for women in leadership, while Tempa's mother was against it, a pattern I've seen rather often in Evangelical churches.

However, my relationship with Tempa was not the norm when it came to either physical involvement or communication. A relationship I had had just a year before exemplifies both problems all too well.

During my senior year of high school, I was at a church lock-in at another church. Our church had joined with them to have a joint lock-in, but only a handful of people from my youth group attended. I ended up getting to know some other people there, one of whom was a young woman named Harriet (I realize at this point, that I dated two women with rather old-fashioned names, something that had never occurred to me before). I liked Harriet immediately, so I began flirting with her in that immature way I always used. At the bonfire, I threw marshmallows in her direction, pretending that it was someone else, for example. Oddly enough, such behavior worked, and she seemed to show an interest in me, as well. Later that evening, I went to sneak up on her and scare her when she was in a room where someone was playing guitar. She came to the small, maybe two-feet by two-feet, window to look out, and I went to hit the window to scare her. The window actually broke, sending glass flying into her face and onto my hand. Luckily, the only injuries were to both of our hands, though, as one might imagine, I felt awful, not only for breaking the window in her face, but also for breaking the window, in general. I often tell my college students now that, if they want advice on how to meet women, they should talk to me, as I know ways to get their attention. I spent a good deal of time after that alone, as I felt quite guilty about what I had done, and no one really came to support me and tell me I had simply made a stupid mistake. However, Harriet and I ended up sitting on a set of steps outside of the church later, along with a couple of people she knew. We had a great time talking, so I gave her a call after the lock-in was over. Her mother, though, would not allow her to date, so I went on with my life and ended up dating Angela later that year. The next year, though, she and I saw each other again at a Christian concert, and we got back in touch with each other and were finally able to begin dating.

We could not have dated much longer than a month, perhaps two, if that, before I had to break things off. It wasn't that the relationship was not enjoyable, as it was, but the problem was that it was too enjoyable. Harriet and I could not keep our hands off of each other, doing as much as I had done with any girl all the time. Once, we were at a local state park, Bays Mountain, walking through some trails. When we would get over a hill or around a curve where no one could really see us, we would start at it, and I had my hand up her shirt in a hurry, breaking it off only when we heard someone behind us coming over the hill or around the curve. After a play at Milligan, where I was now going to college, we started kissing before we got into the car, and things became fairly hot fairly quickly, so we got into the car, drove to a more secluded part of campus, and kept things going. As with Angela, Harriet pulled off her shirt, giving me more of a view than I was used to getting. One day, though, she really worried me with a comment she made. We were at my church's fellowship hall, as I had a key and could get in at any time. We were on a couch in the youth room, and, as always, we were enthusiastically going at it, and she paused and said, "If sex weren't wrong, I would love to have it with you." I overreacted, giving her a self-righteous reaction about how she should not even say such things. I cannot believe that my reaction was based on any kind of theological reasoning, as she was clearly still within an orthodox view of sex; she was simply stating what her emotions and hormones were clearly conveying. The truth was that I was scared, as Harriet clearly had interests that went beyond what I was used to when it came to girls. Also, she voiced them, while everyone else I had dated remained quiet. She was a girl who was clearly interested in the physical side of our relationship in a way I had never seen before, and she made me nervous. While I used Christianity to defend my fear, I certainly did not allow it to keep me from what I wanted in a physical relationship, the epitome of hypocrisy.

We did not break up that day, as my self-righteousness passed, and we seemed to go back to normal. However, not long after that, in a phone call I made while on break from work at Kroger, I began to end things. I simply hinted that we should see other people, and it went downhill from there. She wanted to talk about matters, and I went to visit her, so we could, but it was clear we were finished. For the first time, though, a girl I dated wanted to talk about what was happening, but I was already through with the relationship, running away because I was scared of what was going on, what was clearly out of my control. I later tried to get back together with her, talked to her a couple of times, but she made it clear I was going to have to work to do so, and, being who I was, I passed on that opportunity.

It is easy for me to blame the church for their lack of education and information when it came to sex, as it is clear none of the congregations or organizations I was in when I was a teenager helped me make sense of the physical feelings I was dealing with. The books I read were little help, as well, giving me out-of-date information and not admitting the realities of the situation I was struggling with. However, I know a good deal of the blame lies with me, as I simply wanted what I could get out of each relationship without being aware of what the girl might want or need. In this way, I am sure I was little different than most teenage boys, many of whom use girls in ways much worse than I did; however, that does little to comfort me now. My guilt was often focused on what I was doing wrong as far as crossing physical lines in those relationships when it should have shown me what I was doing wrong in how I treated the girls, leaving them whenever I grew bored, using faith only when it was convenient.

4

Answers to Questions That Didn't Matter

When Wayne invited me to visit the youth group to return the Accounting book for school, I felt like I fit in almost immediately. It helped that I knew a few people there, even if loosely, but, mainly, I just felt welcomed. I convinced my parents to let me begin attending there, despite the fact that I would have to borrow one of their cars to get there, as it would be another six months before I found a job and was able to get one of my own. At the beginning, I could not quite make it to every event, but I went to everything I could. However, there was one way in which I did not fit, though I certainly was not aware of it for the first few months. One night, at a lock-in, I was talking to Allan, the youth minister, and he asked me if I had been baptized. I had, I assured him, as Presbyterians practice infant baptism, and my parents had often told me I had received such a baptism. In my mind, that should have ended the discussion, but Allan was clearly not happy.

It seems that Central was part of a denomination (though they would probably prefer to call it a movement, given the history of the group of churches) they referred to as the Christian Churches/Churches of Christ, but which most people who write about or discuss the denomination call the Independent Christian Church. Either name is meant to distinguish them from the Church of Christ, a group that takes the New Testament as their guide so literally that they do not have instruments in worship, some of them do not practice Christmas as a religious holiday, and some of them will not have dinners on church grounds, all based on what is literally in or not in the New Testament. The Independent

Christian Church is similar in many ways, in that they, too, claim to be following the New Testament literally, calling themselves followers of the apostolic tradition. While they disagree over the above issues, they also do not have women in leadership, do not answer to any higher denominational structure, and, importantly for me, practice adult baptism by immersion. By *adult*, they really mean that the person should be of an age to make such an important life decision. There is no particular cut off, as some of my friends were baptized before they were twelve, the age of accountability from Catholicism, but some of the others waited (or their parents forced them to wait) until they were teenagers. The other key is immersion, as they point out that in Mark 1:9–10, among other gospel accounts, Jesus came "*up out* of the water," which clearly implies he had to be completely immersed in it, ignoring the fact that this passage probably refers to Jesus' coming out of the river onto dry land. There are also some scholars within the denomination who argue that the Greek word for baptism, which is simply *baptizo*, literally means immersion, as it comes from the word used when talking about dyeing a garment or drawing water by dipping one vessel into another. I did not qualify on either of these important points.

Allan took the time to point this distinction out to me, taking me verse by verse through passages in the gospels and the book of Acts (especially the book of Acts, as that's the best description of the church, or, the apostolic tradition) to show me why I needed to be baptized to be saved. Such an approach led to some odd discussions during my time in the denomination, by the way. We often set up hypothetical examples where someone would accept Jesus as their savior, but then get hit by a dump truck walking across the street to the church to get baptized, leaving open the question of whether or not that person would go to heaven. When I was attending a college within the denomination, our church history professor once hinted in a talk that one *might not* have to be baptized to be saved, and we talked about it for weeks, parsing his words for whatever hidden meaning might be there. Allan was doing exactly as he had been taught to do. Despite my recent rededication, and my clear devotion to the faith, there was something missing in my life, and he took close to an hour to make sure I knew what I needed and why I needed it. I remember being a bit surprised at his fervor over the subject, but it clearly had an effect on me, as I did decide to get baptized, or rebaptized, depending on who I asked. And the two people I most needed to ask were my parents, as I was only sixteen, and I felt I needed their permission to do so.

After a few days of preparation that I needed both to make sure I could answer any questions they had and to muster up the courage, I planned to talk to them. For some reason, I chose the time right before they went to bed, going into their bedroom where they were both reading. I often chose this time for such conversations, but I don't know why. The only explanation that makes any sense to me is that, if they said no to something, I wouldn't have to face them until at least the next day. Regardless, I went into their room and asked them if I could be baptized. Their answer was simple: I had already been baptized, and I didn't need another one. Since we did not discuss theology, I didn't take that approach with them, despite my preparation. I didn't take any approach with them; I simply said okay, then left. After all, I was the good kid who did what he was supposed to do. If my parents said I couldn't be baptized (again), I was not going to argue with them, try to win them to my side through either theology or sheer force of emotion. That discussion took place on a Saturday night, and I went to church the next morning and did not get baptized.

However, the following Sunday morning, I did, without their knowledge. Being the good son, I saw that as my only option, as I would not openly defy them or argue with them, but I would do something behind their back, though even that was rare. I was worried they would find out, even having to hide a card that a couple in the church mailed to me congratulating me on my baptism, putting it in the back of the top shelf of my bedroom closet. Knowing my parents as I now do, I have a feeling they knew I would get baptized and they know that I did; I sensed it even then. To their credit, though, they never brought the subject up, even in indirect ways, nor did they question me about it. They were never particularly happy with my newfound devotion to religion, but they let me pursue it in my own way.

Now newly saved, I felt completely at home as a member of the church and the youth group. Oddly enough, though, a new theological issue would become a problem, but this one would come from one of the other members of the youth group, and I would simply get dragged along with him. Chad was one of the most active members of the youth group and the son of one of our more active elders. He was one of the people I was at least familiar with when I began attending the youth group, as I had met him at a birthday party for Kenneth a few years before. My first summer in church there, we became good friends, as we spent most days in his basement trying to lift weights with another friend of his, also named Chad, or at the mall wasting quarters in the mall arcade, the Gold Mine, playing Joust. Sometime during my junior year, he became interested in the spiritual gift of speaking in tongues, which I had never really heard of. He described it to me, but I didn't have a good deal of interest. Since most people don't often deal with this issue, let me give just a bit of background. Almost every Christian knows about the day of Pentecost when the disciples were in Jerusalem after Jesus had ascended to heaven, but they did not know what to do next, as they are often described as afraid, fearing for their lives now that Jesus has been killed. However, a wind blew through where they were staying, tongues of fire rested on their heads, and they were able to speak in languages so that everyone visiting there could hear the gospel of Jesus Christ in their native tongue.[1] Later, in a few letters, mainly 1 Corinthians, Paul discusses speaking in tongues as a spiritual gift, clearly laying out some ground rules for how it should or should not be used in worship, leading to one of the major disagreements about tongues, as it's called. Paul says that there must be an interpreter so the speaker is speaking to the edification of the congregation, not just to himself, as he says in 1 Corinthians 14:27–28: "If anyone speaks in a tongue, two—or at the most three—should speak, one at a time, and someone must interpret. If there is no interpreter, the speaker should keep quiet in the church and speak to himself and to God." However, some other people read verses, such as Romans 8:26, where Paul writes, "In the same way, the Spirit helps us in our weakness. We do not know what we ought to pray for, but the Spirit himself intercedes for us through wordless groans," and say that tongues can be used for individuals. Paul also mentions at the beginning of his most famous chapter, 1 Corinthians 13, the "love chapter," that tongues is nothing without love, and he also says in 1 Corinthians 14 that there are several other spiritual gifts, including prophecy and love, that are more important than speaking in tongues. The debate in the Pentecostal church centers around whether or not one must speak in tongues as evidence that the person has received the Holy Spirit or if there are other ways to receive that gift from God. Outside of the Pentecostal denomination, though, people argue about whether

1. Acts 2.

or not tongues happen at all anymore. Many denominations believe that tongues ceased after the time of the apostles, arguing that they are not needed anymore, that they were simply a phenomenon of the early church, as they needed them to spread the gospel to a diverse world when they were uneducated. Some people would even argue that simply learning a language these days serves the same purpose and is still a gift from God, though they have clearly separated out any connection to the Holy Spirit or the miraculous.

I was quite satisfied with the development of my spiritual life, but Chad was not; he clearly felt he was missing something. He asked me to take him to a Christian concert at East Tennessee State (the Culp Center, again, as it continued to play a role in my development, it seems), as a band I enjoyed would be playing. The band's name was an attempt to be a clever pun, as they were Bash-n-the-Code (or, Bashing the Code, using "the Code" as a synonym for "the law," perhaps, or maybe simply the normalcy of the world; I'm not really sure). It turns out that Chad was not that interested in the band, though he enjoyed them well enough. Instead, he wanted to meet with several members of another church, Abundant Living Christian Fellowship, after the concert so he could begin speaking in tongues. In today's society, we hear about Pentecostals and non-denominational churches on a regular basis. When I was seventeen, I had never heard of either, though I had certainly run across the slang term "holy rollers," but I had no idea what types of behavior that term referred to. With Pentecostals running for political office or broadcasting their services on television these days, and especially with the influence that style of worship is having throughout the Evangelical community, they are one of the fastest growing denominations, and no one is worried about them, as they used to be. However, people still do not talk about speaking in tongues on a regular basis, though most other Christian denominations do not view them with the same fear and skepticism of the past.

When we went into a hallway, then, I had no idea what to expect. One of the leaders asked me if I wanted to participate, but I told him I wasn't particularly interested, mainly because I didn't know what it entailed. He pulled out a Bible and began showing me verse after verse, explaining why God would give me the Holy Spirit, why I should want the Holy Spirit, and what speaking in tongues would look like. I probably knew all of these before he started talking, as we were studying Acts and

1 Corinthians in Bible Bowl (more about this later) that year, but I could not have laid it all out as he did; I had no real answer for why I should not take this opportunity. When Chad began speaking in tongues, they moved on to me, and put me under a bit of pressure to participate, as well. I certainly should not have done so without any advance preparation, but, in the midst of everything, I decided to jump right in. I had much more trouble than Chad, as he just went with it. He had been waiting for this moment for weeks, so he had begun speaking almost as soon as they laid their hands on him. For me, it took several people praying and speaking in tongues around me, laying their hands on me. The man who had taken me through the biblical background stood beside me and coached me, told me to say the word "hallelujah" over and over again until something came. Finally, after what felt like at least fifteen minutes, but probably was not that long, something came out of me, and it was not a language I could have identified then or now. This description leads to another debate on this issue. Some people argue, drawing on the story from Acts, that the language must be a human language, that the purpose it serves is to allow one to communicate with others. However, others argue that the language may very well sound like nonsense, but it is a prayer language, serving as a special conduit between the speaker and God. I certainly fell in the latter category, as there was no interpretation, just the group of us all speaking in our own tongues.

Chad went home thrilled, and I went home confused. While Chad talked about going into the woods, speaking in tongues, and being "slain in the spirit," another term he had to describe to me, as it was when the spirit so overwhelmed him that he would collapse in religious ecstasy, I simply kept trying to use the newfound tongues at home. I eventually became convinced that this approach was useful, so the word spread through a small group of us, as several leaders of our high school prayer club also practiced the gift of tongues. One night, we had a meeting of the prayer club at our church's fellowship hall, and it led to someone else wanting the gift of tongues. Brian was a year younger than me, a big guy at around 6'4" and 250 pounds, who, not surprisingly, played football, but, surprisingly, not very well. He had become more and more interested in the prayer club as he was growing up, and he had been asking about tongues, having heard us talk about it. That night, he was down on all fours in the floor of our youth room, while several of us knelt around him, laid our hands on him, and prayed for him to receive the gift of tongues, often using our spiritual tongues in our prayers. We were doing all of this praying and laying on of hands with the door shut, while others who were not interested stayed in the main part of the fellowship hall on their own. However, one person was in the room who was not interested in participating, but interested in watching. Gordon was skeptical of the gift of tongues, so he wanted to see what took place. Even after Brian began speaking in tongues, which he did as easily as Chad, Gordon kept talking to people about it, questioning them, and it was clear he did not approve. I was at the fellowship hall the next day, and I saw Gordon's car drive down toward Wayne's house, which surprised me. They were not close friends, but I did not think much else of it.

After church the following Sunday, the elders said that they wanted to talk to a few of us in the youth room. They brought me and Chad in to meet with all of the elders. They told us they knew about what had happened in the youth room, so I knew immediately where Gordon had been going that Saturday, as Wayne's father was one of the leading elders. I was not overly fond of Gordon at that minute. However, I was impressed with the elders, as they handled that meeting with a care and tact that is not often found in any organization, even churches. They began by telling us that they loved us, that they would love us, no matter what we did, even if they disagreed with it. They said that they were not telling us not to practice speaking in tongues, that they would never tell us what we could and could not do. However, they did state that they disagreed with it, and they asked us not to practice it on church property. I thought that a fair request even then. After they talked to us, they hugged us and prayed with us and for us, not with any passive-aggressive comments about our getting on the right path, just an honest prayer for our spiritual growth. It was one of the most moving moments in my Christian development, as it showed me people acting out of pure love, even while they were in disagreement with what we had done. Needless to say, I did not show the same type of love to Gordon, as I accused him of ratting us out, but he argued that the elders needed to know what went on at the church. He was right, but, at the time, I was too young to see that. It didn't affect our friendship, and we went on as normal. Chad was not as pleased with the situation, and he actually left the church the next year, leaving the faith, as well. I never learned all of the details, as he and I seldom saw each other, but he proclaimed that he was an atheist, and I'm fairly certain he does not attend church even now. My life simply went back to what it was before, leaving tongues behind, as I had never had much of an interest. At least, though, I had seen that Paul was right, that speaking in the tongues of men and of angels means nothing if one does not have love.

What most people would not expect, though, is that those are the only two theological incidents I can recall from my teenage years at Central. I cannot remember a single lesson from all of the youth group meetings we had, though I'm sure I found them meaningful at the time. I can remember times I taught the youth group when I was in college or even discussions we had in the college group once we started that; however, no youth group class times come to mind. I'm also sure we had theological discussions among ourselves, friends from the youth group at each other's houses or in the youth room, arguing about some important doctrine, but I also cannot recall any of those. The idea that Christian teenagers sit around discussing abortion, same-sex marriage, or the role of the Holy Spirit certainly does not apply to our group, nor to most others, I would guess, as we, like most Christian teens, were mostly interested in hanging out with each other and enjoying our time in high school.

What I can remember, then, are moments and events where that was the focus, spending all night at church at a lock-in, going on a trip to Gatlinburg for a teen convention, or simply an outing to Dairy Queen after a youth meeting, what we called an afterglow (we had no idea of the sexual connotation). One summer, when the youth were helping with the Vacation Bible School program, we would go to Milligan, the local Christian college, after we were finished with our work and play volleyball on the sand volleyball court they had there. We almost installed one at our church, shifting instead to making our own portable poles that we could use. We only used them once or twice, as the moment had passed; it was the trip to Milligan that somehow made it special, and we could not recreate that at the church. At one of our lock-ins, Sherri and Sheila—twins who had recently moved to our church, as their father was a missionary who had been working in Thailand, but who had come back to the U.S. to work on a seminary degree—began a magic marker fight with me. We chased each other around, simply marking on each other. It was a silly game, if it was even a game, but it has stayed with me long beyond any Bible study we all participated in. We played sardines, where one person hides and everyone else tries to find him or her, the reverse of hide-and-go-seek. When one finds the person hiding, instead of telling others, the discoverer is supposed to hide with the person, leading to eight people in a closet or under a table or, as in one case, in a baptistery, thus the name of the game.

    The teen conventions were probably the most enjoyable, however, as it gave us all a chance to get out of town without any real parental supervision and simply be teenagers. We would walk around Gatlinburg, visiting the tourist traps, spending money we had worked hard for. We went to Ripley's Believe It or Not, which I referred to as "Believe It or Not, You Just Got Ripped Off," clearly stating my opinion on our time there, as well as a house that sort of pretended to be haunted, but was designed with cheap scares, such as a balcony with a hinge, moving just enough to make us think it was collapsing. What was most enjoyable was the fun we created on our own. For some reason, on one such trip, I decided to see how many twelve-ounce cans of Coke I could drink in one day. From Johnson City to Gatlinburg, an hour and a half trip, I drank a six-pack, and I ultimately put away twenty-four in an eighteen-hour period. Whenever I tell this story to people, I add that I had my gall bladder removed when I was only thirty-one, which makes some sense. My caffeine intake might also explain what happened in our hotel room that evening. Somehow, everyone ended up in my hotel room, and, somehow, a wrestling match broke out involving everyone in the youth group, roughly twenty teenagers. If one can imagine a teenage version of a free-for-all in the WWE, that might give a picture of us that evening. What is amazing is that nothing was broken and no one was injured. The worst injury happened when I tried to jump on a bed, using it as a spring to jump on someone else, and my head hit the ceiling. We took people and threw them from one bed to the other. The twins, who were relentless, would run at my stomach with their heads, while I would catch them and throw them behind me on a bed, only to turn around to see another one running at me. Our youth minister, Scott, was new, so he was not involved, as he sat in a side chair watching the melee. I thought it would be nice to involve him in the activity, though, so I put ice down his back. I should point out that Scott was not small. He was not fat at all, and he was probably no taller than me, around 5'8", but he was strong. I had never seen biceps as large as his, and, yet, that did not prevent me from including him in a wrestling match with teenagers. He threw me on the bed with one arm, jumped on top of me, then began pulling other kids on top of him, leading to a pile up of close to ten people. I was on the bed, so I wasn't hurt at all, and we all laughed about it the next day. Essentially, we were teenagers without any drugs, alcohol, or sex, and we didn't miss those things. We could not imagine having more fun than we were already having, even if our afternoons or evenings were spent at a fast food place, out at the only Christian bookstore in town, seeing a movie, or simply sitting at the fellowship hall, talking. Our faith was always present, in the music we listened to and in the conversations we had, but it was not an oppressive one, despite all the restrictions we allowed it to place on us (or, more accurately, that we placed on ourselves).

The one activity that influenced my life at that time more than any other, though, was probably Bible Bowl. When I first joined the youth group, Wayne simply told me to stay after our Wednesday night meeting and play Bible Bowl. He did not explain what it was, and, like almost everyone, I had never even heard of it. While it clearly sounds like some conglomeration of Bible study and bowling, it is actually an adaptation of high school quiz bowls. I can still remember the word that effectively ended my Bible Bowl career: *wrap*. I can no longer remember the question, but it essentially asked for the two times that the word is used in the book of Acts. I am still able to give the answer to the question, though I missed it then, was too late buzzing in, actually. In chapter five, the body of Ananias is wrapped up and carried out by men after he has been struck down for lying to Peter. Then, in chapter twelve, Peter is in jail when an angel appears to him, tells him to wrap his cloak around him, then follow the angel to safety. I do not think I will ever forget these two incidents. This question was not the last one I had a chance to answer, though, as the loss in this game only knocked us into the losers' bracket. In that game, we were fairly well defeated, ending my two years of Bible Bowl in the first two rounds of the national tournament, definitely not the way we had expected to end our years of playing.

Most people, even within the Evangelical subculture, have never heard of Bible Bowl. Each denomination has their own version of competition when it comes to the Bible, but none are really this complex. Baptists, for example, tell me about sword drills, where one has the Bible by his or her side until a verse is called. The person must then open the Bible and find that verse as quickly as possible. The point is to encourage children and teenagers to know the Bible so well that they can find verses before anyone else. In Bible Bowl, however, much more is demanded of participants. Each year, a particular book or books of the Bible are chosen for the text. In the two years I played, we studied Exodus one year and Acts and 1 Corinthians the second year, about forty chapters each year. There are local tournaments that teams participate in, usually meeting once a month. Each month, more of the book is covered, so the first meet may cover chapters one to seven, the second, eight to fourteen, and so forth. By February or March, tournaments cover the entire text. By this time, regional tournaments have begun, almost always hosted by colleges and universities within the Christian Church/Churches of Christ, the denomination that sponsors Bible Bowl. The colleges use these tournaments to recruit potential students, as the prizes often involve scholarships to the schools. Then, in July, everything culminates with the national tournament, which rotates from city to city and is always a part of the North American Christian Convention, a time for leaders from the denomination to come together to hear speakers, worship, share ideas, see product exhibitions, take in workshops, and have Bible studies together. It is not quite a revival in the Pentecostal sense of that word, but it was a type of combination of a business meeting, expo, and revival, as best the non-Pentecostal denominations can do.

The game is similar to academic bowl games that go by various names, including Scholar's Bowl, Quiz Bowl, or simply Academic Bowl. There are fifteen toss-up questions that are open to either team; players answer by buzzing in. They can interrupt the question at any time and attempt to answer, but they cannot give any information that goes beyond what is in the question; otherwise, they can be accused of fishing and the opposing team can contest their answer. Toss-up questions can be better guessed by studying lists of once- and twice-used words in the text. In my example above, *wrap* would show up as a once-used word, while *wrapped* would show up there, as well. The better players would have such lists memorized, making the competition more about who could buzz in faster than the other. If a member of a team answers a toss-up correctly, the team receives a bonus question, ranging from twenty to forty points. On these questions, they can confer together, then relate their answer through a captain. Bonus questions almost always come from lists in the text. The ten commandments in Exodus was certainly a good bonus question, but, the farther one progresses in tournaments, the more challenging they become. For example, one might be asked to name the six proper names that begin with J in a particular text or portion of a text. There is also a fifteen-minute time limit to each game. At the end of the questions or time, the team with the most points win. If there is a tie, there is a bonus toss-up to decide the winner. In some tournaments, especially the national tournament, games consist of twenty questions and have a twenty-minute time limit, with a halftime after ten minutes.

Note that there are only two real skills required to succeed in Bible Bowl. The one that people seldom think of has to do with reflexes and quick thinking. As with *Jeopardy!*™, there are people who win who do not know the most about a subject, but who are gifted at beating other people to the buzzer. Such a skill does not convey any sense of intelligence or depth of knowledge, but simply a quick ear-to-hand coordination. The other skill similarly does not imply any intelligence or creativity, as it simply involves memorizing vast quantities of information in a way that it can be easily recalled. The best players in Bible Bowl are those who can, first, memorize the entire text for that year's competition. If one were to ask what Exodus 20:15 says, they could respond with, "You shall not steal." If one were to try to trick them, as I once did with a player named Phil, and ask about 20:27, they could respond that no such verse exists, as there are only twenty-six verses in chapter 20. However, the great players go beyond simply knowing the text in such a comprehensive fashion. Instead, they move on to other ways of viewing the text, such as computer-generated lists that separate out phrases and verses based on certain criteria like once- and twice-used words. For an additional fee, teams could order lists from the Bible Bowl office. If I would have taken the time to memorize such lists, I would have known that *wrap* or *wrapped* was only used twice in the book of Acts. Then, as soon as I heard the word, I would have known that the question focused on that word, buzzed in, and quoted those two passages. Instead, because I only knew the text, I was beaten to the buzzer. I knew the answer to the question, but I did not have the narrow knowledge required to answer it quicker than the opposing team. We would often create such lists on our own. If, in our studying, we noticed that there were few names that began with G, we would start a list in the margin and try to compile as many of them as we could. We noted any reasonably important phrase (and by "reasonably important," I mean in the context of the game, not in the context of actual Bible study) that was alliterative, as those were always popular questions. They might ask about rhyming words or words with no vowels (*myrrh*, for example) or other rare occurrences in the text. To illustrate such a question and the difference between the great players and the merely good, which is what I was, I'll relate a question from a game early on during my career in the game.

We were playing First Christian, Johnson City, the best team in our league and one of the top teams in the nation. We were a solid team, so we could always give them a good game, but we usually lost to them, as they often went undefeated at our meets. Since I was still quite new, I thought I was better than I was, which often led me to buzz in to answer questions too early, often leading to trouble. This time, the question was asking about rhyming words, but I buzzed in after only hearing a clue about the first word, which was *ring*. I stumbled about, thinking of any word that rhymed with it, and guessed *sing*, which turned out to be correct. Our best player, Gordon, was impressed by my getting the question right, especially in such a close game with First Christian. Afterwards, he was talking to Phil, their best player and one of the best players in the country, and Gordon was praising my ability because of that performance. Phil, who clearly knew the text better than either of us, simply responded, "What other word was there?" He knew that *sing* was the only other word in the text that rhymed with *ring*; I had simply beaten him to the buzzer.

It's clear, then, that the focus of Bible Bowl is memorization, not any kind of interpretation or understanding, which was reflected in the way we studied. We never debated what one of the ten commandments might mean in our world, how the use of the word *kill* might be different than *murder*, for example, or what that commandment might mean to someone from a military family. We did not discuss the spiritual gift of speaking in tongues that Paul wrote about in 1 Corinthians, about whether such gifts were still in existence today, about why our denomination did not believe they weren't and why, in fact, our denomination seemed afraid of such phenomena. Instead, our job was to memorize the parts of the Bible for that year, then spit them out more quickly than anyone else could do. Such a focus easily leads to a reinforcement of a literal interpretation of the Bible, as the model we were following did not invite discussion, but regurgitation. Such an approach lends itself to creating young Christians who know the Bible so well they can use (and misuse) it in all kinds of discussions, quoting chapter and verse in arguments about any political or social issue, but without knowing any kind of historical, theological, or sociological context. We could become automatons who, like a baby doll, could repeat the same phrases over and over, could repeat the verses we had ingrained inside ourselves, but could not understand them. We did not see the conflicts between various passages of scripture, nor were we encouraged to do so by anyone in the game and certainly not by the rewards of the game. Success went to those who did not think, but to those who responded without thought, who reacted by instinct and retrieved what they had crammed into their heads over the course of a year.

Lest it sound as if I do not appreciate my time in Bible Bowl, let me quickly say that it had several benefits for my life. The main one, especially for someone who now lives in the mainline world, is that I actually know the Bible quite well, as I augmented my time in Bible Bowl with reading of the other parts of the Bible. When I am in Sunday school discussions now, I am appalled at how little mainline Christians know of the Bible. They seem the mirror image of the Evangelicals who only know enough verses to argue for or against a few particular positions on certain issues, as the mainline Christians know the verses that bother them and that they want to do away with. However, even this trend seems to be changing for the worse, as my Evangelical students often admit that they have never even read the entire Bible (usually five out of twenty-five or so in a class have done so), the book that they claim is the center of their lives, that is the inspired (and inerrant or infallible, to some students) Word of God.

Despite that benefit, I had a few other troubles within Bible Bowl, the main one being a simple lack of fitting in. These kids had been playing Bible Bowl together since they were in seventh grade, for the most part, so they had seen each other at least once a month for four or five years before I became a part of Central's team. Many of them had played in Junior Bible Bowl, adding to their years of togetherness. Also, they had attended denominational conventions and events, in addition to their Bible Bowl activities, and they had family connections, as any subculture does, that went beyond even those. Even those players who were on different teams knew each other quite well, leaving me a clear outsider. I also simply refused to conform to the typical expectations of how one dressed or behaved while playing the game. Since this competition was within a church denomination, it still had a formal church feeling to it, with players dressing up for meets. While I was certainly willing to wear a coat and tie for Sunday morning church services, any other time I would wear a t-shirt and shorts or blue jeans. When I began playing Bible Bowl, I fought against the expectations. At the previous year's national convention, for example, our team had worn matching pink dress shirts with baby blue ties (it was the 1980s, after all). I had never owned a pink dress shirt, and I certainly was not going to wear one in any sort of competition, a point I made early in the season. I found some other rebellious souls on our team, and we proceeded to take our attire in a completely different direction. For one meet, we all decided to wear camouflage clothing—largely based on watching Arnold Schwarzenegger movies—which I also did not own. Because it was such a good idea, though, I at least borrowed some from Wayne, who was roughly my size. However, we did not tell Gordon, our captain, so he came dressed in a suit. Adapting as we went, we told people he was our manager, which satisfied him well enough. Later, I went even farther, as I was a fan of what was then called WWF wrestling, especially Hulk Hogan and Randy "Macho Man" Savage. I began emulating their attire for meets, making shirts with Centralmania (as opposed to Hulkamania) on them, wearing athletic tape wrapped around the ends of my fingers, and even using MM (for Macho Man) as a note on my score sheet for inspiration. A few years later, at college, I met a young woman who had seen us at a tournament, but she was having trouble remembering if it was us or not. The one thing she could remember, she said, was someone dressed in ripped up clothes with a bandana on. My friend and I chuckled, as she was clearly referring to me.

Before I had begun playing, the oddest attire belonged to one of the best players, Phil, who wore shorts all year long, even to tournaments where it would clearly be snowing and he would have to walk from one building to another in between games. The fact that Phil was one of the best players, though, seemed to earn him an exemption from too much conversation, though people still commented on his wardrobe on a regular basis. My experiences, though, with attire and Bible Bowl did teach me that I and other people could get away with wearing whatever we wanted, as long as we could play the game quite well. People may have talked about Phil's shorts or my odd ensemble, but most of them would have taken us on their team without question. They would have taken me because of the one aspect where I did clearly fit in to the Bible Bowl culture: I was extremely competitive. Having grown up in a neighborhood where we played a different sport every season, I was used to playing hard and often losing, as we had one neighborhood kid who was clearly better than the rest of us, and his team almost always won. Also, my father had played college basketball and had a chance to play major league baseball. I grew up playing both sports, but without the skill (or height) he had, though I still had the same competitive drive. The top players in Bible Bowl shared that competitive fire, as they studied for hours in order to become the best, knowing that the odds of winning the national championship were so slim that one question could decide the final match. Phil, for example, played every year he was eligible, placed in the top ten on the individual exam every year, but never won a championship. Players often threw copies of their texts after losing matches, and no one spoke to the losing team while they were on their way out. Even local meets had the feel of local high school sports, especially in the games between the top two or three teams. The pressure was intense for those of us who wanted to win. My competitive streak led me to get placed on the top team from our church, as we had two. I quickly became the second best player on the team, behind only Gordon who had played every year he was eligible, as well. Gordon was clearly smarter than I was, as his reputation at school proved. Even though he was a year ahead of me, I saw and heard what other students and teachers said about him. He was the type of kid who took the encyclopedia with him to the bathroom, so he thrived in a game like Bible Bowl. I came to every practice I could, any one that did not conflict with work, essentially, and I learned everything he could teach me, though certainly not with any sense of humility. I pushed to become the team captain, even though I had only been on the team for a month or two, and I was not even aware of all the rules.

Gordon is the person who kept me on the team when I almost quit in the winter of my first year. I had wanted to be the best player in the league or at least on the team, and I was clearly not. Gordon was not only better at learning the material because he was willing to work harder than I was, he was faster at buzzing in, having had six years of experience. We were sitting in my car outside of the church fellowship hall, and I told him I was thinking of quitting. He told me how Phil had been talking about me, about how much potential he saw in me, and he essentially flattered me into staying. He wanted someone to help him win, and he knew that I could do so, so he was not disinterested in having me stay on the team. I never completely got over my arrogance, my unwarranted desire to be the number one player on the team, but I at least learned to channel it, which prepared me for the next year when I would be the number one player on the team, the year where I learned how difficult such a position was. My competitive drive led me not only to want to be the best player, but it also had its dark side. Like those players who threw books, I, too, behaved in such a manner. At one practice, I threw my book across the room, where it bounced off a couch, pages scattering throughout the floor. I had arguments with teammates at halftimes of tournaments, where we debated whether or not I was hurting the team with my aggressiveness, leading my friend Mike to suggest I sit out the second half of one game. It was clear I had the most knowledge and was the best player, but the team was willing to lose the game, or at least run that risk, just to get me out of the game. At times, though, my anger and energy took the form of righteous indignation, as I could recognize when other people were behaving as I did. Once, at a tournament at Kentucky Christian College, we were playing against a team from Largo, Florida. It was a close match, and we were playing well against a team that was clearly better than we were, so they were as tense as we were. After they had gotten a question right, they were asked a bonus question. One of their players turned to his girlfriend and said, rather sharply, "You learned these; you better know them." I came about halfway out of my chair, as I thought he was going to become a bit more violent. Even Wayne, who was as non-confrontational as anyone I knew, shifted forward in his seat, as he thought something was going to happen.

It is this level of competition that raises the question of what players learn from the game. While it's true that they learn the Bible, and many of them do gain insights into what it means to play on a team, especially as many of them will never have the chance to do so athletically, the competition also leads to such conflicts within and between teams. I never saw the player from Largo the same way again, even after he and I attended the same college, and he never behaved that way again. People saw me as a hothead, someone who could not control his anger, especially in tense situations, a description that defined me even through most of my college years. There doesn't seem to be anything particularly Christian about this sort of competition. Yes, the games begin with prayer, and, yes, the questions are about the Bible, but, otherwise, one would often have been hard-pressed to distinguish the competition, especially at the higher levels, from any other academic quiz bowl or even local sports. Players may say that they loved getting to know the Bible much better or that they enjoyed the community they built during those years, both of which are true for me, as well, but most of us wanted, first and foremost, to win. We wanted the scholarships that were available at tournaments; we wanted to be voted all-stars; we wanted to place on the tournament and national exams; we wanted the trophies that came at the end of every meet and season; and we wanted others to see how good we were at this event. As with almost every other competition, when we were honest with ourselves, it came down to pride. Or at least it did for me. Perhaps other players really did want to do well solely because it was the Word of God they were studying. Perhaps they were much more enthusiastic about the friendships they made along the way than whatever accolades they collected. I didn't talk to other players that much about such things. I can say, though, that, for me, it was another competition, another chance for me to try to prove I was better than other people at something. There's nothing Christian about that, but I didn't recognize that at the time, and no one ever questioned my motivations. As with my extremism in music and my struggles in physical relationships, I could blame the church or those around me, but the fault lay clearly with me. I wanted recognition and acclaim, the exact opposite of what I was reading about in the Bible, but I never thought about what I was supposedly learning.

What I take away from all of these memories is that Central's youth group was one of the few places in life where I felt like I fit in. Even during my senior year of high school, where I became one of the most recognizable people on campus, I never felt like I was a part of something larger than myself. The youth group gave me that feeling, as I always wanted to be at the church or out with one of my friends from the group. When I was married a few years later, the four men who stood with me were four members of that youth group, nobody from college. I know we had disagreements and struggles along the way, and I know that I now no longer share their theology, but this group best exemplifies for me what Christianity could and should be. We were one in a way we did not understand at the time, working together to help one another and support one another in quiet ways. I cannot think of another way I would want to have spent those years of my life.

5

Finding the (Hot) Buttons to Push

When I said we were normal teenagers who did not sit around talking about abortion or same-sex marriage, I was not exaggerating. Our youth group did not discuss politics that I can ever recall. That might have something to do with the fact that I began attending there in 1986, in the middle of Reagan's final term in office, and there was no major election until the Bush-Dukakis election, which did not occur until I had begun college. It might also be because we assumed we all agreed with one another on politics, so there was nothing to discuss. It was also a different world then, with no Rush Limbaugh on the radio, no political blogs on the internet, no Fox News, just Dan Rather or Tom Brokaw, though CNN had been around for a few years by that point. However, I really believe that it was because we were teenagers, and most teenagers do not spend their free time talking about upcoming elections. That has changed since I was in high school, I know, especially within Evangelical churches. More and more of my students come to college having spent their past few years obsessed with a particular issue of the day, often abortion still, but more likely same-sex marriage, though stem cell research was a fad topic for a few years. They have clear leanings to the political right, often the extreme political right, even if the candidates do not espouse Christian teachings. However, they are still not the children of *Jesus Camp*, the documentary that discussed the Christian equivalent of groupthink, one woman's response to the supposed brainwashing camps that Muslims use to raise their true believers who turn into terrorists. Instead, they are simply teenagers who believe what their parents and pastors have told them, much as almost all of us did, whether we were raised on the political left or right.

My politics came from my parents before I entered into the conservative Christian world, but those politics were apolitical, apathetic, even. If we did not discuss religion often, we never discussed politics, as I could not say with any kind of assurance who my parents voted for or even whether or not they voted until probably 2004, when I was in my mid-thirties. I never noticed if they went to vote on Election Day or if they simply went to work, like any other Tuesday. I asked my parents a few years ago why they were not more interested in politics when we were growing up, and my mother responded simply, "We were too busy trying to pay the bills to worry about such things." Now, many political activists would say that our poverty is the reason they should have been interested in politics, but I completely understand my parents' approach. They needed to work to feed three children, so that's where they spent their time, energy, and money.

Oddly enough, the only political act I ever saw my parents perform was a negative one, and it did have a rather profound impact on me. For most of my childhood, our neighborhood was outside of the city limits. I went to county schools, and all of our services were provided by the county. When I was about twelve, the city began trying to annex our area; many people in the neighborhood did not want this to happen, largely because of property taxes, I now understand. Some people circulated a petition through the neighborhood, and I saw it sitting on our kitchen counter. I asked my parents what it was, and they told me. I asked, "Are you going to sign it?" They told me that they were not. I then asked, "Do you want to be annexed by the city?" They said that they did not.

Now, given our lack of conversation on politics, I did not follow up and ask them why they would not sign a petition against annexation when they were clearly opposed to annexation. However, it clearly registered with me as a disconnect; I could not make sense of such an action. Perhaps they would have said they were too busy to get involved; perhaps they would have argued that they did not want to get on the bad side of certain people in the neighborhood or city, as they knew a good deal of people; or perhaps they would have said that one just should not get involved in such matters. Regardless, what I took away from that event was that, if I ever saw something I disagreed with, I should speak up, not remain silent. Our neighborhood did get annexed, and, even though I never saw any ill effects of that action, I also wondered if a bit more of a fight might not have changed matters.

Even though there was no Rush Limbaugh of my teenage years (though he was broadcasting at the time, as I later learned), I was eventually influenced by outside sources, those that went beyond my family and church group, though my denomination was actually involved with one of them. First, when I had my rededication event at the Christian concert, I sought out everything Christian I could find. I eventually found my way to the *700 Club* with Pat Robertson. There was no Trinity Broadcasting Network when I was growing up, but Robertson's show was the closest thing I could find to Christian television. There were other shows on the Christian Broadcasting Network, but I cannot recall watching any of them; my focus was on Robertson and his guests. It often came on at odd times, though, so I would have to record it and watch it after school or before or after work, whenever I could find the free time. Fast forwarding through the advertisements for such programs as Compassion International, though, made me feel a bit guilty. Watching the program on a recording gave rise to other questions, the main one of which involved prayer. Throughout the show, Robertson would pray for various people or things, and he encouraged his viewers to pray along with him. I wondered, though, if I should pray with him when I was watching a taped show. He wasn't actually praying at that moment, but I also knew that the prayer would still mean the same thing. Sometimes I did pray with the tape-delayed him; sometimes I didn't. I'm sure there is some theological argument about such concerns, but I seldom raised them with other people, which I'm sure only helped my social life, such as it was.

I just happened to be watching the *700 Club* during the late 1980s, which is when Robertson was running for the Republican nominee for president. My interest in his show quickly sparked an interest in politics. My only connection to national politics before this time was when I was in fifth grade, and Jimmy Carter flew into our small airport, gave a speech, then flew out again. We got to go and hear him, though from a considerable distance. We made signs, though they were not allowed to relate to peanuts in any way, which disappointed me greatly. When we had a mock election in that same fifth grade class, Reagan won by a considerable margin, as I was the only Carter vote, a sign of where I would ultimately end up. However, I had now clearly switched to the Republican side, as I was now a devout Christian, and the two quickly became equated in my mind. I fully intended to vote for Robertson, should he win the nomination for president. Because of when my birthday fell, though, I was not old enough to vote in the primary, which prevented me from helping him get to that point. However, I followed his policies much more closely than I had followed anything else. The one that still sticks out to me is what we often call a "sin tax," as he argued that we should tax alcohol and cigarettes at a high rate to pay for the health care costs that those two products contributed to. I'm sure that his primary motivation was actual sin, which he would have equated with those two products, but his logic made perfect sense to me at the time. Oddly enough, I do not recall any specific programs he had in mind that connected religion to politics. Instead, he focused on typically Republican ideas, such as reforming the educational system, partly by doing away with the Department of Education, and passing a constitutional amendment to require a balanced federal budget. He focused on small government, though he worked in some moral issues, such as pornography and that "sin tax." I'm sure he talked about school prayer, as that was always a major topic of Christians at the time, but I don't remember thinking that he would help lead us to a theocracy. I could not have even articulated such an idea, nor could I have envisioned what a Robertson presidency would have looked like. I simply saw a Christian who was running for the top office in the United States, and I thought I should vote for him. Unfortunately, politics and faith have not greatly changed since the 1980s; instead, that connection has simply gotten stronger. The religious right has equated the evils of big government with moral issues, such as abortion and same-sex marriage, leading Evangelical Christians to vote for people who say they stand on the same side on moral issues, while those same Christians do not question the economic policies (or much of any other policies) of the candidates. Instead, they vote for the "more Christian" candidate based on a few key points.

The other event that helped guide me deeper into the intersection of politics and faith happened at the North American Christian Convention in the summer after my senior year of college. In addition to the Bible Bowl tournament, there was a huge exhibition section, where a variety of vendors would set up. I always came back with a stack of books, usually from someone like Charles Swindoll, whom I was fascinated with at the time, since we couldn't buy such things at home. My future alma mater, Milligan College, had a booth set up, so I picked up a sticker for my car, becoming one of those students who shows up to campus with paraphernalia already put on, something I would never have guessed I would do. The one booth, that caught my attention that summer, was simply selling pins, such as one might wear as a tie tack or on a lapel. The design was simple: two tiny feet. Given that it was the late 1980s, fifteen years after *Roe v. Wade*, and that I grew up in the Bible Belt, one would think I would have known something about abortion, but I can only remember two other times I had even heard it mentioned. In my junior year, Gordon was talking with a group of us about a paper he had written, where he compared Jonathan Swift's *A Modest Proposal* to our current society's legalization of abortion. I had neither read Swift, nor heard of abortion, so I did not know what comparison he was making, nor did I know how clichéd such an approach actually was, though, given that he was a high school student, it was fairly original. When I was much younger, Kenneth asked me if I supported the ERA. He didn't explain what it stood for or give me any details beyond the fact that it would enable women to have abortions, which I didn't understand, given that I was around ten. At the booth, though, the members of whatever organization sponsored the booth told me about abortion, what it was, when it had become legal, and what I should do to try to reverse that situation. They did not use the graphic pictures that some groups use, and, I do not even recall what group they were with. I ended up buying a pin, which I wore for several years, including at work, as I slowly began my move toward an even more conservative political stance, driven by the hottest button topic of them all.

When the 1988 election came around, I voted for George H.W. Bush, not because of any of his policies, which I could not have even listed, much less explained, but solely because of abortion. I became the one-issue voter. Then, in January 1989, three friends and I went to a local abortion clinic to protest the legality of abortion on the anniversary of *Roe v. Wade*. We were the only four there, but that did not dampen our enthusiasm. Scott, who would become my roommate my sophomore year and who was the one who had set up the protest by obtaining the necessary permits and by making signs, also contacted the local news station. A camera crew came by and filmed us marching, while Scott answered a few questions. I was living at home that semester, so I was eating dinner that evening in one room, while my parents were in another. I was watching the news, trying to see if we actually made the cut. When the reporter was there, I knew full well that we might make the news, and I knew how my parents would react to my being there. Every time I walked past the camera, the sign blocked out my face, hiding my presence from them and everyone else. After the segment aired, they asked me if I had seen Scott on the news. They told me I should not get involved with such things, never asking if I was there or not. As with my baptism, I'm sure they knew I was; my attire had probably given me away, a fact I had not considered, as I had not changed clothes since the protest. The sign covered my face, but not my clothing. Their comment was their way of telling me not to do something like this *again*, not just that I should not do something like this, in general. Over the next summer or two, as Scott and I kept in touch with letters, abortion often came up during our discussions. In 1989, there was a Supreme Court decision that I thought gave us hope that abortion might be overturned, and I remember writing to Scott about it. In *Webster v. Reproductive Health Services*, the court did not overturn *Roe v. Wade*, but they did encourage states to pass laws that banned abortion, which would give the court a chance to test *Roe* specifically. Scott's response was much less hopeful than mine, but he had been following the subject much longer. While I was the wide-eyed idealist, he was the realist who would continue to work, knowing full well his work might not amount to anything.

I was still wearing my pin with the little feet, both at work, when I could get away with it, and at school. One day, a friend and I were at K-Mart, and I saw an employee who had a larger button, one that had a picture of a fetus on it and the first part of Jeremiah 1:5, often quoted in the abortion debate: "Before I formed you in the womb I knew you." I commented on the woman's button, told her how much I liked it, and she simply gave it to me. The only condition, she said, was that I needed to wear it so that people could see it. It found a home on my jean jacket with all of my band buttons.

Once I started with abortion, I became involved in more political organizations, though my involvement was limited mainly to writing letters and signing petitions. When I was a senior in high school, the movie version of *The Last Temptation of Christ* was released, and I joined in the protest against it. I don't believe it ever showed in our home town, or I'm sure that some of us would have gone to protest it, but I did bring a petition to church to have people sign. There was not a great response, as people in our church were oddly apolitical when it came to such issues. They were conservative, it's clear, but they were conservative in the traditional Southern sense of not wanting the government to tell them what to do. They seemed fine with people making whatever movies they wanted, just as long as they were not made to see them. The question I always come back to is what drove me to become so interested in these issues when the Christian community I was a part of was largely indifferent to them. I was not in a church where the preacher told me what to believe and who to vote for, nor where we took trips to Washington, DC, to protest on the anniversary of *Roe v. Wade*. Even our youth group, where idealism lived in so many other areas, never talked about what we might do to change the political landscape we lived in. Instead, I worked up the energy and enthusiasm about such subjects on my own, drawing from Pat Robertson and *The 700 Club* and any books I might find that led me along that path. For some reason, I was (and am) simply drawn to extremes; when I found conservative Christianity, I found the conservative political scene that was on the rise, and I left others behind in my move toward it. Luckily, I talk more than act, so I never joined groups like Operation Rescue, an organization so devoted to the reversal of *Roe v. Wade* that they would lock themselves together, blocking entrance to abortion clinics, ending up arrested. Their leader, Randall Terry, was dealing with several court cases while I was in high school and college, showing me what others were willing to do. As I moved through college, my politics changed rather dramatically, leading me away from the one-issue approach I had used in my first voting opportunity, led me even to vote for a third party candidate in 1992 when Ross Perot came along. I was not yet ready to vote for a Democrat, and Perot captured the dissatisfaction so many people had with politics at the time. I was ready to become an independent who would not vote for a major candidate until 2004, as my extremism took a different turn, even leading me to become a member of a socialist group while in graduate school. Though the groups changed, I moved from one fringe to another, trying to find a place where I could make a difference, all without getting too involved.

6

The Questions Come Quickly; The Answers Do Not

IF ONE IS EVER inclined to see the hand of God working in someone's life, my arrival at Milligan would provide that person with plenty of material:

- I met Wayne, my future high school best friend and had every class with him our sophomore year without our planning it.
- He and I worked together on an Accounting project, which necessitated my giving him the book over a weekend.
- He invited me to church and was unwilling to listen to my excuses, an action completely out of character for him.
- He then forced me to stay for Bible Bowl practice without my even knowing what it was.
- I almost quit Bible Bowl, but Gordon talked me into continuing with it.
- I then placed in the top twenty on the individual test at the national tournament, something no one from our church had ever done, earning a scholarship to Milligan, a college I was not considering at the time.
- My father met a recruiter from Milligan at a high school college fair.
- I did not call King College back to confirm that they were offering me a full scholarship.

- I met with the Milligan recruiter who gave her card to my father.
- I put no rational thought, then, into the decision to attend Milligan and not King.

Really, nothing about this decision makes any sense to me, a trend I continued throughout my years there.

And I was miserable when I arrived. There were several causes for my unhappiness, but I certainly can't ignore the one I was most responsible for, my own immaturity, both in thought and action. Despite the fact that I had been one of the better students in high school, I really was not a mature thinker. I still read everything I encountered at a literal level and did not understand any type of metaphorical writing. Poetry was extremely difficult for me, but all types of literary writing were. Not surprisingly, this limitation spread into my reading of the Bible, as I certainly would have qualified as a fundamentalist, even though I would have had no idea what that term meant. My lack of maturity in thought led directly to my lack of maturity in action, as well. I still clearly behaved as if I were a high school student, especially in my one-on-one relationships. I thought I was funny when I was simply rude, and I thought I was deep when I was simply obscure. While everyone else was finding friends, my roommate was complaining because he had requested a single room, but ended up with me. To be fair to myself, though, my roommate was even more socially awkward and actually made me look relatively well-adjusted. Further complicating this problem was that I had chosen to attend Milligan at all, as there was only one other person from my high school there, and she was not someone I knew well. While many of my friends were attending East Tennessee State University, the public university ten minutes away, taking classes with people they had gone to school with for over a decade, I was in orientation groups and classes with people I had never encountered before. Many people would point out that college students often experience this situation, especially those who go any distance away from home to school. However, I had not encountered this situation before because I had never moved locations or schools. We had lived in the same house since I was two years old; I had never had to make new friends in a new neighborhood, new school, or new city. I had gone to school with almost all of the same people my entire life. I had absolutely no experience with how to make friends for the first time, yet another way I was simply not mature enough for my freshman year of college.

The fact that I chose a denominationally-affiliated college also led to my feelings of isolation. I had only attended Central for the past two years, so I had not grown up in the subculture, as many of my peers at Milligan had. I had played Bible Bowl, but only for those two years. When I attended orientation events, I recognized a few faces from tournaments we had played back in the spring, but the other people who had also attended those tournaments had done so for the past six or seven years of their lives. They had played in local, regional, and national tournaments with many of these people while my only friends were the ones in my neighborhood. They had attended denominational events at the state and national level, creating a spread-out version of a church youth group. They all had a built-in group of people they were rather familiar with, even if that group had lived several states away, while I looked around and wondered where I had seen that person before.

Oddly enough, I also found I was too conservative for Milligan. In my first few weeks, I found I was the only student who listened exclusively to Christian music, watched only Christian movies, and did not watch television (as there was no Christian alternative). Instead, I heard students who cursed, saw students smoke or dip tobacco, and learned there were even people who drank alcohol, sometimes in copious amounts. What was truly outrageous to me, though, was that these people considered themselves Christians. The climate was so far from what I expected, I was considering transferring to Johnson Bible College, the college that had hosted our monthly Bible Bowl meets when I was in high school. Since I was considering going into the ministry, I didn't really need the liberal arts part of Milligan, and I was sure that JBC, as it was called, would be a much better fit. My best friend during my first few years of college, Scott, disagreed with me. I found out later he was one of those Christians who dipped tobacco and cursed, but, for now, I knew simply that he was from Pennsylvania where his parents ran a Christian camp. They did not make much money, certainly not enough to attend Milligan, but Scott had cobbled together enough scholarships and grants to be able to attend. He was always one of the smartest students at Milligan, which would certainly help me later. One day, around the time I was seriously considering transferring to JBC, Scott had a friend visit whom he wanted me to meet. Scott's friend was attending

JBC, so meeting him would give me an opportunity to see the benefits of the school. The conversation took place in Scott's room and was much more casual than its effect on my life would seem to call for. The friend was actually reclining on Scott's bed while I borrowed a desk chair. I laid out my predicament to his friend, which just led him to laugh. He then proceeded to tell me how students at JBC acted, and it sounded remarkably similar to Milligan. He said that such behavior went on at every Christian college, and there were people who were not Christian at all at such institutions, including JBC. I could not understand why anyone would attend a Christian college, especially a Bible college, if they were not a Christian, but I did not grow up in the subculture, did not know the pressures that parents placed on their children, the expectations that came with being the child of an elder in the Christian church or, even worse, being a preacher's kid (PK) or missionary's kid (MK). Scott praised the virtues of Milligan's liberal arts program, as did his friend, all in an attempt to convince me to stay at Milligan. Though they never explicitly argued that I could only control my behavior, that assertion was underneath everything they said. Since I could not be responsible for how others lived their lives, I should make the best choices for mine and get on with living how I should live. If only I would have learned that lesson then, perhaps I would not still be struggling with it two decades later. But most ideas in life are like that. We continue to struggle with who we were at twenty, then thirty, and on and on, wondering when we'll get it all right.

Academically, I also found ideas I did not expect at a Christian college. When I was in high school, I assumed I was smart, that I knew how to think. The fact that I did not make the grades I should have was simply indicative of my laziness. While that logic may be true, I was definitely not as smart as I thought I was. As has happened to many students before me and will happen to many after me, as I witness in my freshman classes year after year, college was the place where I discovered my lack of intelligence, especially as it relates to my faith. Scott was one of the main gadflies in my theological thinking, as he was clearly a much better thinker than I was. Luckily, though, we both enjoyed the discussions, even when they led nowhere, the epitome of late-night dormitory discussions. Scott would often come into my room and announce, "I'm God. Prove me wrong." I would ask him to perform some miracle, only to be met with, "Do not put the Lord your God to your test."[1] We would circle round and round such exchanges for a good hour with him shaking his head on a regular basis, saying, "You could do this so easily." It took over a year before I was able to stand toe-to-toe with him on such arguments, but I spent my freshman year falling back on weak Christian logic. Once, for example, we were debating cursing (or *cussing*, as I would have called it then) and being a Christian. He sat with his back against my dorm door, while I walked around the room, laying out my arguments. I'm sure I pulled out Matthew 15:10–11, "Jesus called the crowd to him and said, 'Listen and understand. What goes into someone's mouth does not defile them, but what comes out of their mouth, that is what defiles them'" (taken completely out of context, of course) or Philippians 4:8, "Finally, brothers and sisters, whatever is true, whatever is noble, whatever is right, whatever is pure, whatever is lovely, whatever is admirable—if anything is excellent or praiseworthy—think about such things," focusing on the *pure* and *lovely*. However, what caused me to "win" the argument was a statement that, in a different form, would become outrageously popular in the late-1990s. As he kept pushing for the acceptability of cursing, I finally said, "Yeah, but would Jesus do it? That's the bottom line." I had just pulled an early version of the WWJD? (What Would Jesus Do?) craze. Scott actually conceded that argument, whether because he actually could not think of an appropriate response or because he knew I was not ready to hear the type of response that was needed to counter that claim, I'm not sure. It would be a few years before I would be ready to begin considering such a counter-argument, so it was better that he let me have this one.

Courses were also raising questions I had not considered before, even in the most conservative classes. Dr. Roberts, for example, taught my Old and New Testament classes in my freshman year. One of the early assignments in Old Testament was for us to look up an article on the ten plagues God performed against Egypt in *The Interpreter's Dictionary of the Bible*. The *Interpreter's Dictionary*, as it's called, was and is one of the best commentaries on the Bible, one I still use today, for which I can partly thank Dr. Roberts. While I do not remember all of the article's arguments, the one that stands out is one that I commented on in my paper for Dr. Roberts. The *Interpreter's Dictionary* argues that nine of the ten plagues (the one on the firstborn being the clear exception) were

---

1. Deuteronomy 6:16 or Luke 4:12.

physical occurrences in Egypt on a regular basis, all of which could be explained naturally. There was some sort of bacteria that could get in the water, for example, making it look like blood. I was appalled by such an argument, as it clearly took away from the miraculous power of the plagues. If they were nothing more than natural occurrences, God had no hand in the liberation of the people of Israel. I wrote much the same in my paper for Dr. Roberts, though I certainly did not phrase it as such an alarmist reaction, though that is clearly what I thought. He did not mark a great deal in my paper, but he did comment on that section. In the margin, he wrote something along the lines of, "Yes, but couldn't God have caused those physical events to happen at just that time in order to free His people?" I did not think Dr. Roberts was undercutting the authority of the Bible or attacking my faith. I thought his argument made some sense. I wasn't sure that I was willing to change my belief to fit his, but I also did not discount his argument. What I have found in my years of theological thinking and especially my teaching is that changes in belief do not happen immediately and certainly not because of some grand challenge to a theological idea. Rather than pushing me to accept a more radical idea (which he may not have even believed, probably did not, knowing him as I did later), he took me one step along the way. I now, whether I wanted to admit it or not, took one step away from a literal reading of the Bible. Even though accepting his belief did not necessarily make me do so, this one question opened up just a crack of an idea that everything might not be as it is literally written in the Bible.

Other classes helped reinforce this belief, even when they were not about the Bible itself. I was in a freshman Humanities class with Mrs. Kiser. There were a number of facts about Mrs. Kiser that could have led to my questioning my version of Christianity, as she was both a vegetarian and a feminist, two beliefs I had never really encountered before outside of reading about them. I was so sheltered in my thinking that I could not have even used the term *feminist* to describe anyone, and it was only years later that I thought of her with that term. I made jokes about her vegetarianism, as I joked about anything at that time, and certainly anything I did not understand. It was in a discussion of *Beowulf*, though, that she helped to chip away at some of my assurance about my thought process. I had been taught in high school that *Beowulf* was not merely a Christian text, but that it was an allegory for Christianity. Beowulf clearly represented Jesus, while Grendel represented evil, in general, and the dragon was a clear reference to Satan, especially given my knowledge of the book of Revelation. My high school teacher had read the work this way and taught us to do so. What I thought was my ability to think was simply my ability to parrot what someone else had given me. When we were discussing the work in Mrs. Kiser's class, and she brought up the debate about whether or not *Beowulf* was produced by Christians or pagans, I was adamant that it was a Christian work. Mrs. Kiser laid out two columns on the board, one for the Christian argument, the other for pagan. If I was not the only voice for the Christian argument, I was clearly the loudest, and we spent the entire class period debating the issue. Given what I now know about the history of the work and simply having read the text more closely, I am not surprised the list for the pagan side was much longer and much stronger. I would not admit this reading, though, and kept arguing for the Christian interpretation, showing my inability to hear and weigh opposing evidence for something I believed. At the end of the class, Mrs. Kiser turned to the board and wrote in large letters over both lists, P-A-G-A-N. I actually cried out against her doing so, though it was clear that I was doing so in a humorous way (at least I meant it so, though I'm sure professors tired of my antics). I was not greatly bothered by her changing the interpretation of a literary work, as I did not have anything invested in it. I did not appreciate literature at the time, and I certainly would not have argued that it mattered at all in my life. I had argued so strongly because I could not admit that I was wrong, that I always wanted to be right, especially to prove that I could think at the same level as others in the class. However, what her revision of *Beowulf* did for me was to show me that what I had been taught might not always be right, what I thought I believed might not be right. The fact that I was simply replacing one reading I had been taught with another reading I had been taught did not occur to me at the time. I still had not begun to think for myself, but incidents such as these occurred often enough in my freshman year to slowly erode confidence in my ability to think. I was not where I needed to be at the end of that year, but I was much further along than when I had matriculated ten months before.

My sophomore year was much more difficult academically, partly due to my lack of interest. I see this problem in my students all the time, though now it usually happens in the second semester of their freshman year. They come to college with a healthy dose of fear, as they have heard all through high school about how difficult college will be. They do all of the reading and homework those first few weeks of the semester, asking whether or not they should bring every book for the class every day. They are dutiful, and it usually pays off for them. However, in the second semester, that fear has largely evaporated. They see what this college thing is all about now, and they know they can be successful here. They put in less time than they did the first semester, cut corners on the reading for classes, and begin skipping minor assignments, as well as classes. They also get more involved on campus, joining a variety of organizations that further pull on their time, in addition to the friendships that have developed over the previous semester. If they're seriously dating someone, they have even less time. Their grades tend to suffer. I often tell my students that that semester is the worst one for almost every student I see. I fell into the same pattern in my sophomore year. I had my best semester of college in the second semester of my freshman year, so I thought I could revert to my high school habits of simply doing the bare minimum. This attitude, combined with a more difficult course load, almost led to my leaving Milligan, largely due to my Humanities course. All students at Milligan, at least when I was there, had to take twenty-four hours of Humanities courses, six hours each semester for the first four semesters. Those hours were divided into three hours of discussion groups that met three days a week and three hours of lecture that met on Tuesdays and Thursdays. The Humanities curriculum covered all of Western culture: the art, literature, music, philosophy, and history from the beginning of civilization to the present. They also incorporated a writing aspect to help us improve in that area.

I was not a particularly strong student in these areas, having focused on math and science in high school, so I had to work fairly hard in my freshman year. The writing portion caused me significant trouble. In one of the first writing lectures, the professor (either Mrs. Iles or Mrs. Nipper, I can never remember which) told us that our first assignment was a paragraph we would write from a list of topics. I chose why we should not study ancient history, setting a trend of rebellion that would last for the next decade or so. What was significant about that first lecture, though, was when the professor told us any sentence fragment or comma splice would cause us to lose one letter grade per error. After the first essay, that penalty would increase. I did lose a letter grade on that first essay because of a sentence fragment, which I already knew about, but I somehow never lost any points for a comma splice, which I did not learn until I was teaching freshman composition in graduate school. I often tell such stories to my students to show them how ignorant I was as a student. One of my favorites actually takes place the next year, as we were assigned a major research paper in Sophomore Humanities, a class that was certainly more challenging than my freshman class. We were given a list of topics, and we had to go by Mrs. Nipper's office to sign up for a topic. Given my typical procrastination at that point, I was one of the last to sign up, so I was left with W.E.B. DuBois, someone I had never heard of before. I wrote the paper when the format for papers was changing from the old system of footnotes to the new, parenthetical method of citing sources. I used the old footnotes, not because I knew that system better, but because I believed it would make my paper look longer, and I needed a good deal of help there. I made a D on that paper, but only because Mrs. Nipper allowed me to re-write it. Her actual question when she called me into her office was, "Kevin, what is this?" Like many students before and after me, I responded, "I don't know." I was lucky to get away with a D, actually.

When I walked into the discussion section of Humanities, I first met Dr. Dibble. One of his opening lines that semester was, "This class is designed to weed people out." He was almost right about me, as I was almost one of the weeded that semester, doing so poorly that I should have lost my scholarship. He was probably the most interesting looking man I had ever met, reminding me of an Old Testament prophet. He had a white beard that came halfway down his chest, and he had lost most of the hair on his head. He wore thick, black-framed glasses he would take off when making a particularly difficult point, rubbing his nose with his index finger and thumb. He would then begin his answer along the lines of, "Well, what Kant would say is . . ." I would love to say that I was impressed with him that first semester, but the truth is that I hated him. He was unlike any teacher I had had until that point. He took roll, but he did not give or take away any points for attendance, which led to days where there were only two to three students there. His style of discussion was often confrontational, especially when theological matters came up. Since I was a Bible major, he and I often argued about whatever issue would come up. The fact that I often did not do the reading led to my losing almost every discussion. Near the end of the semester, we were supposed to read Thomas Hardy's *Tess of the D'Urbervilles* over

Thanksgiving Break. I laughed to myself, knowing I would not spend my break reading a novel. Because I came to class and paid attention, I passed that exam by one point. By the end of the semester, I had decided I would not spend my last semester of Humanities in Dr. Dibble's class.

Fate or God or chance or providence (or Providence) or whatever you would like to attribute such events to had other ideas. Registration at Milligan was still done by hand in those days, so we would all sit in the theater, waiting for our turn to go into the registration area. On a large chalkboard, they would write classes that were closed, and we would furiously adjust our schedules. The order of registration was decided by alphabetical order by last name. In the fall, they began at the beginning of the alphabet, so I always got the classes I wanted. In the spring, they reversed the order, and I was often left with a schedule I would not have chosen. When I went to register for that last semester of Humanities in the spring of 1990, I had few choices left to me. I could choose an eight o'clock section with another professor, but I hated eight a.m. classes. I only had one my entire time at Milligan, and it was during a spring semester. My other option was to choose Dr. Dibble for a ten o'clock section. I went with him again, despite how I felt. For the early part of the semester, nothing was different. I was doing a better job of reading, though, as my performance the last semester had almost cost me my scholarship. My GPA had dropped below the required level to keep the award, but I received a letter informing me that they would give me one semester to pull that number back up to where it needed to be. Losing that scholarship would have led to my leaving Milligan, as my parents were already less than pleased that I had turned down a lower tuition at East Tennessee State University to go to Milligan.

Oddly enough, this type of generosity happened several times at Milligan. At the end of my sophomore year, I received a scholarship for Bible majors. However, over that summer, I changed my major, which should have caused me to lose that scholarship. Mrs. Nipper, the woman who managed the scholarship program, found a general education scholarship for me that was almost the same amount, surprising me at the beginning of the fall semester with it. Also, in the second semester of my sophomore year, I needed to get the registrar to sign my insurance form to allow me to receive the Good Student Discount. I needed a 3.0 to receive that discount, but I had earned a 2.5 GPA the previous semester. However, I was close to a 3.0 with my overall GPA, as I ended with a 2.975 for my first three semesters, so I was hoping she would be generous. She told me that they were supposed to use the previous semester's GPA, putting me a long way from the 3.0, but she signed the form anyway, telling me, "I know you'll pull it up this semester."

I was not so sure. I was still struggling with Greek, as I had the previous semester, but, more importantly, I was in Dr. Dibble's class again. I was doing a bit better, though I was still not enjoying his teaching style or the material. However, I was not smart enough to sit quietly in his class, always taking the bait he laid out for me, rising to the argument he was hoping to engage me in. In his class, we often took off on digressions, not really knowing how we moved from one subject to another. At Dr. Dibble's retirement dinner, one student described his class as one where we wandered off into the forest, sometimes returning, sometimes not, and that Dibble seemed to want it that way. The fact that I can recall talking about Adam and Eve in class, but not remember the actual subject matter of that particular session is not surprising to me. I do, though, clearly remember talking about Adam and Eve. This day was not the first one that found us discussing theology that only tangentially related to the reading assignment. We had discussed Judas earlier in the semester, wondering whether or not he truly had a choice to betray Jesus, so when the class got around to the creation story, I was not surprised.

As he often did, Dibble brought up the story with a simple question, asking us why Adam and Eve were kicked out of the Garden of Eden. Being a Bible major and being someone who cannot resist answering questions in classes, I immediately raised my hand. Since many people skipped his class and others almost always sat quietly, I did not have a great deal of competition. He called on me, as he often did in his booming bass voice, "Brown! What do you think?" I responded with the answer I had been given time and time again over the years: "They were kicked out of the Garden of Eden because they disobeyed God." I had no doubt that my answer would end the discussion. The answer was so blindingly obvious that everyone knew it. Everyone except Dr. Dibble, it seemed: "You think so?" he asked.

"Of course," I responded, a bit surprised that he even asked.

"You don't think that it's because God was afraid that they would become like him?"

I had never heard such an idea before, and I wasn't sure what he was trying to prove with his argument. Certainly he was espousing a theology I was not familiar with. Thankfully, though, I knew my Bible, and I knew he was wrong. I did not hesitate to argue with him.

"No. It's clear that it's because they disobeyed God. The serpent even uses God's words to try to trick them. God tells them that if they eat of the tree of the fruit of good and evil they will surely die. When they eat of the fruit, God has no choice but to kick them out of the garden where they will then die."

"You sure the Bible doesn't say anything about God being afraid they would become like him?"

"Of course I'm sure."

"Perhaps you should look up the end of Genesis 3 when you have some time."

And he left it there. He did not continue the argument, did not quote a chapter and verse that I'm sure he knew quite well. Instead, he just returned to the day's subject and left me to wonder what I did not know. At some point later that day, maybe even later that week, I went and looked up Genesis 3 and read it. The story is familiar as it is the well-known telling of how and why Adam and Eve are kicked out of the Garden of Eden. As I read along, I was not surprised by anything I was reading, as I knew the story quite well. However, when I came to the end of the chapter, I read something I had never noticed before. The end of Genesis, chapter 3, verses 22 and 23 read, "And the LORD God said, 'The man has now become like one of us, knowing good and evil. He must not be allowed to reach out his hand and take also from the tree of life and eat, and live forever.' So the LORD God banished him from the Garden of Eden to work the ground from which he had been taken." He was right. God had kicked Adam and Eve out of the garden because they (God in the plural form) were worried that man would become like him/them.

Note that I had never heard about a metaphorical reading of the creation and fall; I still took whatever the Bible said absolutely literally. Therefore, if God said that Adam and Eve would become like him if they ate of the tree of immortality, then I believed they had the possibility to become gods right in front of them. Why they did not eat of this tree earlier did not occur to me. Dr. Dibble was not trying to get me to think about that question; he simply wanted me to question what I had been taught, to look into matters for myself, and I had done that. I wish I could say I recognized it at the time; it changed my behavior, but not as much as I would later claim it did. I have told and re-told this story so many times I have worn the rough edges off of it, made it into the perfect pearl of a story, an epiphanic moment worthy of a Flannery O'Connor short story. Life does not work that way, I know, but the story is now clearly that, a story, not an actual memory with the fuzzy places that exist in all of our memories. I have filled those places in with narrative that help shape my life. However, regardless of how much I have altered, the core of the story still stays true, and it is still the moment where I truly changed as a student, but, even more, as a thinker, as a Christian, and as a person. Whenever I tell my story to my students I point to this moment as the one in which my life changed. I tell people that Dr. Dibble did not simply cause me to change my major; he caused me to change my life, the way that I see the world, the way that I think. All of that is true, but it did not happen on this day. This event did not cause me to run to the Registrar's office to change my major, did not cause me to begin reading all of the assigned material for my classes, did not cause me to re-read the Bible and re-think all I had believed. However, it did begin to make me realize that what I had been taught might not be true, that I might not be the thinker I thought I was. It caused me to pause, if only for a moment, and doubt my faith in my knowledge, and that was all the crack I needed to begin to make progress.

With any step forward there are numerous steps backwards. I'll give one such example from the following fall to show just how far I had not progressed. I was still listening to only Christian music at this point, despite a roommate the year before who balanced the two musical influences quite well and another one in my junior year who listened to secular music much more than Christian. It was through him that I was beginning to broaden my musical tastes, as he played guitar and was a fan of musicians who were experts at their craft, not just fun for me to listen to. I had been listening to more and more musicians and bands who were not Christian, even going so far as to begin watching MTV's afternoon show devoted to heavy metal music, which I had become a fan of only after converting to Christian music. At the time, AC/DC had a new album out, *Thunderstruck*, which was getting a good deal of airplay. I had always enjoyed AC/DC, having grown up with a brother and sister who loved KISS and alongside of friends who owned *Back in Black*. After hearing the title song several times, I decided to buy the cassette tape. I bought the tape from a record store in our local mall over the Thanksgiving weekend, so I was staying at home with my parents. I also had gone to the mall the day before Thanksgiving to get glasses for the first time, which might have an impact on what happened later, though I'm not sure. What I do know is that, for some reason, almost every Thanksgiving break during college, I got sick, usually from the flu. This year was no exception, as I spent much of the break lying in the bed from my teenage years, trying not to throw up. I could have blamed my illness on the new glasses, as I have heard that some people get sick from the transition, or simply from a flu bug that often struck me around the same time. However, at the time, I blamed the purchase on the AC/DC tape.

Such cause and effect belief is common in the conservative Evangelical world. God wants to keep us on the straight and narrow path, so he punishes us when we begin to slip off of it, all for our own good. I had become a Puritan in the mold of Anne Bradstreet, who wrote in "To My Dear Children,"

> Among all my experiences of God's gracious dealings with me, I have constantly observed this, that He hath never suffered me long to sit loose from Him, but by one affliction or other hath made me look home, and search what was amiss; so usually thus it hath been with me that I have no sooner felt my heart out of order, but I have expected correction for it, which most commonly hath been upon my own person, in sickness, weakness, pains, sometimes on my soul, in doubts and fears of God's displeasure, and my sincerity towards Him, sometimes He hath smote a child with a sickness, sometimes chastened by losses in estate, and these times (through His great mercy) have been the times of my greatest getting and advantage; yea I have found them the times when the Lord hath manifested the most love to me.[2]

I still believed that people got sick because God let them get sick, even made them get sick if it was for their ultimate benefit. I threw away the tape in the same way I had burned the records and tapes, even the *Sports Illustrated* Swimsuit Edition from years before. That was the way I dealt with evil, even after such an insight from the previous semester. Any kind of religious development was going to take some time, it seemed, and my thinking clearly needed some work.

---

2. Bradstreet, "To My Dear Children," 273.

William Golding, best known for writing *Lord of the Flies*, has a short essay about his development as a thinker I have often used in my freshman composition courses. In it, he lays out three levels of thinking that most people pass through. Grade Three thinking is not thinking at all; it is simple prejudice. He gives the example of several of his teachers who can only be described as hypocrites: Mr. Houghton, who praises the clean life, but who smokes and leers at any woman who walks down the halls, and Miss Parsons who claims that her students are her children, but who desperately wants a family. He then progresses to Grade Two thinking later in his education, describing it with Pontius Pilate's question to Jesus, "What is Truth?" In the story from John's gospel, Pilate does not actually seek an answer to this question; instead, he uses it as a means of ending discussion, clearly implying that such an idea does not exist. Golding describes a few of his actions from this level, as well, such as when he argues religion with Ruth, a young woman whom he has a crush on. They are debating the trustworthiness of the Bible, and she tells him that the King James Version is clearly reliable, while he argues for St. Jerome's Vulgate. She tries to use numbers as her next step, arguing that all those millions of Methodists could not be wrong. He says that, if it's a question of numbers, he would go with the Buddhists. The fact that he slips his arm around her at this point does not help his argument. His parents receive a phone call from Ruth's parents that evening, as Ruth is quite shaken.[3]

Golding's point is that he does not believe any of what he is arguing. He has become a pure Grade Two thinker, someone who sits back and pokes holes in everyone's else's beliefs, but who believes nothing of his or her own. Almost all teenagers progress through such a stage, acting on nothing but radical skepticism and investing in nothing. Most people, from Golding's description, stay here or slip back into Grade Three thinking, as Grade One thinking takes a good deal of commitment, and it offers few rewards:

> Political and religious systems, social customs, loyalties and traditions, they all came tumbling down like so many rotten apples off a tree. This was a fine hobby and a sensible substitute for cricket, since you could play it all the year round. I came up in the end with what must always remain the justification for grade-one thinking, its sign, seal, and charter. I devised a coherent system

---

3. Golding, "Thinking as a Hobby."

for living. It was a moral system, which was wholly logical. Of course, as I readily admitted, conversion of the world to my way of thinking might be difficult, since my system did away with a number of trifles, such as big business, centralized government, armies, marriage. . . .[4]

Now that I had begun thinking, it was not surprising that I would end up in Golding's Grade Two, as I had begun to question the beliefs I had long held, while I was clearly still holding on to many of those beliefs. I began to act with the radical skepticism of Grade Two, questioning professors and students alike without really knowing what I believed, though my questions ultimately helped me discover those beliefs.

In my senior year, I was taking an introductory education course. I had decided late in college to major in English (influenced by Dr. Dibble's class), and I was trying to rush through the education certification process to graduate with the credentials I needed to teach high school English. I should have taken such a course two or even three years before, and many of the other students were freshmen and sophomores. The professor was not a skilled instructor, as she tried to talk about classroom management at one point, and she was clearly unable to manage a college classroom, not to mention middle or high school students. One day, we somehow came to the topic of teachers who were homosexual. I cannot recall why we should have been talking about this subject, but I do remember one older student sitting in the front row who was very engaged in the discussion. She was adamant that she would not allow her children to be in a classroom led by a homosexual teacher. I was sitting in the back, not paying much attention to the class, as I seldom did or had to in order to do reasonably well. However, I could clearly see a flaw in her argument, and I questioned her about it. I wanted to know what she would do if a homosexual parent refused to allow his or her children in her class. She was flustered and could not come back with a logical argument. She simply grew angrier and angrier, repeatedly saying, "Well, I don't care. I'm just not going to have my kids in their class." No one else seemed interested in the discussion, and the professor let the class end without any serious conversation on the matter. The other student left rather angry with me, and I don't recall our talking much the rest of the semester. What is most interesting to me, though, is that I could not have articulated what I felt about homosexuality at the time. My roommate

4. Ibid., para. 40.

from my sophomore year had been working at a gay bar, and I was fairly certain that he was "becoming" gay. He clearly came out after he was expelled from the college, and we kept in touch the next few years. I was certainly not comfortable talking with him about the subject, and I was definitely not accepting, though I would not have condemned him, either. It took several more years before I began to truly understand what I believed on the subject. My argument in class had nothing to do with my beliefs on the subject. I was not defending homosexual parents' right to have their children take any teacher in any school. I was not standing up for the children's right to receive an education that was equal to everyone else's. No, I was arguing simply because I saw a flaw in her argument, and I took great glee in being able to point it out. The fact that she had no response, that she was flustered by my comments, simply made me happier. I did not want a conversation; I wanted to point out her hypocrisy.

A similar event happened later in my senior year when a debate began to spread across the campus. The part of the student government that was in charge of entertainment had invited Henry Lee Summer, a musician who performed secular music, to Milligan. What complicated the matter greatly was that the only place musicians performed on our campus was the chapel stage. Not only was he performing non-Christian music, he was doing so in our chapel. There were articles and editorials in the student newspaper, and then a young woman in my graduating class wrote a letter to the editor arguing against his coming. I decided to weigh in with my own letter. The bulk of the letter, from what I was told, was well-written and well-argued. However, I had begun my letter with a biblical paraphrase that was clearly designed to offend. In her letter, the young woman, Jen, had argued that churches that supported our college might be angry at our inviting someone like Summer, that they might withdraw some of the funding upon which our college depended. I thought this argument was the weakest portion of the letter, and I decided to attack it, though not in a terribly logical manner. Instead, I remembered a passage in Acts 8:20 where Simon the Sorcerer tries to buy the Holy Spirit from Peter. In most translations, Peter's response is rather tame: "May your money perish with you, because you thought you could buy the gift of God with money!" (NIV). However, in *Today's English Version* (also known as the *Good News Bible*), Peter replies, "May you and your money go to hell, for thinking that you can buy God's gift with money!" This version was the one I used.

It was clear that my intention was not to convince Jen or anyone else of my position; instead, my point was that I thought her (and, by association, everyone who agreed with her) argument was dumb, and I refused to engage it. I did not care if Summer came to Milligan or not. When the college decided to bring him to campus, someone stopped me and asked if I was coming to the concert. He seemed rather surprised that I was not, as I was clearly one of the loudest voices in support of him. Again, though, I did not care about his coming; I simply wanted to prove Jen wrong. During the final in my Contemporary literature class (again, Dr. Dibble), my friend Monica informed me that Jen had cried when she read my letter. I told her (and the class) that I didn't particularly care, that if one were going to debate such matters, he or she needed to deal with people who did not agree. The secretary to the academic dean, for whom I worked, had read my letter and told me it was a good argument, but that I should cut the opening paragraph. She was clearly correct, and I wish now that I would have. But, when one lives in a Grade Two mentality, pointing out other people's foibles is much more fun than self-reflection.

I had not left the church by the time I graduated from Milligan, but anyone who knew me well should have seen the signs. It would take another year for me to get to that point, but I was well on my way to that departure. I could blame the college here, as they made a mistake that many Christian colleges that emphasize the liberal arts make. They did a great job of teaching me to ask questions about my faith, important questions I had ignored until that time. I certainly did not know why I believed what I believed when I entered Milligan, and the emphasis on true thinking helped me to see that. The problem was that I also did not know what I believed when I left. I was taught and taught well how to see logical problems in arguments, how to take apart an illogical assertion, how to question assumptions, including mine. I had begun to take apart my faith. However, no one tried to teach me how to put it back together, how to reconstruct a belief system that could withstand the questions that would surely assail it. I see too many of my students graduate with the same problem. We have given them the tools to question everything about their lives and how to craft arguments about political, religious, literary, and historical ideas in clean, clear prose. We also help them dismantle their faith, to question all they have been taught. Like at Milligan, though, we often do not give them the tools they need to reconstruct what they have lost. I see students who leave their college years angry at the church, not having attended their last year or two. They are often even angry at their college, usually because they see the school as behind the times. Now that they see their previous beliefs as shallow, they wonder how anyone can still believe what they once did. Having helped them tear down the fortress of their faith, we have left them on a now-empty plain with no defenses against the questions life will bring against them. In the same way no one showed me how one can be a thinking Christian, we often do not show our students, even though almost all of us who teach at such colleges clearly practice such a life. Our Christian colleges and professors do not do a very good job of showing students that there are other ways of being Christian. It would take me close to a decade to learn that on my own, almost half of which was spent outside of the church.

7

Questions Not Allowed

AFTER I GRADUATED FROM college, I got married, which was not surprising, given that I attended a Christian college, and probably half of the students who graduate from Christian colleges are married by that time, but it was surprising considering I had often said I had no interest in marriage. That relationship will not come up often, but it is the backdrop for many events that occur, so I should say just a bit about it. My wife and I had begun dating during my senior year of college, having met at Kroger, where we both worked. She was four years older than I was, and she was working there at night, working as an accountant during the day. We got engaged after only four months of dating, and we were married just thirteen months after our first date. It's difficult to explain why I changed my mind on marriage or why I moved so quickly, but my main guess for why I did both was that I was living with another college student whom I had also met through working at Kroger. He had been engaged three different times, and it looked like he might be on his path for another. The fact that none of them had worked out did not seem to occur to me. Also, DJ, one of my best friends from Milligan, had been married for almost two years, and he seemed happy. The problem with a Christian college, especially in one's final two years, is that almost everyone seems to be getting married. Engagements and marriage were simply in the environment where I was living. Since I was supposedly growing up, and she was already grown up, I felt it was the next step to take. If I'm honest, though, there was also the physical aspect of our relationship to consider. Though we did not have sex, as

I continued to insist on not doing that, despite my changes in religious thinking otherwise, we had done more than I had done with any other woman. Given my lack of knowledge and experience to that point, I'm sure that my hormones helped to carry me along to my decision.

Even though she was in her mid-twenties, and I had begun graduate school, we were still attending the college class at Central. There was no young adult class, and the college class had grown considerably during our time there. When I and a few friends started it at the beginning of our college career, there were three to four of us, sometimes hitting five or six, but that was considered a great turnout. Now, we could often fill up our minister's living room, coming closer to twenty people on a regular Sunday. The church seemed to be changing in other ways, as it was moving more toward an imitation of the larger churches, with more elaborate Christmas cantatas and pageants, despite our small size. Theologically, it also seemed to be moving along the lines of the country at large, as there was a continued shift to the religious and political right, even though Clinton had just been elected president, perhaps *because* Clinton had just been elected president. After the twelve years of Reagan and Bush, the religious right had felt fairly secure, but Perot's entrance into the 1992 election had thrown them off, and they were now reacting against what had happened. The church had hired a new minister during my time in college and had recently added a new youth minister, and I did not know either of them well. I knew Bob, the pastor, much better than I knew the youth minister, as he had been hired during the end of my college career and the beginning of my transition to graduate school when I was not as involved as I had been, as I had been focused on the college class. I cannot even remember his name, which is odd, considering he is one of the main reasons I ended up finally leaving the church, though he was merely a symptom, not the cause, if I'm honest.

I had been attending more sporadically as I moved into graduate school, a point that was causing conflict between me and my wife. It had actually begun before we were married, so she should have seen something coming, but, in such a short engagement, much of the focus is on the wedding, and those early days of a relationship blind almost all of us to truths we should see. She was unwilling to attend without me, as it still felt very much like *my* church to her, as everyone asked about me when I wasn't there, which made her feel less welcome. One Sunday, though, I was there, and we attended the college class for Sunday school.

Somehow, the idea of predestination came up, at least in passing, and I was unwilling to let it pass. I had been fascinated with the idea since my junior year of college when I took Dr. Dibble's American Literature I class. There is no way to study the first half of American Literature without discussing the idea, as any understanding of the Puritans is incomplete without an understanding of their theology, and predestination is a key tenet. Since Milligan was connected with the Churches of Christ/Christian Church, the theology of almost all of the students was focused on free will, not predestination, so, as was his wont, Dibble tried to push us to think the other way.

He created a thought experiment to argue that we actually do, or at least should, if we're intellectually consistent, believe in predestination. He told us to imagine that we were looking at a refrigerator in our dorm or apartment, where we had both a can of Coke and a can of Pepsi. His question was simple: If God knows you're going to drink the Coke, can you drink the Pepsi? There is no way to answer this question without either arguing that God is wrong about what he supposedly knows or that we are forced to drink what he knows we are going to drink. It's a simplistic approach, but it at least points out a common contradiction in Christian thought, as most Evangelical Christians try to have it both ways, saying that God has a plan for people's lives, yet arguing that God's plan does not limit our free choice, an argument I heard throughout my college career and still hear from my students. When the subject came up in the college Sunday school class, then, I was ready to talk about, and talk about it, I did. I raised all of these questions and more, trying to point out this contradiction that I now saw, behaving like a good Grade Two thinker, where I could point out the flaws in other people's logic, but not put forth anything of my own. I even drew on Mark Twain's question of who was responsible for the fall of Adam and Eve. He argued that, if God knew Adam and Eve would eat of the tree, then created them anyway, the fault was with God, not them. I was raising issues many of these students, especially the younger ones, had not yet encountered in college and certainly not in church. The youth minister, though, eventually cut me off, and he did so by using the Bible, which has always struck me as the worst part of his behavior. What I wanted was an honest discussion of the ideas, as that's what I had been doing for four years in college, and I truly was puzzled by the church's approach to this subject. I wanted church to be a place where those discussions could continue, but he made it clear that it was not. He quoted from the end of the book of Job, after Job has spent the entire book suffering. Job's friends have all come to him with various accusations and solutions, especially pointing out that Job must have sinned to make God this angry with him, which was not true, and telling Job that he should curse God and die, which was also clearly not good advice.

Job, while not portraying the patience that is often ascribed to him, as he was clearly angry throughout parts of the book, did not at least take the extreme step of condemning God. However, he did ask a number of questions of God throughout the book, especially near the end. God finally appears to answer Job, but he does not give him the answers he wants. Instead, he gives him questions:

> The LORD said to Job:
>
> "Will the one who contends with the Almighty correct him?
>   Let him who accuses God answer him! . . .
>
> Would you discredit my justice?
>   Would you condemn me to justify yourself?
> Do you have an arm like God's,
>   and can your voice thunder like his?
>
> Who then is able to stand against me? . . .
> Who has a claim against me that I must pay?
>   Everything under heaven belongs to me."[1]

The message was clear: I was not allowed to ask questions. I was supposed to respond as Job did:

> Then Job replied to the LORD:
>
> "I know that you can do all things;
>   no purpose of yours can be thwarted.
> You asked, 'Who is this that obscures my plans without knowledge?'
>   Surely I spoke of things I did not understand,
>   things too wonderful for me to know.'
>
> You said, 'Listen now, and I will speak;
>   I will question you,
>   and you shall answer me.'
> My ears had heard of you
>   but now my eyes have seen you.

---

1. Job 40:1–2, 8–9; 41:10–11.

> Therefore I despise myself
> and repent in dust and ashes."[2]

The implication was that I was asking questions of God, wondering why God worked the way he did or didn't work the way I thought he should. What I was really questioning, though, was their perception of God, the ways they talked about him and, more importantly, the ways they didn't. I wanted people to admit that they changed their views on God based on what was more convenient at the time, to say they were inconsistent in their interpretations of God. While I was questioning the idea of God's sovereignty, it was their creation of that interpretation that bothered me, not the fact that it might or might not be true. However, the youth minister pointed out quite clearly that this question was one I was not allowed to ask, and, by implication, there were others. That was not the last day I attended church, but, both mentally and spiritually, it might as well have been.

Oddly enough, my friends in graduate school, most of whom were not Christian or, like me, were leaving or had left the church, tried to talk me into staying or, at least, continuing to use the traditional Christian morality to guide my life. This behavior surprised me a bit at the time, but it would surprise me even more now, given what I know and hear. Almost every conservative Christian I talk to who has attended graduate school talks about some sort of abuse he or she received while in graduate school: professors who mocked anyone who believed or who went even further and actively tried to punish students who were openly Christian, or peers who did the same. I have always thought such assertions were exaggerated, as I have only seen two or three such incidents in the seven and a half years I spent in various graduate schools. East Tennessee State was clearly the exception to these stories I would later hear. The professor I worked for was a Sunday school teacher in his congregation, and several of the other students were clearly Christian and did not receive any open or subtle abuse I could ever discern. The only incident I saw was when a student gave a presentation in an Arthurian literature course about how Christians had co-opted the pagan holidays and turned them into the major Christian holy days we still celebrate. The subject matter is clearly not controversial, but she presented it in a way that was clearly hostile to Christianity, as if her subject matter

2. Job 42:1–6.

proved without question that Christianity was a fraud. DJ and I talked about it later, and we were both surprised she would think we didn't already know that information. We were not offended at all, just a bit amused at her fervor over something so inconsequential.

When I began talking about leaving the church or at least questioning some of the basics of morality, the graduate students immediately tried to convince me otherwise. Once, in an American Humor class, before it began, I was talking with a few students about this issue. I was wondering what would keep me from doing wrong if I gave up my faith. It's easy to see now how I was slowly taking one step after another out of Christianity, but every step was a difficult one to take, so I was moving cautiously. Here, I was clearly concerned about how I would live my life without the moral compass I had counted on for so long, which was especially troubling to me, given the extreme beliefs I had held for the past six years or so. When I raised this issue, I did so with a hypothetical example that was direct and not nuanced at all. I asked a simple question, "Without any type of external controls, such as a religious faith, what would keep me from pulling out a gun and shooting someone in the head?" We did not have much time before class, but one person did take the time to answer. Jennifer—who was clearly not a Christian and was known for making outrageous comments, such as "Adultery isn't adultery if you don't get caught"—was the one who responded: "You cannot impose your personal beliefs on another person. They have rights and freedoms, and you have no right to take them away." My response was swift and short, "Why not?" I expounded, "What keeps me from taking away their rights and freedoms?" She fell back on the Constitution, but I pointed out that was an external control. Unfortunately, we had to begin class, but she had helped me take one more step away from the church. Neither she nor anybody else could have talked me into staying in the church or at least keeping some sort of faith, but at least she tried.

One other person who made an effort, but who was not a Christian, at least at the time, was a young man we called Kerley, his last name. He had been a philosophy major when he was an undergraduate, so he loved to sit around and discuss abstract ideas. His office adjoined mine and DJ's, so I often spent afternoons with him (and often included Jennifer) in such long discussions. He was a methodical thinker, taking the time to prove his points, even after I had granted his givens, so he was a good person to discuss such issues with. When I was considering taking up both drinking and smoking, as I needed something to solidify my role as an English graduate student, but I did not enjoy coffee, I talked to him about it, as he did both of those. I enjoyed spending time with him and other students in what we called Smoker's Alley, liked the conversations there, the sense of being outside of the norms of society, and I even liked the smell, having grown up with my mother's smoking before she quit. Kerley actually talked me out of smoking, as he laid out everything it would do to my body in fairly clear detail, then told me he wished he had never begun. His argument was compelling, so I remained alcohol- and tobacco-free, as I had wanted both to create my image, and I had just been talked out of one of them. One afternoon, we were sitting around the office, and the subject of morality and faith came up. I never explicitly laid out my concerns with the church, but we did talk about the same idea I had raised with Jennifer. I was honestly struggling with how I would live a good life if I did not have a faith to guide me through it. Kerley quoted Kant and a few other philosophers in his defense of at least a basic morality, but this subject was not like tobacco. I used the same argument with him that I used with Jennifer: "But why should I listen to them?" I kept on with my argument that those people were simply another form of external control, and I was trying to give that up. If I were going to live by something outside of myself telling me what to do, then it might as well be the Bible. Since I was giving that up, though, I wanted to give anything up that looked like it, so I continued chipping away at any type of external authority.

Before I left ETSU and Johnson City, I was successful at getting rid of such an approach, but it terrified me. The realization of how terrifying it was came in a church, though it was almost empty, occupied by only me and my wife at the time, as we were there on a Saturday night. We were cleaning the church, as we had been hired by the congregation to be the janitors for a year. Central actually had a wonderful system for their custodial work, as it sought to benefit people who needed financial help. Anyone related to the congregation could apply for the position, as they simply needed to write a letter explaining why they needed financial assistance. The elders of the church would then meet to consider all the requests, then try to give the job to the person most in need of help. Since I was in graduate school, we could certainly use the income. My wife worked as an accountant, but she was not a CPA, and she worked for a small oil and gas distribution company, so she was not making enough to support both of us. I had a graduate assistantship that covered my tuition, but it only paid a $5000 stipend. Even though it was the early 1990s, $5000 still did not cover very much. We applied for the janitorial position, and the elders decided to give it to us. I felt guilty about taking the job from someone like a single mother who might need the money more than we did, but we were the only applicants that year, which comforted me greatly. The job was not onerous, as the church was not large, and we quickly learned shortcuts. Since the building was only used a few times a week, there were parts we did not need to clean every week, leaving those for monthly cleaning, and we even learned there were weeks we did not need to vacuum, as we could pick up any major debris, and the rest would go unnoticed. Close to the end of our time as custodians, the church actually collapsed in a snow storm, as Wayne's father, one of the main elders, let me know. He called and asked me to come over to the church to clean up, as there were some piles of dust. Given that we had received a few feet of snow, and we lived in a town that was ill-equipped to handle a few inches, I was surprised he would ask me to come out. He then laughed and told me that the roof had caved in. For the rest of our year, we only needed to clean the fellowship hall, where we held services from then on, which lessened our load considerably. To the church leaders' credit, they voted to keep our pay at the same rate, as they were helping us out more than they were paying us to clean. I felt guilty about that, as well, as my attendance was becoming more and more sporadic. We would go to the church on Saturday night, clean the building, then sleep in on Sunday morning and skip church. It was clear we were not sick or out of town, as anyone who lived near the church, especially the minister, who lived in the parsonage next door, could see when we had been there. People then knew we were simply not attending church, though almost no one said anything about it, at least while we still showed up periodically.

It was on one of those Saturday nights I realized the path I was beginning to take, moving away from the faith that had defined my life for the past six or seven years. I was upstairs vacuuming, so I was also thinking while I was doing that work, and I was thinking specifically about the question I had been asking my peers at ETSU about, about how one lives a life without any kind of external definition of right or wrong. I realized I would be completely free of such a definition if I left the church, left my faith behind. There would be no universal definition of right and wrong to either guide me or constrain me from then on. Rather than any type of elation, I felt fear and terror, and I realized I had been looking for such a guide with all of my questions to my peers. I wanted someone to tell me another way to live my life now that I was giving up the one that I had known. But no one was able to provide an answer, and I certainly had not found one. My only comparison to this feeling is the one the Existentialist philosophers come up with when they talk about *angst*. Existentialists argue, in short, that we have no inherent meaning in our lives, that we are here, but we do not know why we are; we have to define our own meaning. We do so through the choices we make, but those choices are completely and utterly free; there is no god, no fate, no devil, no determinism whatsoever limiting or guiding our choices. Thus, we are completely free, but that means we also have complete responsibility for our choices. They argue that these conditions lead us to *angst* or anxiety. While freedom sounds like a wonderful idea, the responsibility that comes with it is so overwhelming that we often create ideas or beings, such as fate or god, to avoid responsibility for our choices. On that evening, I felt the weight of that anxiety. I knew I was giving up any external system I had used to define my existence to that point, that I was going to have to take full responsibility for my choices should I choose to give up my faith. I knew I needed to leave that faith behind, but it utterly terrified me. Even with that knowledge, though, I did it, anyway. I made a conscious choice to leave my faith behind. It would still be a year or two before I would stop referring to myself as a Christian, but the decision had been made. After our time as custodians was up, I stopped attending church altogether, shifting my focus to graduate school and turning literature and reason into my guiding principles. If I could not find faith in religion, where there were too many unanswered questions, then I would look to reason, to think through the problems of life and come up with rational answers.

There were a few people, though, who tried to keep me in the church, but, despite their sincerity, they did not know the approach to take or how to show me another way to believe, which is what I truly needed. Our minister at Central, Bob, had tried to keep in touch with me, even calling me at my office at school on a fairly regular basis, but I did a fairly good job of avoiding him. The one time I did actually meet to talk with him, though, he was not able to convince me to remain in the church. He mainly told me about his struggles when he was younger, even made the comment one is not supposed to make in such situations: "I know what you're going through." As with most people before me, I thought he had no idea what I was going through, as my situation was completely different from any that had come before me. While that's true on one level, as every situation is unique, shaped by our particular backgrounds and biases, as I've taught several rounds of college students, I'm finding that the questions they ask and the struggles they face are almost always the same. Not only are they similar to each other, they are also similar to the questions I had when I was their age. We both came to college with our faith clearly defined in a narrow sense, then encountered information or ideas that caused us to question our interpretation of that faith. When we did not see another way to be a Christian, we believed that the one way we knew was the only way; since it is not correct, Christianity as a whole must be wrong. It is no surprise that so many people who attend Christian colleges end up leaving the church. Bob at least tried to identify with my struggle, and he did try to tell me his story. However, his story did not sound like my story; there was nothing in it I could identify with. His struggle had come after college, and his seemed even more theological than mine. His solution for my problem was a book, but not one that was easily accessible for someone with limited theological training. Instead of giving me a memoir or biography or even a book along the lines of *Mere Christianity* by C.S. Lewis, he gave me a book by Karl Barth, a German theologian. I never read it, though I did flip through it a few times. I only remember seeing a chart on one page, which did not inspire me to read it. Any book that needed complicated charts to lay out a defense of Christianity was not a book I wanted to read.

The real problem was that I simply did not want a defense of Christianity at that point. I wanted that time of rebellion, that time of freedom from the faith that had shaped me for so long. Once I had made up my mind to pursue the path away from it, I needed to follow that path to see where it went. I would probably not have heard anything Bob said, no matter how appropriate it might have been. I can't really fault Bob, then, for not keeping me in the church, though I've always wondered if there would have been a way for him to break through to me. He had not inspired me with confidence in the past, though, as he was the minister who did our pre-marital counseling. As in many such sessions, he had us fill out worksheets that contained basic information about us, but also asked us more open-ended questions. We were supposed to do these separately, then talk about them with him. The main question I remember centered on goals, especially the one thing we would like to accomplish in life. Given that I was in graduate school, mine focused on attaining the PhD and finding a job teaching college. My then-fiancée responded that her focus was on family. When she made that comment, she immediately turned to me and said, "Not kids. Just us and our extended family." Two problems should have been apparent to us and to Bob. First, our goals were not in synch with each other, and, while they did not contradict, it was clear that they could lead to conflict. We did not discuss this possibility of conflict or even the apparent divergence of our primary goals in life. Second, and more importantly, was the defensiveness she brought to her response. She and I had talked, and I was quite clear on the subject of children, as I did not want any. She seemed fine with that, but her answer clearly shows she had other ideas she had not shared with me (I found out later that both her mother and my mother had told her I would change my mind on the issue). She gave her answer, then immediately clarified it in such a way that I would not respond either with simple anger or even calling the relationship off. I did not take note of her response or her behavior as I should have, nor did Bob notice or comment on it. Given that our relationship was in trouble by the time I left the church, I had already recognized that Bob was not the best person to give advice, as I thought he should have suggested we not get married. Even though I would not have listened to him at that point, just as I probably would not have listened at this point, I still faulted him for not recognizing the disconnect in our answers. Though I would have left the church anyway, given how I felt by this point, not having a minister I trusted to help guide me certainly did not help my situation.

    Bob was not the only one who tried to help, as Wayne also put forth an effort. Even though I had gotten married and gone to graduate school in English, while he was still single and pursuing a graduate degree in Accounting, we still saw each other on a fairly regular basis and spent time together. Even outside of church, he and I had both started trying to play golf, so we would see each other then. Wayne and I never had serious conversations during these outings, sticking to safe subjects, such as school or our families. When I began drifting away from the church, Wayne did not raise the subject. However, once I left the church, he did try to have a serious conversation with me about it, a challenge for him, as he was introverted and non-confrontational. We had gone out to lunch just a few months before I and my wife were moving to Mississippi, so I could pursue a doctoral degree, and we were driving back to the office where he was now working. He said simply, "I wish you two would come back to church. We miss you when you're not there." It was clear and direct, and it conveyed his true feelings. It was one of the most sincere comments he had ever made to me. The problem for me, though, was that I did not feel I could have this conversation with him, as there was too much back story that I would have needed to explain. I felt I would have to go through the past three or four years of thought that led me to this point, the theological concerns I had and the questions I could not find answers for. He and I had simply never had that kind of relationship, despite our having spent so much time together for so long. He had been my best friend in high school, but we had never shared our struggles, never talked about difficulties with girls or school and certainly not religion.

Six months into my marriage, my wife and I almost divorced. That weekend also happened to be the weekend Wayne and I were traveling to Indiana to be in one of our best friend's wedding. We were in the car for several hours up and back, and we spent a good deal of time together there. I had told him she and I were having trouble and it looked like things might come to an end. Even though he told me later that no one was surprised when we actually did get divorced, he was honestly surprised this weekend. We barely spoke about it, but he did express his disappointment and shock, but that mainly came from the fact that he wanted to be married himself, so he could not understand why someone would give it up so quickly. He wanted the life I seemed to have, which is what surprised him. Then, as now with religion, though, I felt I could not explain the situation clearly enough, so we let it drop. I avoided the question, told him that I appreciated his concern, but that we were fine, we would be fine. I did not believe I would be fine in the way he wanted me to be fine; I simply did not know how to tell him how and who I would be from then on. Even when we kept in touch while I was in Mississippi, seeing each other from time to time when I would come home to visit, I did not tell him about my religious struggles, and he did not ask if I was attending church. On the way back, we simply faced forward in the car, never looking at each other, and moved on. He did, though, before he said goodbye, tell me he wished we saw each other more often and that he wished we would come back to church. I still appreciate the effort it took him to have that conversation, and I wish I could have spoken honestly, but I missed the opportunity to have a real conversation with someone who had played such an important role in getting me to where I was, though he did not appreciate that place.

One other conversation spans the time between Tennessee and Mississippi, both literally and figuratively, as it took place on the move between the two states, and it took place between me and DJ, who was quickly becoming my new best friend, as I moved away from Johnson City, Central, and Wayne. The trip down was largely unremarkable, as the conversation consisted of general subjects and DJ's pointing out how often I-40 crosses the Tennessee river. However, the trip is a long one, as we drove the entire state of Tennessee from Johnson City to Memphis, then down to Oxford. Not surprisingly, our conversation eventually turned to more serious subjects. DJ introduced the topic by mentioning his wife's concern for me. I had gotten rid of a good deal of belongings before the move, mainly items I had accumulated in high school and college, so some of them related to my devotion to Christianity. What began the conversation was something I gave to DJ: my collection of Christian music tapes, both originals and copies, as I did not know what else to do with them. He told me they could use them with the youth group at the church, which made sense. I kept a few of them I still enjoyed, but I gave him the rest a few weeks before we moved. Then, as we were driving along, he said simply, "Tammy's worried about you because you gave away all your Christian music." That began a conversation that lasted the rest of the trip and the next three years while I was in Mississippi. This protracted exchange was a conversation I had been wanting to have with someone for some time, as DJ had the same educational background I did, so he had encountered the same questions and concerns. He had a deeper religious background than I did, but mine had certainly been more fervent. He was not closed-minded, though, knowing that life was more complicated than conservative Evangelical Christians often made it out to be. When I mentioned the problems I was going through with my marriage, he not only understood, he also argued that there were times when divorce was the best option, which was not an opinion I expected him to have. He was the person I needed to talk to, as I felt he, if anyone, could understand my concerns.

We talked the rest of the way to Mississippi, then all the way back, including our stop at a Shoney's for lunch. It was clear that Tammy was not the only one concerned about my religious development, as he clearly wanted to convince me to stay in the faith, to keep asking questions, but to stay in it. I assured him I would be fine, which sounds exactly like what I had told Wayne, but there was a distinct difference now. What I meant by that comment was that I would ultimately end up in the place where I needed to be, though that might not be back in the church. I told him that, as long as I kept asking questions, he had no need to worry, that it was only when I stopped asking questions that the situation would be truly dire because that would mean that I had ceased to care about religious questions at all. I still find this approach to be true in people I meet. Those who are unwilling to consider the questions are the ones who cause me concern, even if they are still practicing their faith, as it seems to have no life to it. Those who leave or have left the church, but still engage people in discussion are the ones who will ultimately come to some sort of belief, as they clearly want to believe in something; they just don't know how to do so yet. They have not found the way they need to engage with the divine. I was in the same situation. Even though DJ was diligent in his arguments, he could not convince me to come back to my faith because he did not have the path I needed to find my way back. I had already been down the path he was suggesting, and it did not lead me where it led him. Instead, it lead me to a dead end, a place where I could not believe anything I had been taught, a place where I seemingly only had two choices: believe that way or believe nothing, and neither of those appealed to me. I knew I wanted to believe, but I did not know what.

When I was in Mississippi, DJ even suggested I read *Mere Christianity* by C.S. Lewis. My students are always surprised by my disdain for Lewis, as he continues to be held up as a paragon of Evangelical Christianity, but my lack of respect for him comes from this time in my life. Since I was reading the book as an outsider, as one who needed to be convinced of his arguments, I came to it with a different approach than my students and DJ do. And Lewis did not convince me, at all. His arguments were weak and shallow, and they assumed ideas that were not necessarily true. For example, one of his most famous arguments centers on the divinity of Jesus. Lewis argues, "A man who was merely a man and said the sort of things Jesus said would not be a great moral teacher. He would either be a lunatic—on the level with a man who says he is a poached egg—or he would be the devil of hell. You must take your choice. Either this was, and is, the Son of God, or else a madman or something worse. You can shut Him up for a fool or you can fall at His feet and call Him Lord and God. But let us not come with any patronizing nonsense about His being a great human teacher. He has not left that open to us."[3] Leaving aside the problem of what Jesus means by the term "Son of God," which is a term much more complicated than many Christians want to admit, what bothered me then and continues to bother me is Lewis's approach to the Bible. Lewis assumes that all the comments of Jesus are what Jesus actually said. Even before doing any serious reading in textual criticism, I had come to doubt that approach, as there were simply too many contradictions for me to believe that. Where Lewis argues that Jesus says he is the Son of God, I saw a text, written by people who believed Jesus was the Son of God, which is a very different view. Lewis never admits that such a belief might even exist. Therefore, he gives his readers a false choice, arguing that there are only two approaches to the subject, not realizing or admitting that there is another major one, along with several others that could also be equally valid. This thinking was what drove me from Christianity in the first place, as I wanted there to be rational answers, and here Lewis, supposedly one of the great thinkers of the faith, makes simple errors that I, a person with advanced degrees in English, but certainly not theology, could catch. DJ would try to counter my complaints by pointing out that Lewis originally gave these talks on the radio, so they were for a different audience, but I insisted that his arguments should at least make sense, especially as he is trying to argue people into the faith. This lack of consistency in Christianity led me to try to find a faith that was much more rational.

It was only several years later that I realized how quixotic my search for a rational faith was, given the basic definition of faith as something that is not based on reason, but, at the time, my faith in reason was so strong I believed it could solve any problems. When that faith in reason was combined with my natural desire to find something to believe in, it was no surprise I ended up with such a paradoxical view of the religious world. I read around in a variety of religious traditions, looked at the basics of Hinduism, Islam, and even the Baha'i faith, but none of them

3. Lewis, *Mere Christianity*, 41.

seriously caught my attention. Instead, the one religion that seemed most interesting to me was Buddhism. I will readily admit the irony here in that I went searching for a rational approach to faith, and I ended up becoming interested in Buddhism, a faith largely based on paradox and contradiction, one that argues that the world we see is an illusion that blinds us to the real truth of who we are and how we attain enlightenment, a faith that argues we only truly attain the truth when we remove all ego and desires whatsoever, including the desire for enlightenment. However, that was the religion that somehow drew me to it. It had begun when I was still at ETSU, and the beginning was not rational in itself. Since I grew up in the 1980s, I missed many of the television shows of the early 1970s, as syndication was not popular yet, and I was too young to have seen them during their first run. I missed the *Kung Fu* movie and TV series the first time around. However, when I was in graduate school, another series began, which was based on the original, if loosely, called *Kung Fu: The Legend Continues*. I had had a passing interest in Eastern approaches to life, as I grew up watching television shows and movies about ninjas and various forms of martial arts— including *The Last Dragon*, a movie that is often described as one of the worst of the decade and one that I still own, as it is still one of my favorite awful movies—which is probably where my interest truly began.

I took my interest in the television show and pursued it, even reading a book by David Carradine, the star of the new and old series. However, I did not know where to go next, but I ended up talking with one of my professors at ETSU about it. I had taken a class in 1960s American Literature, so I asked Dr. Waage, my professor for that class, if he knew anything about Buddhism. Given the interest in Eastern religions during that decade, he made the most sense to ask. He did not have a great deal of knowledge or interest, but he told me about a professor who taught speech, Dr. Kirkwood, who had actually gone to the East to study with a guru. Oddly enough, I had taken a class with this professor a couple of years before, as I took my speech and science classes at ETSU over the summer, partly because they were cheaper, but also partly because I had heard those classes at Milligan could kill a GPA. I went to talk with him. He was encouraging, asking why I was interested in the subject, and he even responded kindly when I presented my case through self-deprecation, admitting that my interest in Buddhism came from a television series. He suggested a few other books for me to read, especially

Zen Flesh, Zen Bones, compiled by Paul Reps and Nyogen Senzaki, and anything by Alan Watts. I would love to say that I took his suggestions to heart and went forth and read what he suggested; however, I was a graduate student in literature, and I was more interested in reading novels when I had the free time. I later went back to see him one more time, but he was busy grading finals that week, so we did not talk. I'm not sure what I expected from him, but, at that point, my interest was not enough to compel me to do any work to follow where my interest was leading. I probably expected him to give me some basic information, to tell me that my ideas were on the right track, that Buddhism was a rational approach to the divine, but he certainly did not support my thoughts in that direction. He talked about contradictions in the approach and even the different branches of Buddhism and where they differed, which I had not known about. I wanted him to tell me I was right, that Buddhism was better than Christianity, but, he did not, and I was not interested enough to dig into it myself.

However, I did at least ask one more professor about Buddhism, and his comment is the one that helped me as I became more interested later in life. I was having trouble understanding the seeming contradictions that Dr. Kirkwood had mentioned and that I was seeing in the little reading I had done on my own, so I was talking about these problems with Dr. Dibble. I knew that he had an interest in religions, in general, and I would go visit him at Milligan from time to time to talk about a variety of subjects. On this day, we were sitting in the student union grill, and I raised my concerns about what I had discovered. He suggested I read the *Tao Te Ching*, as Buddhism came from Taoism, and that text might help me make some sense of what I had been reading and thinking. This book is the one that began to help me make sense of matters and kept my interest alive, even if only in passing. I cannot truly say it helped me understand Buddhism on a rational level better than I had been doing, but I at least understood where the ideas were coming from and what the terminology meant, at least somewhat better. Also, the ideas just struck me as true and important, and the writing was beautiful, poetry I did not find in the prose of Christianity, which appealed to the more aesthetic side that I was developing as I continued to study literature. I read and re-read the *Tao Te Ching*, letting it sink in, as I was finishing my time at ETSU; however, I did not pursue any other reading in Buddhism until I was at Ole Miss. There, I did begin to read the books that Dr.

Kirkwood had suggested, especially those by Alan Watts. As before, I did not understand all that I was reading, but it was making sense to me in a way that religion had not for the past few years. If I would have thought clearly about it, though, I would have recognized that it was not because there was a rational basis for it; instead, it was simply because I sensed there was something true about it. What also should have connected for me, but did not, was that, what I liked about Buddhism, was mainly what it had in common with Christianity. I loved the idea of ridding oneself of the ego, which clearly connected to Jesus' frequent comments to give up the self, an issue I struggled and still struggle with. The Buddhist idea of right thought and right action appealed to me, as I believed that religion should, at its most basic level, answer the question, "How, then, should I live?" which is why Micah 6:8 was one of my favorite verses: "He has shown you, O mortal, what is good. And what does the LORD require of you? To act justly and to love mercy and to walk humbly with your God." However, what was also appealing to me was the main difference I saw between Buddhism and Christianity, though I could not articulate it yet. Christianity, at least as I had known it to that point, was a religion of dualities, which forced me into choices I disagreed with, much as the Lewis book had done. People are either in or out; actions are either sinful or righteous; music was either Christian or secular. In Buddhism, however, dualities are the major part of the illusion we see around us, so we must learn to see past them to see the truth of the world, which is that there is no right without wrong, no good without evil, no righteousness without sinful behavior. The second passage of the *Tao Te Ching* says clearly,

> All the world knows beauty
> but if that becomes beautiful
> this becomes ugly
> all the world knows good
> but if that becomes good
> this becomes bad.

This approach struck me as true at a deeper level than the dichotomies I had been presented with thus far. It dealt directly with issues I had with ideas, such as predestination and free will, as a Buddhist simply accepts that both are true and that both are false, as there is a truth behind them that we must get to that cannot be defined in words. The idea of there being a moment where humans went from being completely innocent and pure to being sinful, stained creatures, as the traditional interpretation of the Garden of Eden argues, begins to break down, the dichotomy shown to be false. Instead, the idea represented by the *yin-yang*, that we all have good and evil inside of each of us, that everything in existence does, helped show me that there were other ways of seeing sin and evil.

    I did not know any of this at that time; I simply felt that here was something that would help me see the world in a way that I needed to see it. Oddly enough, though, I never practiced meditation, nor did I seek out anyone in Mississippi to discuss the subject with. Since I was still focused on a rational approach, I was looking for religion in books I could read, not in actions I could perform. My understanding of Buddhism still came from the outside, not from a lived experience, which is the core of any religious tradition. It helped change my thinking and understanding, but it did not change my life, could not change my life, as I would not let it. It did, however, change my knowledge of Christianity, but not in the positive way that one might expect. I did not make the connections between Buddhism and Christianity, allowing one to influence my views on the other, learning from both. Instead, as the expression that is often applied to math tells us, "use it or lose it" can also be applied to religion. Since I was not reading the Bible or attending church, my basic knowledge of Christianity was beginning to fade rather rapidly, causing me to forget a wide swath of information I had known throughout my high school and college years. The best example of this decrease in knowledge came in my literature classes, as the works we read contained numerous allusions to the Bible. In my first year at Ole Miss, I was taking a course called Recent American Fiction. As much as I loved that time period, I was not enjoying the class. As my friend Geoff put it one day as we were leaving the classroom, having just discussed Ralph Ellison's *Invisible Man*, "I liked that book before we started discussing it." We felt that way about almost every book we read in the class, which was disappointing. However, one book we read that I did not lose my enthusiasm for was Toni Morrison's *Sula*. I had read it before as a senior in Milligan, but I did not remember much about it, given that I had spent the three years since then reading many more books, and I did not particularly like it then. On the second read, though, I really appreciated what Morrison was doing. In the discussion, we were talking about the novella's approach to death and the fear of death, especially as seen in the character of Shadrach. Our professor asked if anyone knew anything about the biblical character of the same name. I was on the verge of raising my hand and pointing out that that was the legendary name for one of the three wise men who came to visit the baby Jesus. Luckily, someone else was able to give him the correct answer before I had time to speak, saving me the embarrassment of missing a basic biblical character. Shadrach was one of the three men in the book of Daniel who refused to bow to the statue of Nebuchadnezzar and was put into the fiery furnace to die. When he and his two friends, Meshach and Abednego, were put into the furnace, they did not die, and there was a mysterious fourth person in the flames with them (whom some people have speculated was Jesus, making an early appearance in the Bible, which is odd theology, but interesting, otherwise). The three wise men did have legendary names, but they were Gaspar, Melchior, and Balthazar. This incident seems harmless enough, as these three characters aren't major biblical figures, showing up in only the first three chapters of the book of Daniel, but this story is one of the better known stories in the Old Testament and certainly one I was taught numerous times growing up. Preachers and Sunday school teachers often used the story to show how people were willing to stand up for their faith, even to the point of death, to show children or youth how important belief could be and how God would protect those who believed. The fact that I had forgotten it made me wonder what else I had forgotten in those few years.

However, I could still use what knowledge I did have and the logic I possessed to talk about Christianity and argue about it well enough. DJ and I continued to talk via email, as my views on the existence of God and the truth about Christianity and Buddhism continued to change, almost from week to week. My wife and I would not really talk about Christianity, as we didn't talk about anything that was serious, but we would talk about church attendance, at least. She continued not to attend church, even though she said she still believed. One evening, as I was getting ready to head upstairs to read, the subject came up. I was standing on the stairs of our townhouse, while she was sitting in a chair in the living room, getting ready to watch television. She said that she would not go to church, and I questioned her about it. I kept asking, "If you believe it's right, why won't you go?" Her response was simple and unchanging, "That's not the way I was raised." It sounds like she was raised by her mother, step-father, and father to attend church together, but that's actually not the case at all. Instead, she often attended church alone when she was growing up, as one or the other of her parents would drop her off at church, then pick her up or allow her to ride home with someone else. When she said she was not raised that way, what she meant was that she hated having to grow up that way, and she did not want to live that way now. She believed that being a part of a family meant attending church together, so she did not want to relive her childhood years of going to church alone. This approach bothered me greatly, as I believed people should act on their beliefs, if they have them. Since I no longer believed, I no longer acted as a Christian, nor even called myself one, a step that was certainly difficult, but important for me. I pushed my questions even more in our discussion that night, even asking, "So, if you would go to hell for not attending church, you still wouldn't go alone?" She responded the same way, "That's not the way I was raised," and left it at that. Needless to say, her approach frustrated me greatly, which is part of the reason we did not talk about the subject often, as I had little respect for her views on the subject. I often wonder if my lack of feelings for her by this point affected my views of religion, not in the fact that I had no respect for Christianity because I had no respect for her, but more that I stayed out of church longer than I would have because I did not want to attend church with her or even that I wanted to be as different from the person she married as possible. I'll readily admit that such an approach is passive-aggressive, but I was certainly taking that approach in the marriage by then. I was too much of a coward to simply get a divorce, as I had tried the direct approach before, only to get pressure from almost everyone in my life not to do so, and I did not have the courage to simply stand up to everyone about that. I felt I could simply become a person she did not want to be married to, and she would be the one to leave, even though she had clearly stated that she would never file for a divorce. Her continued desire to attend church may simply have strengthened my resolve not to go and not to believe. If I would have been single, I may have given Christianity another chance. I cannot prove the two are related, but, given how many other changes I made in my life, I cannot discount it, either. However, I was doing what many people did in college and graduate school, as I was trying to figure out who I was and who I wanted to be; my unhappy marriage may have had nothing to do with it. The more I think through this time in my life, the more I realize that pulling out one strand and saying that it was the cause of my behavior is too simplistic. All of these aspects of life kept me from believing, and none of them encouraged me to give Christianity another chance.

One drawback to where we currently were is that I really didn't have many friends who had any faith, so I had few people I could talk to. Granted, I could still talk to DJ, but that was mainly via email and phone calls, so I didn't get those chances on a regular basis, but he was mainly it. There were two other people in Mississippi I talked about religion with, but not often and not as deeply as I would like, mainly due to my own immaturity. When I was working on my doctorate at Ole Miss, I found a graduate assistantship in the library, a place I had never really considered working, but my dissertation director was friends with the dean, so it worked out well. While there, I met Stephanie, a woman who was a year or two younger than me, but a year or two further along her career path, as she had gone to school for a Master's in Library Science, and her position at Ole Miss was her first job out of graduate school. Since we were roughly the same age, we often had conversations about music and movies, but we occasionally drifted into talking about religion. Like me, Stephanie was also struggling with issues from her younger years, though I only found out a couple of years later how much she was dealing with and how much she was not able to tell me at the time. The one moment, though, that showed me just how far I had come from five years before was when we were talking about terminology. Stephanie later told me that she did not like labels, as she found them limiting, and our conversation at Ole Miss hinted at such. When we were talking about religion, I said simply that I did not consider myself a Christian anymore, as I had made up my mind about that a year or two before. She looked surprised and commented, "You know, I could never say that." She had made her doubts abundantly clear throughout our conversations over the past year or so, and she clearly was as far away from the Christianity of her youth as I was from mine, but she could not take that last step. The fact that I could showed me how seriously I was taking this drifting away. I have doubted at times that it was as serious as I believe it was, now that I'm older and have more perspective on it, but this conversation always reminds me how difficult a struggle it was, how challenging it is to give up a major piece of our identities, as Stephanie clearly could not do that. The moment in the church where I felt like the floor had fallen out from under me was not just the realization that I had no moral guidance, I now see; it was that I no longer knew who I was, and I had nothing to put in its place.

There were other students at Ole Miss who were also struggling with their faith, and I was able to talk to them, at least on a superficial level. My best friend in the department—my only friend, if I'm honest—was Geoff, a Master's student who began his program when I did mine. We had two of our classes together the first semester, and he is the student who made the comment about Recent American Fiction and our discussion of *Invisible Man*. He didn't have much interest in religion, simply saying that we couldn't know if any of it was true, so we shouldn't expend the time or energy to try to figure it out. His wife, Sharon, however, was interested in religion, so she and I talked about it from time to time. My wife and I often went over to their apartment to watch movies, and one night, the conversation turned to religion. Sharon asked us why we didn't attend church anymore, as she at least knew that much about our religious behavior. I gave my standard response about irrationality and how I was looking for a religion that made sense, raising the main concerns I had about Christianity. My wife, to my disappointment, said her reason was pretty much the same. That response simply was not true, and it didn't help our already unsteady relationship, as I wanted her to answer honestly, but I didn't raise that issue at the time. Sharon, it seemed, was interested in religion, but she didn't seem happy with traditional Christianity. At the time, she seemed much more interested in Judaism, as she was reading about the various rules and rituals of Orthodox Judaism. She was even beginning to practice them, if in minor ways. She once called me and asked me to meet her for lunch, an odd invitation, as she had never done it before and never did it again, but that may simply be because she wanted someone to talk religion about, and she was hoping to make me that person, though that didn't work out due to my awkwardness at that lunch. I had a tendency to be rather abrasive, and Sharon was rather soft-spoken, more interested in really exploring ideas than I was, as I was much more willing to simply pontificate and hold forth about issues. When we were ordering, though, she ordered a hamburger, then told me about how and why she made her choice. Orthodox Jews, she told me, do not mix dairy and meat; thus, she could not have a cheeseburger, which would have been her traditional choice. Oddly enough, that's the only aspect of the lunch I remember, as our conversation truly was stilted due to my awkwardness. The same problem had come up when I would talk to Stephanie, a problem complicated by the fact that I only saw her during work hours; she would be trying to get work done, and I would stop by her cubicle and talk to her for long stretches of time, a practice that eventually got her into a bit of trouble, as she was the full-time employee.

Both of these situations were complicated by the fact that I was a young man in an unhappy marriage talking to two women about my age. Despite my having left my faith behind, I certainly would never have considered having an affair, especially as Sharon was also married, and I both liked and respected her and Geoff. The morality that Christianity instilled in me was still there, whether or not I would admit it. However, I was also not mature enough to have a relationship with women my age where I wasn't at least thinking about what it would be like to be single and have the opportunity of dating again. There were two opportunities to honestly discussion religion with people I respected that I did not take advantage of, simply because I was not mature enough to do so. I was left in this odd place, where the people I was able to talk to, such as DJ, were trying to point me back to the Evangelical Christianity I had left. While conversations with him were helpful, they were not the direction I needed to take, and I did not capitalize on the few opportunities I had to talk to people who might have helped me find another direction. I also did not pursue other paths within Christianity, as my knowledge was limited, and I had no one to show me another way to live in that tradition. My move away from the church always reminds me of a song by a Christian musician that was released just at the time I was beginning to make that move. Since my listening tastes had changed to more heavy metal and alternative Christian music, I did not know the song as well as I had other ones. Steve Taylor was on the fringe of Christian music, satirizing the church as much as anything else, which is why so many young Christians liked him. He was clever and funny and wrote songs that made us wonder about the church, which is what we needed at the time. I had listened to all of his early tapes time and time again, even his one album where he and a few other musicians moved to a secular label and recorded a non-Christian album under the band name Chagall Guevara, a tape I still own, as I still argue it's his best work. In 1987, though, just before he made that move, he released an album called *I Predict 1990*, which was most famous for the controversy it caused for a song called "I Blew Up the Clinic Real Good," told from the point of view of an ice cream truck driver who blows up abortion clinics because they're going to hurt his future business. It is clearly satirical, attacking both those on the anti-abortion side who take such extreme approaches, but also the pro-abortion side who argue that a fetus is not a child. People who did not pay attention to the song, though, and only heard the title and the general premise, condemned Taylor's supposed support of violence. It is no surprise that he left Christian music for his next album, though he ultimately returned after his one stint in Chagall Guevara. The last song on the album was a quiet song called "Harder to Believe Than Not To," a song that explores the doubts many young Christians have and argues that it is harder to believe in Jesus than not to. He says simply, "Don't you know by now / Why the chosen are few?" At one point in the song, I can now find the best description of what I should have done when it came to my faith, but that I was ill-prepared to do so:

> Shivered with doubts
> That were left unattended
> So you tossed away the cloak
> That you should have mended[4]

I needed to mend the cloak of faith that I had, to sew up the holes and patch it with new ideas instead of tossing it away, but no one had ever shown me how to do that. I had not seen that there were more progressive denominations within Christianity that might help me live with my doubts instead of allowing them to overtake my faith. I had been told that there was one way to be a Christian, so once that way stopped working, I assumed that Christianity must be the problem, not the particular approach to Christianity I had chosen.

At the end of my time at Ole Miss, then, my situation was not looking particularly hopeful; all aspects of my life were suffering. Despite the fact that I had just finished my doctorate in December of 1996, I had not enjoyed my program, and the job market for tenure-track college English professors was not promising. My marriage was almost over, which was a positive development, but still stressful and an event that showed me how I had become a person I did not much like. The divorce was clearly my fault, as I had not put forth any real effort to solve our problems or to simply be a decent human being. I had taken a passive-aggressive approach to our difficulties instead of simply dealing with them. When my

---

4. Steve Taylor, "Harder to Believe Than Not To."

wife got an opportunity to move back to Northeast Tennessee because of a job opening, she broke her own rule and went to a lawyer to begin the divorce proceedings. I wasn't even a decent enough person to do that for her. Religiously, I was learning much more about Buddhism, but my knowledge of any religious tradition was strictly intellectual. Buddhism's emphasis on right action, for example, had no effect on the way I treated my wife, though it certainly caused me considerable guilt, as I knew my actions were wrong; I simply did not care. My hypothetical questions about morality had become a reality. While I did not kill anyone with a gun, arguing that there was nothing to stop me from doing so, I had caused my wife a considerable amount of emotional pain. Reason certainly had not made me a better person, and religion was having no impact on my life. Clearly, the path I had chosen to take away from my religious roots was not a path that was bringing any joy to my life. There had to be another way; I just didn't know what it was yet.

8

Sneaking Back Into the Church

As my marriage was ending, I ended up taking a step backward, not forward, looking to the past instead of the future. Before my divorce was final, I went home to Johnson City for a few days. While I was there, I decided to go see Leeanna. I will readily admit that my intentions in going to see her were not merely to see how she was doing, but to let her know about the divorce and see if there were still any feelings between us. I had actually seen her just over a year before when I was in town on Spring Break. I was visiting Dr. Dibble, and he and I went to the cafeteria to eat and talk. While we were there, she walked by, as she was now a student there, which I had not known. We talked for just a few minutes, mainly about her brother Erik, whom I had been good friends with when we were in the youth group, and she told me they had his email address at home. I told her I would stop by and get it the next day before leaving to go back to Mississippi, knowing even then that that was simply an excuse to talk to her longer and more privately. Since I was still married, though, I did not want to do anything that would lead Leeanna to think I was trying to start an affair, and I did not want to put myself in a situation where I would be tempted to do so. The one positive action I can take from the time when my marriage was clearly falling apart was this moment, where I clearly could have cheated on my wife, yet chose not to. I'm still amazed at how I was governed by the traditional Christian morality in this way, how, even though I gave it up in so many ways, I refused to perform an awful action, such as cheat on my wife. When I went to see Leeanna the next day, we spent the time outside by my car in their driveway, simply talking.

However, I did try to make it clear in my comments that my marriage was not going well, to let her know, without clearly stating the fact, that it would probably be ending sometime soon. I must not have been successful, as she later told me that she got the impression that the opposite was true, that my wife and I were very happy. My guess is that we both already had our ideas of how my marriage was going firmly ensconced in our minds, so nothing we saw, said, or heard led us to change our minds. She assumed everything was going well, as that was not what she wanted to hear, and my hints did not cause her to think otherwise, while I knew how badly the marriage was going, so I thought my hints were more obvious than they were. When I returned just over a year later, she was out with a friend that night, so I ended up talking to her parents for about thirty minutes. They had known me for over a decade by that point, given that they were involved in the church, and I had joined the youth group just over ten years before. I had been at their house for church events or simply to spend time with either Leeanna or Erik. It did not surprise them that I would stop by, even if Leeanna was not home, nor did it surprise me when they asked about the marriage. I told them that we were in the process of getting a divorce, which certainly surprised them both. We did not go into detail, though, as it was late, and I did not feel that comfortable talking with them about the situation. The next day, I went back to see Leeanna, and we talked by my car yet again. We started with general subjects, as she was graduating college that weekend, and I had gotten a new job in Indiana, but, as one would expect, my divorce finally came up. I told her a bit about the situation, then talked about telling her parents, which she already knew. I mentioned how everyone seemed to be disappointed by the news, to which she replied, quite casually, "Well, not everybody." At that point, I knew we would at least talk about getting back together, but I had been married for four and half years, so we had become different people, and we would need time to get to know each other again. Also, I was taking a job that nine hours away from where she lived, which did not lend itself to a hopeful beginning of a relationship. However, I agreed to stay in town for a few more days, come to her graduation, then take her out to dinner that night, so we could begin getting to know each other again. Neither of us was surprised by this development, given our previous history of breaking up, then getting back together again, but this time certainly seemed different. We were both much older and ready to make a more serious commitment, talking about whether or not we wanted children, for example. I was not soured on marriage from mine that was just ending, so I was open to considering it. Also, I was not surprised because I had learned that most people look to the past when they are struggling with their future. We like to have some part of our lives that is comfortable in times of uncertainty, and she and I were comfortable with each other.

Getting back together with Leeanna actually led to one of three events that helped lead to my returning to church and, ultimately, to faith, though a new kind. However, I hesitate to talk about the first two, as they come from a place I do not understand, and they do not exemplify my more intellectual approach to religion that now guides who I am. I have only shared these events with a select few people, as I am almost embarrassed by them, but I need to share them to truly relate what helped lead me back into the church. The first event came while I was still living in Mississippi, though my now soon-to-be-ex-wife had already moved out, and I was dating Leeanna. I had encouraged my ex-wife to take everything we owned with her, as I could at least acknowledge that she deserved some material possessions for the suffering she had endured. I was sitting in a living room that only contained an old couch and chair, with a lamp on a pressboard table beside them. I was reading a book, though I cannot remember which one, and I had set it down on my lap to take a break from the reading. It was night, and it was fairly late, but, given that I had just finished graduate school and did not have a full-time job, I was often up late. As my mind drifted from one idea to another, out of nowhere I saw a scene of Leeanna and me standing on their front porch, and we kissed. Given that we had done so hundreds of times, that scenario was not difficult for me to imagine; however, in this case, the scene was so real that I felt her kiss on my lips, as real as if she would have been standing in front of me giving me a kiss at that moment. Needless to say, I was a bit shaken by the reality of the event, so I took a longer break from reading before getting back to the book, though the occurrence stayed with me for several days. Not long after that, no more than two weeks, I was in the shower upstairs when I dropped the bar of soap I was using. In the time that it took the bar to slip from my hands to the time when it hit the shower floor, I was somewhere else. The scenery in front of me changed, and I was not standing in the shower. I could not have told you what I saw, even immediately after the moment passed, but I knew I was not in that shower for those few seconds. As before, the event shook me rather severely.

In both cases, there might be logical explanations that scientists, psychologists, or philosophers could provide to explain what happened. In the case of the kiss, I could have drifted off to the half-dream state we often inhabit where things feel real when they are not. I could have simply been suffering from the emotional stress of the divorce and getting back together with someone from my past, causing me to feel in a way I had not done before. Given how I had to turn my emotions off for the previous few years, turning them back on so quickly could cause an extreme reaction. In both cases, it was late at night, and we often imagine such events in the odd hours of the night and morning; Edgar Allan Poe certainly proved that in his writing. There are probably even more explanations that might explain these two events. However, it is the *might* that caught my attention even then. I knew there were probably ways to explain what had happened, but I also knew that the *might* that was implied in any of those approaches would always exist. For the first time in several years, I began to doubt my faith in reason. I had to admit that reason and logic and science and philosophy could not explain everything. If one talks to most scientists and logicians, they will readily admit their limitations, but, in the popular portrayal of such people and especially in the view of conservative Evangelical Christians, those who put their faith in reason believe that they will ultimately solve all the questions of the universe. I could not explain everything in my life with reason, and my admission of that fact opened a crack wide enough for me to begin to consider faith as a way to deal with the world again. Neither of these events caused me to believe Christianity was true, nor did I even believe they were the hand of God in any way. I believed even then that there might be perfectly rational reasons for why these two events happened and for when they happened. However, the simple fact that I could not explain them was enough for me to begin to turn toward a more serious exploration of faith in an attempt to view the world in a more holistic sense, not turning from reason, but using reason and faith together to see a wider world than I had seen during my time in the church as a teenager and college student and during my time outside the church as someone who believed reason was the solution.

The third event came shortly after, as I moved to Indiana to take my job at Culver Academies (made up of Culver Military Academy and Culver Girls Academy), a private (or independent, as they prefer) boarding high school that used the military model to provide a leadership system for its students. Since Culver was a boarding school, they provided chapel for the students, and they required them to attend once a week. On Friday nights, they had a Jewish service, then both Catholic and Protestant services on Sunday mornings. These services provided the perfect opportunity for me to get back into attending church, but without any type of commitment, as I could simply show up for the service, which lasted less than an hour, then go home again. It had the added benefit of helping me connect to the life of the school, but I really did not think about that when I made my decision to attend. Since the service I attended was focused on Protestants in the broad sense, the chaplain stayed away from dogma of different denominations and focused much more on key issues within Christianity. I could remind myself of the parts of the service I enjoyed, such as the music, without being overly concerned about questions that might trip up my rational hesitations again, such as predestination and free will and how that question affected my view of God.

However, our chaplain, whom the students and faculty referred to as Chaps, helped me in a couple of other ways. First, he was influenced by the Quakers, and he tried to bring some of their ideas into the worship service, incorporating large sections of silence and times for reflection, something I had never really seen in a service before. When I attended the Independent Christian Church, we were supposed to use communion as a time for reflection, but that was always geared toward making sure that we were "right with God," as one was not supposed to take communion otherwise. That time was not reflection in the sense that this time was, giving us time to simply sit in silence and *be*. Without my knowing it, Chaps had opened the door to the idea of mystery that comes from the mystical tradition in Christianity, an idea I had never encountered before, but one that would become increasingly important in my development. Before, I had always sought answers to questions that arose, needing to find the one right answer to the question I had before I could be satisfied. Here, without my consciously thinking that it was so, I began to sit in the midst of mystery, not seeking any answers at all. My readings in Buddhism helped prepare me for such an experience, as they repeatedly focused on sitting in meditation, though with a different emphasis. The combination of Chaps's approach and my reading, though, began to open me up to new ideas.

Second, Chaps's sermons also helped me on my path back into the church, but not because of the subject matter. I do not remember any of his sermons, which is surprising, given that I can still recall sermons from Central. I have always been rather harsh on sermons; thus, when I hear good ones, I tend to remember at least a part of them. However, what I do remember about Chaps's sermons is the tone behind them. It was not one of confidence, but one of doubt, implying Chaps did not have all the answers to the questions he was raising. He and I never spoke about this tone, so I have no idea if he purposefully took this approach, if his sub-conscious doubts simply worked their way into the sermon, or if I merely heard what I needed to hear in his sermons. When I mentioned that tone to some students, they were surprised by my suggestion, as they had never heard such implied doubts, but, then again, they were sitting in a required chapel service, so I'm not sure they were paying the type of attention I was.

There was still one step I was not willing to take, though. The Protestant service did not have communion as part of it, and, as a non-Catholic, I was not allowed to partake of the Eucharist when I visited that service. However, Chaps did offer communion once a month after the Protestant service for those who wanted to practice that sacrament. I never stayed for that portion, as I still did not feel comfortable with such a commitment. Communion still stood for me as a central act of the Christian faith, and I was still struggling enough that I could not make such a declaration of faith. I had trouble saying The Apostles' Creed, as I was not sure enough of what I actually believed to say so publicly, and communion seemed much the same. Students even noticed my absence there, and one in particular, Jenny, often commented on it. I gave her an evasive answer, but even their notice would not provoke me to attend. The students' confusion about my religious background worked well in the classroom, as I could put on whatever religious guise I needed in order to provoke the students' thinking about a particular subject. When a student made a slightly anti-Semitic comment in a class one day, I could easily respond, "You should watch what you say about others. You never know who might be Jewish. One of your teachers might even be so," causing a look of fear that I enjoyed then and now. I could talk about Buddhism or Judaism or various groups within Christianity as the literature we studied alluded to all of these, and the students never really knew where I stood. One student once declared that he knew I was not Methodist. I asked, "Joe, what makes you think I'm not a Methodist?" He responded without hesitation, "My sister's a Methodist, and she tells me I'm going to hell all the time." Everyone laughed, and I went one step further: "Joe, there's no reason for me to tell you you're going to hell all the time. Everyone knows that already." One sees the benefit of teaching in a private institution in comments such as this one.

I had used the religious confusion before in teaching, even before I had begun returning to the church. While I was finishing my doctorate at Ole Miss, I was teaching part-time at a community college in West Tennessee. Given that we spent a good deal of time talking about short stories and poems, religion came up a good deal, as we talked about Philip Roth, Bernard Malamud, and Flannery O'Connor, just to name a few. I would talk about Mithraism in "Greenleaf" or the difference between the Talmud and the Midrash in Malamud. Such conversations are clearly what confused students, as several came to talk to me after class one night. They begin simply and straightforwardly: "What denomination are you." As one who loves to play with language, I could not refrain from responding, "A ten-dollar bill." They missed the joke, but it helped me stall for time. I asked them what they thought, and their guesses ran from a variety of Christian denominations to a "non-practicing Jew." I asked what led to the final comment, and the student commented, "You said that it had been a long time since you had thought about the Midrash, so it made sense." It was good logic, and it certainly taught me that students listen more than we think they do. As at Culver, I did not answer their question, leaving myself a flexibility I greatly enjoyed.

The religious diversity at Culver, though it was certainly less than one would find in a more urban, public school setting, was what I needed as I began my journey back, as I could draw from a variety of sources. I supplemented these institutional sources with the reading I was doing on my own. I continued with my interest in Buddhism, and I spent some time re-reading the *Dhammapada*, the collected sayings of the Buddha, to further my knowledge of that primary text. At the same time, I was also reading through a book that collected the non-canonical gospels. This collection focused on the more serious of these works, not the Infancy Gospel of Thomas, where Jesus raises a childhood friend who falls off the roof (to clear Jesus' name, oddly enough) or smites a peer who hits him with a stone. I was exposed to works like the Gospel of Thomas and the Gospel of Mary, and the Jesus I found there was very different than the Jesus I thought I knew. Reading the Buddhist text alongside the non-canonical gospels was the best approach I could have taken, mainly because of the confusion it caused. There were times where I would have to stop and remind myself of which book I was reading, as they both sounded so similar. The Gospel of Thomas, especially, presents Jesus as much more Eastern than the Jesus we talk about in American Christianity, which should not have been surprising, given that Jesus was from the Middle East. However, we have changed Jesus to fit our form of Christianity, ignoring the passages where he sounds much more like the Buddha; even the passages where Jesus is clearly Jewish cause us trouble at times.

Looking back at the gospels after reading these works, I saw Jesus through this new lens and realized I had never really seen him in the first place. I only had my Western lens, limiting my interpretation of Jesus, which never went beyond the traditional interpretation of him as the Messiah whose only purpose was to spend some time on earth, then die for humanity's sins, and rise again to defeat death. The focus was always on the end point of Jesus' life, not the life leading up to that point. The similarity of Jesus and Buddha's teaching, though, led me to focus much more on what Jesus did and said before the crucifixion, looking especially at those passages that are the most confusing. For example, Jesus' parables, especially the more obscure ones, are often interpreted only one way, though nuances that surround that one interpretation are encouraged. They are presented as riddles for us to figure out so that we might learn how we should live. This approach begs the question of why Jesus would present such important material in a form designed to cause misinterpretation or simply confusion. I had always read them this way, seeing them as something I was supposed to puzzle out or have someone explain to me so I would know the correct behavior or beliefs. However, Jesus doesn't really seem to present the parables this way, even going so far as to say that he presents material in such a way that people will not be able to understand it. When the disciples ask Jesus why he speaks in parables, he tells them, "Because the knowledge of the secrets of the kingdom of heaven has been given to you, but not to them. Whoever has will be given more, and they will have an abundance. Whoever does not have, even what they have will be taken from them."[1] This passage complicates matters even more, as one now has to wonder why Jesus would come to tell this important gospel message, only to then make it more obscure with parables. The parables don't make sense if one only views them through a Western rational approach—the one I had been taking thus far—or if one sees Jesus' teaching as a proclamation of a dogma he wanted people to believe, as one needs to be able to understand before one can believe.

My readings in the non-canonical gospels and in Buddhist thought, though, showed me a different way to see Jesus' teachings, especially the parables. In Buddhism, there are *koans*, short, parable-like teachings, the most famous of which is probably a shortened version of a longer *koan*: "What is the sound of one hand clapping?" Unlike Christianity, however, Buddhist *koans* are designed not to be understood or at least not understood in any logical, rational fashion. The hearer is not supposed to figure them out; instead, the hearer is supposed to realize the limits of the rational mind, at which point the *koans* actually make some sort of sense, though not in any Western meaning of that word. Jesus' parables, then, can be seen in much the same way and with much the same purpose. The religious establishment at the time had no trouble with rational approaches to religion, as they were known for argument and debate, but they had lost the idea of faith and wonder. Jesus' parables, then, became a way to communicate a faith-based approach to life, not a rational approach to life. Granted, they do teach about the nature of God and the kingdom of heaven, but not in any sense of relating dogma. Jesus knew that God and all that related to him was too much for people to understand, so he gave them glimpses of God's love and grace, but not in a rational sense. He could have done that with a treatise or sermon. Instead, he showed them they could not understand God in the ways they had been trying to, that they needed to let go of their rational approach to God and embrace faith and hope, as absurd as they both are. This truth is the message I needed to hear at the time, having failed at trying to approach religion through a rational lens. Perhaps I was drawn to Buddhism precisely because it was the opposite of what I had been trying to do for the few years before I left the church. Having prided myself on my ability to think, I needed an approach that would show me just how little I could actually understand about the world and anything

1. Matthew 13:11–12.

related to God. Buddhism and the unorthodox gospels showed me there was a way to do so, that there was a mystical tradition I was unaware of, as no one had ever mentioned such a side to Christianity before.

Not with any logical progression in mind, I also ended up buying and reading a book on hermits with a special focus on the desert fathers and mothers. This book actually helped provide the next step in my move back to the church, partly in the way one might expect, given my previous experiences, but also in an unexpected fashion. Given my tendency to focus on extremes, no one is ever surprised to learn that I'm fascinated by hermits or monks and nuns. People who take such a step, especially in our culture, automatically intrigue me, as they are clearly conveying that the dominant ideas of the culture do not appeal to them or, at least, are less important to them than their devotion to their faith. Hermits brought in the idea of extreme devotion to faith, but in a different way. Their focus was not on dogma, but on action. While most of the hermits or monastics were rather orthodox in their beliefs, they did not spend much time or energy writing and teaching about the doctrine of their faith. Instead, they talked much more about attitudes of the heart, about love and humility, especially humility, as they understand Jesus' teaching that true action comes from the heart, as Jesus says in Matthew 15:17–20: "Don't you see that whatever enters the mouth goes into the stomach and then out of the body? But the things that come out of a person's mouth come from the heart, and these defile them. For out of the heart come evil thoughts—murder, adultery, sexual immorality, theft, false testimony, slander. These are what defile a person; but eating with unwashed hands does not defile them." Beyond that, they embrace the mystery of the divine and the work of the divine in the world. Oddly enough, they do not talk about God as a friend or someone they spend time with, which has become the norm in Evangelical Christianity today; rather, they talk about God as a presence that they dwell within, which sounds much more Buddhist than it does Christian, hinting at the idea of being one with everything in the universe.

Beyond that, though, the most interesting idea I took away from the book was that hermits do not remain hermits for their entire lives. While I was fascinated with their devotion, I was also mistaken about it. I assumed that hermits went away from society and lived there until they died, not being found for months or years afterwards. However, what I discovered was that hermits went away for a time to spend time in the presence of God, devoting themselves to prayer, fasting, or other spiritual disciplines, but they did so to learn something that God needed to tell them. Then, they would return to the larger society and try to convey that truth to those who needed to hear it. This picture is not the one we often see of hermits, but it was the picture I needed to help me take the next step back to the church. This shift in perspective was reiterated by an experience that happened not long afterwards, oddly enough, at my former church, Central. I was home for a visit, and I went to the church one Sunday, as I had begun doing when I visited. I wanted to see old friends, and it was a good place to see quite a few in one place. However, the church had clearly changed in the years I had been gone, almost five years by now. There was a new building, as the old one had collapsed in the blizzard several years before, but the important changes were more subtle. The church had moved from being more of a family church, where many people who attended the church lived in the community, easily within a mile or so for most of them (some even walked to church) to being more of a typical suburban church, though not nearly as large. The emphasis was clearly on growth, which had not been much of a discussion when I was there. They had put in a new sound system when they built the new church, and they had begun doing more elaborate Christmas and Easter productions than when I was there. There was more of an emphasis on children's programs and a better nursery. More importantly, though, they had a new minister and youth minister, and the church seemed to have shifted to a more conservative theology, as no one seemed to be talking about whether or not women could be elders or deacons now, as some of us were before I left. That shift may not have occurred in the church, but in me, and I simply ascribed it to the church now that I had moved away from where they were. Either way, the church never felt like home to me again, and I eventually stopped visiting as I moved farther and farther away from where I had been.

However, on this day, while I was visiting, we were taking communion, as we did every Sunday. I had decided to take communion while I was there, as I was trying to participate more in church services, as opposed to being an observer as I had been doing in the chapel services at Culver. Also, I never wanted to be a distraction, and I was always worried that friends would wonder why I had not taken communion, and I was not yet ready to have an honest discussion with them about my newfound religious ideas, which were not fully formed. When communion came my way, I prepared to take it. I was sitting in the same pew as a young father who was holding his daughter on his lap. He had to be rather creative when it came to taking communion, moving the plate around his daughter, who was clearly interested in what he was doing, taking the bread, then passing it along to me. As he passed me the plate, we simply shared a smile, a moment that, along with the book on hermits, taught me one more idea I needed to know. While my time at Culver had been useful, as I had been able to ease back into attending church services without any real commitment, I now needed a community. As with the hermits, I had gone into my desert where I could interact with the divine in the way I needed, but now I needed to go back into the society—Christian society, for me—and learn from those around me. I even wrote an essay about the incident and the book, the first piece of creative writing I had published, which helped me realize I could write about my experiences and share them with other people who might have the same doubts.

As my year at Culver ended, I had decided not to remain there teaching. I enjoyed the job well enough, but I had decided to go back to school to earn a Master's in Library Science. Having worked in the library at Ole Miss, I found I enjoyed the work I did there. Also, I found teaching took too much of my free time, especially as I also worked as a coach, as all members of independent schools are required to do some sort of extracurricular work. I did not have as much time for reading and writing as I would have liked, and I felt that library work would give me nights and weekends to work on both of those. I moved to Tuscaloosa to pursue graduate work at the University of Alabama. I needed to find a new church, as I was now feeling ready to re-enter a Christian community; however, I was unsure of how to go about finding a church, as I had never had to find a church in a new town on my own. I had only attended three churches with any sort of regularity, and I was always invited to them by friends or taken to them by my parents. The internet was still in its early days, so most churches did not have any significant web presence, and the yellow pages simply provided basic information. I knew I needed to go with a more progressive denomination, though, as I had moved too far away from the Evangelical tradition, though I could not have defined my change that clearly. I used what information I could find on the internet about different denominations as a starting point. I would pull up a list of denominations from Yahoo!, which was then more of a directory than a search engine of any sort, and look up the basic beliefs of that denomination. However, I ultimately found my church in a much more random (or providential, as my Calvinist friends would say) fashion. I had begun listening to National Public Radio when I was at Ole Miss, having never heard of it before. Since I had let my ex-wife take our television (forced it on her, actually), as I had decided to give up watching television in yet another extreme act, I needed a source of news, and I found NPR to be wonderful.

When I moved to Alabama, then, I immediately found the local NPR station. I didn't listen to them exclusively, using the more popular music stations for entertainment, but I always listened to the news on All Things Considered while eating supper. One evening, while listening, I heard a blurb from one of their sponsors, University Presbyterian Church. Such snippets do not contain much information, but they did have a tagline with theirs: "The church with the social conscience." This motto or mission statement caught my attention, as did their name. Here was a church that had something to do with education, given their name, and that was interested in social justice, the two areas that had become more of my interest. I looked them up in the phone book, found out they were members of the Presbyterian Church (U.S.A.), the more progressive side of the Presbyterian denomination where I was raised, so I decided to give them a chance. People often talk about what draws people to a church and what causes them to return. Something as simple as sponsoring a news program on NPR with an interesting phrase is what got me to UPC, but it was the people who brought me back, two of them, in particular. When I came to the church, there was a young woman greeting people at the door. Her name was Julie, and she was a professor at the university, where she worked in the Education department. Julie asked a bit about me, then welcomed me to the church and let me inside. Her actions on my first Sunday were not what impressed me; instead, it was the fact that she called me by name on the next Sunday when I came back again. People who study church growth or who worry about such matters often talk about a number of ways to encourage visitors to return for multiple visits. I have found that it is as simple as treating people with courtesy and interest. I got the impression that this church was interested in me as a person, not as one more name they could add to their rolls and certainly not as one more giving unit.

Along the same lines, there was Denise, whom I came to know quite well. She came and sat with me during the service and explained some of the more confusing parts to me. She had no idea I had grown up Presbyterian and could easily follow the service on my own; she simply saw someone whom she did not know and wanted to help. The most confusing part, she told me, was the way they did communion. Instead of the traditional method of passing the bread and juice, we all went forward and served one another by name. We would take the bread, break a piece off, then hand it to the person next to us, saying, "Denise, this is the body of Christ, broken for you." Here was a clear sign this church was interested in community, in knowing one another in a meaningful manner. The one final action that made me want to come back also came from Denise. After the first service, she and I were talking, and the subject of my looking for a church came up. Instead of telling me everything UPC did well, she told me about other churches in town, even saying, "If you're looking for a larger church, you might want to look at Covenant or Trinity Presbyterian." Since that day over a decade ago, I have visited numerous churches, having moved several times. Never, though, have I been to a church where someone suggested I attend somewhere else that might better fit my needs. Denise and the church were not interested in having me there just to have me there. They wanted me to find the best place for me, which convinced me UPC was that place.

As I began attending more regularly, I became more involved and found out more about the congregation that ultimately helped me on my journey back to fully participating in a Christian community. The church lived up to its promise of balancing education and social justice, a combination I had not seen in the churches I had attended, which had always been focused almost solely on the state of people's souls in the next life, not the quality of people's lives in this one. Given that I was in school to collect my second Master's, I also valued the intellectual approach to faith that the church took. Sandy, the minister, had a doctorate, something I had never encountered in a minister before, though the ones I did know were at least seminary-educated. Like me, she had written a dissertation, and she was often reading theology she would bring into her sermons or classes. On one of the first Sundays I attended, she was presenting a rather complex theological argument in a sermon, and I wondered how the congregation would perceive such an approach. I spent part of the sermon simply looking around at the other people there, expecting them to be bored, tuned out, doodling, or something along those lines. Everyone I saw, though, looked intently focused on the sermon, and I found out later that people wanted that level of thought on a regular basis. When I joined the choir, I was amazed at the level of education and musical talent I found there. In the male section of the choir, where I obviously sat, and got to know the people better, there were four other regular attendees. One had a doctorate in physics, one in world religions, one in education, and one had a Master's in social work. Including me, then, there were four doctorates and one Master's-level professor. Our organist was a student at the university who competed in and won national competitions, while our choir director was a professor at the university.

However, the focus on education and an intellectual approach to faith did not limit the church from its social justice mission, as they did a good job of balancing the head with the heart. Even though we were only a few blocks away from the university, we were also near one of the poorer sections of the city; thus, we tried to provide food for those who were struggling. One way of dealing with this problem was that we distributed bags of food once a week to anyone who would come by, though many people simply stopped by during the week whenever they could. We did not have a good deal of money, but we tried to provide people with staples, such as peanut butter, while also giving them meals they could eat without stoves or ovens, as several of the people only had a microwave oven. The church also spoke out on social issues of the day and was open to people who would not fit in at many churches. When a homosexual man, Billy Jack Gaither, was beaten, killed, then his body set on fire, in Sylacauga, a small town an hour and a half from Tuscaloosa, our minister wrote about it publicly and preached about it in our church, talking about how difficult it was for people in the South to deal with this issue, even as we approached the twenty-first century. We had at least one woman in our church who was openly lesbian and who served as a deacon when I was there, later becoming an elder. The church later became a clearly labeled Open and Affirming congregation, one of only a few in Alabama.

Given the focus on an intellectual approach to faith, the study I was able to do there helped me take one more step in my theological shift that had begun when I was in Indiana. One of our Sunday school studies was on a book by the Jesus Seminar, whom I had not heard of before. While they are best known for their attempt to determine what passages of the gospels actually happened or were most likely actually spoken by Jesus with their color-coded system, which they published as *The Five Gospels: The Search for the Authentic Words of Jesus*, that is not the part that helped me the most. The Jesus Seminar, for those who aren't familiar with them, as I wasn't, is a group of scholars, historians, and laypeople who try to establish the historical Jesus, as opposed to what they call "the Jesus of the gospels." They argue that, as with all historical figures, Jesus' story and teachings have been changed over the past two thousand years, sometimes purposefully, and sometimes not. They want to try to establish what happened in an historical sense. Some of them are Christians, but some of them are not, so they argue that their approach is historical, not theological. However, their assertions have serious theological implications, and they often write about those, especially those members who are Christian. They often look at any of the miraculous events that surround Jesus' life, ranging from the virgin birth to his miracles to his resurrection. They examine the four gospels to see similarities and contradictions; study their textual background, including any scholarship about authorship, time of composition, and audience; and they explore the historical knowledge about Israel during the time Jesus lived, all with the hope of discovering as much as they can about events that are so important to so many people, but that also do not make much rational sense, as is the case with the supernatural events.

What would surprise most conservative Christians is that these historians do not automatically throw out any supernatural events, as they stick solely to the historical record, as best they have it. If multiple gospels (or other biblical books, as they look at the rest of the New Testament, when appropriate) tell of an event in a way that seems consistent with one another, and there is nothing in the textual or historical evidence to cause them to doubt it, then they accept it as historical. For example, in looking at the feeding of the five thousand, they conclude that some event where Jesus fed a large number of people through some unknown means probably did happen, though they believe the feeding of the four thousand is simply another retelling of that story. When it comes to the resurrection, they do not argue that Jesus' physical resurrection is an historical event, that Jesus literally and bodily rose from the dead and that people saw him in that form. Marcus Borg, in "From Galilean

Jew to the Face of God," writes, "Thus, in my judgment Easter need not involve an empty tomb or anything happening to the physical body of Jesus. . . . Why do I not think that? A major reason is the crucial distinction between resuscitation and resurrection. Resuscitation intrinsically involves something happening to a corpse, but resurrection in a first-century Jewish and early Christian context need not. Resurrection means entry into a different kind of existence, not resumption of a previous existence."[2] Members of the Jesus Seminar do argue that something happened between Jesus' death and when the apostles began preaching, as all the evidence they see shows them a significant change happened to the disciples during that time. They argue for a metaphorical resurrection, that Jesus somehow became new to the disciples and changed their lives, giving them the courage to preach whereas they were afraid to do so before. Needless to say, most, if not all, Evangelical Christians would not approve of such theology.

However, I was fascinated by this approach. Instead of turning off my brain when I attended church, I was presented with new ideas, and I was encouraged to ask difficult questions, some of which I had been struggling with for years. One such example came from our reading for the Sunday school class. In talking about Jesus' triumphant entry into Jerusalem, Marcus Borg, in "The Historical Study of Jesus and Christian Origins," shows the passage from Matthew, where Jesus comes into the city: "The disciples went and did as Jesus had instructed them. They brought the donkey and the colt and placed their cloaks on them for Jesus to sit on. A very large crowd spread their cloaks on the road, while others cut branches from the trees and spread them on the road."[3] Borg then points out the contradiction in this passage, that Jesus could not have ridden on two animals, and, in fact, did not do so in the other gospels.[4] Borg points out that Matthew's gospel suffers from a mistranslation of the prophecy from Zechariah 9:9, all in an attempt to show how Jesus fits the Messianic prophecy.[5] I had seen such contradictions in the Bible before, but I had never had anyone within a church admit they existed. Instead, we always contorted ourselves into uncomfortable and untenable positions to try to prove the Bible did

---

2. Borg, "Galilean," 16.
3. Matthew 21:6–8.
4. See Mark 11:4–8, Luke 19:28–36, and John 12:14.
5. Borg, "The Historical Study," 135.

not contradict itself. If it did, even in insignificant sections, then the entire work would be false, which would make Christianity itself false. Instead of worshipping Jesus, I had been taught to worship the Bible, as it became the cornerstone of my faith. Once I began questioning it, I had no choice but to question everything I believed, as it all centered on the Bible. Now, I was being shown a way to believe in the Jesus of the Bible, but also to recognize that the Bible is not a perfect document. It is nothing more than, but also nothing less than, an account of people's encounters with the divine and their attempt to document that encounter, which comes with all of the problems people and language bring to such events. I was being shown that the Bible was "the Word of God" in a metaphorical sense, which is much broader than "the Words of God," a literal reading, as I had been taught.

My development was not as smooth as I have presented it thus far. Even after reading Borg's book and several others, I found I could still have my faith shaken by such questions. One Saturday evening, I was reading a copy of *The Atlantic*, and I found an article that explored the historicity of Moses, the Israelites' captivity in Egypt, and the exodus. The author argued that none of these events or people ever happened, that they were all created during the Israelites' Babylonian captivity as a way to provide hope for a people who were suffering. The author used a good deal of historical evidence to make his/her point, much in the same way that the Jesus Seminar did. One would think I would be used to such an approach, but I was not. Despite the fact that I had read a book that argued that the resurrection itself was a metaphor, not a literal act, the idea that Moses and the exodus were, as well, shook me completely. On Sunday, I found Sandy after church, and I told her that we needed to talk as soon as possible. She could tell I was shaken by something, but we did not have time to talk then, nor could we talk until later in the week. I fell back into the doubts I had from the past, questioning everything about my faith, wondering if I could believe anything in the Bible, wondering if I could believe anything at all. For some reason, Moses held such an important place in my life, perhaps because he is a figure whom we talk about so much when we are children, even watching Charlton Heston play him on television, that the possibility of his fictional existence mattered more to me than Jesus' miraculous acts, including the resurrection. Dramatically, it would be a nice moment if I could say I went to my minister's office, and she talked me through my troubles, leaving me on the other side much stronger. However, what happened is much less interesting, unfortunately. By the time I met with her later in the week, I was absolutely fine with the article's argument. The idea that Moses did not exist did not take away the power of the story in the same way that a metaphorical reading of the resurrection did not steal the force of the gospel. What I was learning was that an event did not have to be historically true to matter, something I should have learned in studying literature for the past decade or so of my life. Dr. Dibble had told us about John Fowles's concept of a "necessary fiction," where we believe something we know to be untrue because it provides meaning for life, but this situation was different. I did not believe the resurrection or the exodus were not true; instead, I believed they were true on a deeper level than the historical, that they were spiritually and emotionally true, which was coming to matter more to me. In the same way I could not explain love or grace or any other emotion, I also could not explain how or why such stories mattered to me, whether or not they were factually true, but they did, carrying as much, if not more, weight than before, as I now actually believed the truth of them, not just the factuality.

Sometimes, though, I could go a bit too far with my ideas, as my extremist tendencies continued to push me in that direction. Since I felt so comfortable in the church, I was not hesitant in sharing those ideas, either, especially in the Sunday school class. If we were talking about an idea, I would listen for a few minutes, then let loose with one of my theories, spinning it out as far as I could take it, often coming up with ideas on the spot. When we talked about Jesus' teaching about not worrying about tomorrow, for tomorrow has worries enough of its own,[6] for example, I talked about how we should not have insurance or retirement plans, if we take such teachings seriously. At times, people would become frustrated with my ideas, as one person in the class simply said to me, "You're so young." I actually agreed with her, but I also didn't think that was a valid counter-argument to my idea. The one person whom I would listen to more than any other, though, was Joe. He was a retired minister in his seventies when I was there, but still active. I played doubles tennis with him, one other person from church, and another person whom they knew. He might not return the hardest shots at the net, but he would always get a racket on them, showing he still had fairly quick reflexes. Joe would sit in class and let me stretch my ideas out as far

---

6. Matthew 6:34.

as they would go, then, when I had finished, begin with, "Now, Kevin…" and proceed to reel me back in a bit. He always listened to my ideas, then respectfully disagreed with them, or at least wanted to adjust them a little bit. This approach was especially true whenever we talked about predestination and free will, which continued to be one of my obsessions, especially now that I was attending a Presbyterian church again, as predestination was one of Calvin's main ideas. Joe and I listened to each other and continued to disagree, but, one Sunday, he was preaching. I have to admit that I was not listening closely, as Joe was not that strong of a preacher, but he then mentioned my name, saying, "And, Kevin, *that* is predestination, but predestination of a good kind." I had a slight smile and thoughtfully nodded, as if considering his idea, but I had no idea what I was pretending to consider. He and I often laughed about our disagreements, which was an important lesson for me to learn about the church, that we could disagree even on rather serious points of theology, but still love each other and care for each other.

Even Joe, though, could not completely keep me from my extremist tendencies, as I decided I owned too many possessions. Throughout my years of coming back into the church, there have been a few passages of scripture that seem to haunt me, that seem to be specifically speaking to ways I feel I am failing. One of those is where Jesus tells the rich young ruler (or the crowd, depending on which gospel one is reading) to sell his possessions, give to the poor, then come and follow Jesus.[7] When I had moved to Indiana the year before, taking my first full-time job, I had certainly gained possessions, trying to buy enough to fill a house, beginning with almost nothing. I bought the necessities: a washer and dryer, a table, a bed, and a couch and a chair. However, I had also spent the past eight and a half years in school gathering English degrees, so I had also been gathering books. By the time I left Indiana, I had over 1600 books, needing three six-foot bookcases, two four-foot bookcases, and two each of two different sizes of smaller bookcases. I also believed I needed two desks, one for my computer and one for grading, which I actually ended up doing at the kitchen table, for some reason. Needless to say, Steve, one of my best friends who had agreed to help me move, was not particularly happy to help me move from Indiana to Alabama, as we needed a full-sized U-Haul truck to move everything that I, as one person, owned. Part of the problem was that I owned books it was

7. Matthew 19:21 and Luke 12:33.

clear I would never read. The best example of such a book is *Peregrine Pickle* by Tobias Smollett, a book I bought simply because I recognized Smollett's name. Whenever I would go to bookstores, which was as often as I could, I would leave with bags or sometimes even boxes of books to take home and put on my shelves, fully aware it would take me years to get to them, if I ever did. While working on my Master's at ETSU, I would order books without knowing how I would pay for them, even scrimping on meals to make those payments. If I truly loved books, such purchases would make more sense, but what I really loved was the idea of a life I would or could lead, and I tried to use possessions to define that life. I envisioned having people over for dinner parties, where we would talk about books and ideas, ending with coffee and dessert, the model of the literary life. The reality was that I was not very social with my co-workers, as I'm more shy than people actually believe, and I'm almost terrified to invite people to do anything, as I view their saying "no" as a rejection. I also do not enjoy coffee, though I tried for years to drink it, as I thought I needed to drink it to create this life that I envisioned, much as I once thought I needed to smoke and drink to be an English major. And I was not reading many of those books I bought, using them as props for a life I did not have.

During my time in Alabama, I began to rid myself of my most valued possessions, putting the books in stacks I would allow friends to browse before I took them to a used bookstore in Athens, GA, when I would go visit Steve. I started with those books I knew I would never read, like Smollett's novel, then moved on to books I had read before, but knew I would never want to read again. I also made use of the library collection at Alabama, keeping me from buying a large number of books and simply building my collection up again, though I did buy books I believed I would read. My friends worried about my change, especially Steve, as he saw my move to library science and my ridding myself of books as evidence I was giving up literature altogether. It's ironic that, just two years later, Steve would stop teaching English and go back to school for a Master's of Fine Arts in Graphic Design, but, for now, I assured him I would continue to pursue the literary life, reading and writing as much as ever. We did not talk about my religious concerns behind my owning too much, at least not then, as I was not comfortable talking about my extremist behaviors at that point. I'm sure part of my decision was driven by the reality that I had just moved those books and all the furniture that went with them to Alabama, and I knew I would have to move them the following year when I graduated with my degree. Religious motivations are seldom pure, often influenced by situations in our lives that go beyond what we are taught or read in the Bible.

As my year in Alabama was ending, I was sorry to leave the church there behind, and several people suggested I could find a job teaching in Tuscaloosa—as I had decided to go back to teaching English—though I knew that chance was slim. I also felt I needed to move somewhere else, as I needed to go beyond what I had learned at UPC. I had become more involved than I expected to, having been asked to teach one of our Sunday school classes, something I had not done in almost five years, which, oddly enough, turned out to be on Generation X, fitting, given that I was the only member of Generation X in the class. I also sang in the choir for a few months, something I had never done when I was younger, having been told all my life that I could not sing. In college, though, I took one semester of voice lessons and learned I could sing well enough, though only with other people. I had also become the part-time church secretary for a few months, as the church looked for a replacement. Sandy even joked that she was the only minister with a PhD for a secretary. I was active in the church, there almost every day; however, I was not truly invested in the congregation. Part of that was my transitory status, knowing I was leaving at the end of the school year, but part of it went beyond that. There were significant programs or moments in the church's life I did not take part in, as that would have shown a level of commitment I was not comfortable with. In the winter of my year there, for example, Julie, the elder who greeted me when I first came, was killed while driving on vacation. Someone threw a chunk of concrete from an overpass, smashing her windshield, killing her instantly. The funeral was a large affair, as she was involved with many programs and people in the community, through both the church and the university. I was the secretary at the time, and I helped with the program for the funeral, but I did not attend. Instead, I went with a friend from school to see a basketball game, as my friendships outside of the church were more important to me than the ones inside. Also, the church served the undergraduates at the school through a Monday night program, where there was a free meal for any students who wanted to come. They then often played games and had a Bible study. As a graduate student, it would have been a natural fit for me to attend such events and help with them, but I never did. Given the name of the church, it is easy to see how important this outreach was to them, almost defined them, yet I never chose to participate in any way. I never even joined the church, claiming one should not have to officially join an organization, such as the church, that one is a member simply by attending. This reasoning was simply my way of providing a rational basis for my refusal to commit. While I had begun to find some sort of community and have some level of involvement in a congregation again, I still had some way to go to truly make myself part of a Christian community. My time in Indiana had taken me the farthest step, the one that took me back into a church for the first time in four years. My year in Alabama had taken me one more step, as I explored theological ideas and social justice with a fervor I had not before, as it showed me a path I needed to follow, one I had never seen or heard in my years in the church before. I now needed to walk down that path, follow it and see where it would lead me, having no idea it would, in some sense, lead me back to where I had left the church years before.

9

Finding Faith, Again

After graduating from the University of Alabama with my library degree, I moved to Macon, Georgia, to take a job teaching English at another independent school, though this one ranged from pre-Kindergarten to twelfth grade and was not a boarding school. I had decided to teach English again, as I found I missed it when I was working on my degree in library science. One evening, I was reading an article in *The Atlantic*, and I came across an interesting statistic. My first thought was, "I should share that with my class," but then I realized I no longer had a class to share it with. I ended up teaching part-time at a community college in Birmingham while I was working on my library degree.

When I moved to Macon, my first thought was about finding a church, as I had now seen how important a role it could play in my life. I believed I was finally going to find a place to settle down and call home, and I was excited about my new opportunities. I lived within two hours of DJ and Steve, my two best friends, and I had the chance to get back in the classroom again, but I also had an opportunity to find a new church community, one I could stay at and invest in, which I was finally beginning to believe I was ready to do. However, I had trouble finding a new church in Macon, as I was beginning to realize the difficulties of finding a progressive congregation in Southern towns that were either not large cities, such as Nashville or Atlanta, or were not college towns, such as Tuscaloosa or Athens, Georgia. I really only had two criteria, I thought: 1) the church should be small, as I found I enjoyed attending churches where I ultimately knew everyone, at least by name, and where people noticed if I was there or not; 2) the church should be progressive, theologically and socially. Related to the second one was a dedication to explore one's faith intellectually, but I really did not see those two as separate criteria, as the two almost always went together.

In exploring churches, though, I found there were several other criteria I did not know I had, but which I quickly discovered, if they were lacking in a church I visited. I began with Presbyterian churches, given that I had such a positive experience at the one in Tuscaloosa. Since more and more churches were establishing a presence on the internet, I was using that to feel out a church ahead of time and see if it would be a good community for me. Before I visited my first Presbyterian church in Macon, I had already emailed the minister and talked with him a bit, and the church seemed quite promising. It was a bit larger than I was comfortable with, but certainly nowhere near the megachurch numbers. It probably was no more than 150, but, given that University Presbyterian had been around forty on Sunday mornings, even a church of one hundred seemed large to me. However, my visit did not go well. Part of the problem was that I chose a poor day to attend, as a young man was being ordained into the ministry that day, so the church was flooded with visitors, and members were clearly distracted by the festivities. What really dampened my enthusiasm, though, was when I was asked to wear a name tag, showing quite clearly that I was a visitor on that day. This practice may not have been normal, but just for that day, but it certainly did not set a welcoming tone. If people would have used the name tag as a means of getting to know me, though, they could have redeemed this practice; instead, people simply read my name tag, glanced at me, then walked on without speaking. Besides the preacher, who not only recognized me as a visitor, but remembered our email exchange, no one in the congregation spoke to me that Sunday. I did not return. It seems that community and a welcoming spirit were among my criteria, though I was not aware of it until after that visit.

The next Sunday gave me another opportunity to learn more about what I was truly searching for in a congregation, as I visited another Presbyterian church, this one much smaller than the one from the week before. It was so small that, during one of the hymns, I briefly stopped singing just to make sure others were singing, as I could not hear them when I was singing myself. The church looked to have once been much larger, as the sanctuary could easily have seated 150 to 200 people, yet there were no more than thirty there on that Sunday. They did not have a minister, so several members of the congregation rotated the preaching duties, and the worship service seemed well enough planned. What I found that I missed in this service was the sense that the church was alive. It was not the size of the congregation that bothered me, as there were only a few people less than University Presbyterian; instead, it was the fact that the church simply felt like it was treading water, simply staying alive for the sake of staying alive. There are numerous small churches throughout America that do great work for their communities, taking on one or two projects and making an impact through those, but this church conveyed none of that enthusiasm or vigor. Instead, they seemed to exist for their once-a-week services, which seemed to help some of those in the congregation who were struggling with serious issues (as I discovered during their time of prayer requests), but there seemed to be nothing outside of that hour every week. I could be wrong about the good they did, but there was nothing that morning to let me know that.

The last Presbyterian church I tried seemed to be perfect for me. The size of the congregation was just a bit bigger than the one in Tuscaloosa, perhaps sixty or so people on the Sunday I attended, and there was a life here that was missing in the previous church. After church, there was a brief fellowship time, and several people invited me to stay for it, which I did. People were warm and welcoming, talking to me about the church and asking me about myself. One of the members was an ophthalmologist, and he gave me his card, which gave me a significant discount on an eye exam and pair of glasses. Granted, he was helping his own business, but I could always use a savings on glasses, as I went through a pair every year or two, as my eyesight had progressively worsened since college. During the fellowship time, the interim minister spoke to me for several minutes, explaining not only about the church, but also being very clear that he was an interim minister. He did not want to misrepresent the situation at the church: they were looking for a full-time minister and that it might be a significant amount of time before they found one. I appreciated his candor, as I was not clear on that situation, and I had no idea that smaller churches were having such a struggle finding ministers. He then invited me to lunch with a group from the church, and he even paid for it himself, whether through church funds or his own, I never learned; either way, such hospitality was encouraging.

As I write about these churches, I realize just how picky I seem when it comes to looking for the right church. However, I had realized how important that relationship was for my life, so I treated it like a dating relationship, one that could lead to marriage. I wanted to be sure I would be able to spend years with such a community, and that kind of commitment should never be taken lightly. When I found there was something gnawing at me about my latest church visit, I spent some time that week trying to find out what was missing. This congregation seemed to have everything I was looking for, yet it still just didn't feel right. Over the years, through job interviews, first dates, and church visits, I have learned to trust this feeling, given that, whenever I have ignored it, I have ended up in a job or relationship that did not work out. I turned back to the internet to find another congregation, but I took the approach of looking at denominations again, given that I knew there were still numerous churches without a website. I had no idea where to begin, though, so I simply sat at my computer with the phone book open to the church section. I would find a denomination I did not know much about, then search for them, read about their basic beliefs, then decide which one looked like a good place for me. It was in this manner that I found the Christian Church (Disciples of Christ), an awkwardly-named denomination that would become my spiritual home for the next decade. I had briefly heard about them when I was in college at Milligan, but we had not spent much time talking about them, despite the fact that, for much of their history, the Disciples were a part of the Independent Christian church. Instead, when I was at Milligan, we focused much more on the split between the Independent Christian church and the Churches of Christ, as we were much more interested in the latter denomination's even stricter interpretation of the Bible, which led to women not being able to teach any male over the age of twelve or the prohibited use of musical instruments in worship. The split with the Disciples (as with most splits, who actually split from whom is simply based on whom one is talking with at the time) was only briefly mentioned, despite its taking place over a period of years from the 1920s to the late-1960s or early 1970s through several events. Also, the fact that they were the more liberal branch did not encourage discussion among those of us coming from the more conservative branch, despite the fact that many of us would ultimately be drawn to that denomination or one similar to it. Perhaps it was not mentioned for that reason. I wonder if

I would have been able to remain in the church had I heard about the Disciples at this point and explored them instead of leaving.

What I found about the Disciples, though, let me know I was on the right track. They are a denomination that engages the questions of faith, as they do not have a creed that one must subscribe to. Instead, one of their popular phrases is "No creed but Christ." When one joins a Disciples church, that person is asked only one question, "Do you believe that Jesus is the Christ, the son of the living God?" If that person assents to that question, he or she becomes a member. There is not even any discussion about what any of the terms in the question might mean, leaving that up to the individual to decide. The founders of the Disciples denomination were not trying to create a new denomination at all. They were trying to unify the Christian faith by focusing on what members of the various denominations had in common. They were a unity movement, not a splinter group. They were formed because they wanted to offer open communion to any believer and not limit the sacrament to people of a particular denomination or to those who only believed a certain set of beliefs. Thomas Campbell argued in his *Declaration and Address*, "That the church of Christ upon earth is essentially, intentionally, and constitutionally one; consisting of all those in every place that profess their faith in Christ and obedience to him in all things according to the scriptures, and that manifest the same by their tempers and conduct, and of none else as none else can be truly and properly called christians [sic]."[1] The focus on unity certainly interested me, as did their approach to doctrinal debates, for, while I definitely enjoyed debating such ideas, I also knew that community was more important to me. It was the connection to communion that ultimately drew me to the Disciples, as they still practice communion every Sunday, partly because of how they began, but also because of how they read Jesus' statement that the early Christians "devoted themselves to the apostles' teaching and to fellowship, to the breaking of bread and to prayer."[2] I had not realized it yet, but communion was one of the practices I was missing when I had been attending the various Presbyterian churches since I moved. University Presbyterian was an oddity in the denomination, as they practiced weekly communion. Given their focus on it, with its strong sense of community, it was no surprise I was missing that in worship.

1. Campbell, *Declaration and Address*, 18.
2. Acts 2:42.

While I was enjoying other aspects of the Presbyterian churches I visited, I was missing what was a central aspect of the Disciples tradition. Once I understood that idea, I sought out a Disciples church to attend. Given that I was in a Southern town, where the Disciples are not a major denomination, I really only had two choices, so I chose the only one I could find much information on. My assumption that communion had been a missing aspect of my worship experience was confirmed on the first Sunday I visited. Even though the congregation practiced communion in the more traditional sense of passing the bread and juice throughout the congregation, the simple act of communion was enough to help me realize I had been missing it. Also, the congregation supported that focus on communion by exemplifying true community and hospitality, sometimes a bit forcefully. After my first worship service there, a woman named Sarah took me by the arm and turned me toward the guest book, asking me to sign it, though *asking* was a bit of an understatement. While some people might have been annoyed or offended by such behavior, she did it in such a kind and caring manner, her action made me like her even more. After enough years in the church, I now wonder if it was simply my age that made her so enthusiastic. Churches, especially mainline churches, which are struggling with aging congregations, are desperate for people in their twenties and thirties, especially if they are part of a couple. Despite my having neither a girlfriend nor wife, I was a prime demographic target for any church, so her enthusiasm might have been motivated, at least partly, by my fitting that desired age group. However, after I got to know her better, I believe she simply loved her church and wanted everyone else to love it, as well.

The minister was also warm and welcoming, even setting a standard by which I judge most other ministers by, even now. Mark and I became great friends during my years there, and we continue to keep in touch, despite living eight hours away. On that day, he talked to me for several minutes at the door, introduced me to his wife LeAnne who happened by, then invited me to have lunch with him at some point. He was not forceful or pushy, just inviting, so I agreed. However, it was how he handled difficulties with lunch that made me like him even more. He had an emergency and needed to leave town quickly; however, he did not have my phone number or email address, so he had no way to get in touch with me on such short notice. However, one of the girls in the church attended the school where I was going to teach; Mark asked her mother to take a note to the school to put in my mailbox there, hoping I would be going into school to get ready for the fall semester, which would begin in just a few weeks. When I got that note, I realized I had found a place where people would try to do anything they could to help others out or simply to be polite to one another. My two years there would never change that impression of Mark or the members of the congregation.

Mark played several important roles in my spiritual development, the first of which happened only weeks after we had met. Our lunch had gone fine, though the restaurant he chose was awful, something I did not tell him for over a decade, and which surprised him when I finally let on that I hated the food there. I asked him if we could meet simply to talk about where I had been and where I might be heading in my spiritual development. In that conversation, the idea of discipline came up, as Mark was and is a firm believer in the importance of spiritual disciplines in Christians' lives. People who met me after my time in Macon would never believe that I both claimed and fully believed I was not a disciplined person, but I really led a poorly structured life, accomplishing little I claimed was important to me. In the summers, I would stay up until three or four in the morning, wasting time on the internet, mostly, or playing computer games, then sleep until close to noon, as if I were still a college student. I would write only when I found any sort of inspiration, leading to one or two stories every other year, if that, and no more than twenty poems in most years. I had made poor financial decisions, especially in living off of student loans when I returned to graduate school to pursue my library degree, leaving me with close to $60,000 in student loan debt and $20,000 in credit card debt. Even though I had lost seventy pounds in my last year and a half at Ole Miss, I had now gained almost all of it back, coming in at only fifteen pounds under my heaviest weight. There was not a single part of my life that displayed any discipline.

When I was talking to Mark about the subject, I was clear I did not have any discipline, but I also believed I could use some. Mark asked one simple question, "Do you ever get up on Sunday mornings and go to church, even when you don't want to?" I was incredulous, as I believed everyone felt that way, but that everyone got up and went to church anyway. I responded, "Of course." He smiled and said, "That's discipline." When I have repeated this story to him every few years, he always chuckles, not remembering it at all, but saying, "It must have been the Holy Spirit." It may very well have been; regardless, it changed my life, not immediately, but slowly, as I took that little piece of discipline I had and let it grow into other areas of my life over the next five years, beginning with spiritual practices, moving into exercise and diet, then into teaching and work, and, ultimately, into my writing. Mark had long since moved to North Carolina, and I lived in two other states before it truly sank in, but I always remembered this conversation and used it to help me believe I had more discipline than I thought.

Mark also served to help me shape my theology more clearly, much as Joe had done in Tuscaloosa. However, Mark's approach was quite different, as I learned more from his behavior than from what he actually taught me from the pulpit or in any classes, though he was effective in both of those roles, as well. One Sunday, for example, Mark was preaching on the book of Hosea, where Hosea is commanded to marry the prostitute Gomer as a representation of the way Israel had prostituted herself to other gods. This sermon came around the time that reality shows were just beginning to become popular, and Fox had just begun their program *Who Wants to Marry a Millionaire?* Mark referenced this show in his sermon and in the title of the sermon, as the bulletin clearly read "So Who Wants to Marry a Whore?" Mark's sermon worked quite well, countering the popular culture's ideas of success and God's ideas of success, but it was his brazen use of *whore* that caught my attention. I had not lived in Macon more than a few months at that point, but I had lived in the South almost all of my life, and I knew just how conservative people could be, even in the more progressive churches. Our sanctuary was filled with people in their sixties and seventies, people who grew up in an era where one could not use the word *pregnant* on television, and none of them would have used the word *whore* in their conversations with each other or anyone else they knew. I was surprised he had chosen to use that word. On the way out, I lingered a bit to allow most of the people to file past Mark, giving me a few extra minutes to talk to him uninterrupted. As soon as I got to him, I asked, "How do you get away with this stuff?" He wasn't sure what I was talking about, so I told him about his use of *whore* and how surprised I was no one had said anything to him about it on the way out. He looked at me and said simply, "Kevin, if the people know you love them, they'll let you say almost anything." This lesson was one I desperately needed to learn, as I had not been one to shy away from controversy, either in church or in my job; however, I had not taken the time to love people in the process.

My job was not going well, and part of the reason was that I clearly did not like the students. My excuse was that I wanted to push them to think beyond what they had been asked to do, to think about issues, especially social justice issues, that they had not concerned themselves with before. However, the truth is that I was uncomfortable with the wealth I found in the school. What is odd is that the students in Macon had less money than the students in Indiana, as there, at Culver, for example, our point guard was picked up from practice in a Bentley. The difference, though, was the obvious wealth in Macon, as the school was made up of the important families of the town; they were the proverbial big fish in small ponds, as people in Atlanta would have laughed at their pretensions. When I encountered behavior I thought was wrong, I attacked it. One of the problems I took on was the students' language, as my time at Macon was the first time I heard students use the word *gay* as an insult, as in "That's so gay," roughly equating the word with *lame*. I had made a few comments about the word in class, but that was having little effect, so I decided to take my argument to a larger stage and wrote a letter to the editor of the school paper, where I referred to our students as "intolerant bigots." Our principal Margaret called me into her office and asked me to reconsider the letter, arguing that it would not have the effect I was hoping for and would create a climate where I would have even more trouble communicating with the students. Even though I disagreed with pulling the letter, I did see where the letter could limit communication instead of build it up. It was Milligan all over again, where I was trying to confront people about a real problem, but I was unwilling to do so in a constructive manner. Mark's lesson had not yet sunk in, but it would have an effect in the following years.

Many of Mark's lessons were similar in that way, that they might not have a significant impact at the time, but, several years later, I would find myself drawing on them when making similar decisions. When I was in Macon, for example, I attended church in a t-shirt and jeans (I would add a flannel shirt over the t-shirt, if it were cold). I actually had a theological argument for my attire, as I stated that no one should ever feel under-dressed when they attend church. If I, as someone who was clearly involved and often helped with readings, was dressed about as casually as possible, then no one in the congregation would ever feel out of place. Such an event happened in my second year there, as I was doing a reading during a Thanksgiving service we held jointly with a local Lutheran church who had used our sanctuary several years before when theirs was being renovated. I had played softball on their team the year before, so I knew several of their members fairly well. On this Sunday, one of their members had been out running errands and had run late, so she did not have time to go home and change clothes; thus, she showed up in sweats. She told me afterwards that she almost did not come, but she was glad she did, though she was worried about her appearance. My casual dress set her at ease and helped her to feel more welcome. However, after I had been at the church just over six months, I had the opportunity to preach there, something I had not done in ten years, not since I had changed my Bible major to an English major. Mark and I talked about my wardrobe, as I wanted to preach in the same casual outfit, making the same theological argument about creating an environment where everyone could feel welcome, regardless of their ability to buy and wear the *correct* church wardrobe. Mark, however, argued against such an approach, especially as I was preaching on a subject that was already controversial: money. I was tackling Jesus' teachings from the sermon on the mount, where he argues that people should not worry about tomorrow, for it has worries enough of its own and that we should not lay up treasures here on earth, but in heaven.[3] I was taking the approach that such teachings should affect where we shop and what we buy, bringing in fair trade and labor laws and going after such behemoths as Wal-Mart and Barnes and Noble. Mark's argument was that I should at least look like a traditional preacher in my outfit, but his reasoning went beyond one of simple appearances. He told me, "You don't want to give people a reason not to listen to you." He knew I would be preaching on ideas that would already make people uncomfortable, but he also knew they would tune me out as soon as I stepped behind the pulpit if I were wearing the more casual clothes. He wanted my ideas to at least get a hearing, even if they did not have the full effect I was hoping for. I should have been able to see a trend in Mark's advice, as he clearly wanted to have an effect on people's lives, so he did everything he could to create an environment where he could have that effect, even if it meant compromising on ideas that were less important to him. Given my tendencies to extremes, this approach was one I needed to pay attention to.

3. Matthew 6:19–21.

However, I also continued to read and study those who were on the extreme sides of issues, and I learned that, even when I disagreed with them, I could continue to learn from them, as they all had something to teach me. Mark suggested we split the one Sunday school class that he taught into two, with my teaching the old one, and his creating a new one. I wasn't fond of this idea, as I liked being in his class, but he believed such a decision would help increase attendance. He was right, as several new people did begin coming to Sunday school, largely because they wanted to support me in my new role in the church. I was always looking for something interesting to teach, so I thought I'd try to find a book we could work through. In looking around the internet, I found a book by John Shelby Spong, called *Why Christianity Must Change or Die*. The description I found online sounded quite good—"An important and respected voice for liberal American Christianity for the past twenty years, Bishop John Shelby Spong integrates his often controversial stands on the Bible, Jesus, theism, and morality into an intelligible creed that speaks to today's thinking Christian. In this compelling and heartfelt book, he sounds a rousing call for a Christianity based on critical thought rather than blind faith, on love rather than judgment, and that focuses on life more than religion"—and I was certainly at a point where I would agree with the title's assertion. What I did not know before I began teaching the book, though, is just how far Spong went in his theology, as I did not bother to look him up or find out more about the book. Before the first few chapters were finished, Spong had already argued that none of the supernatural events in the gospels had taken place, going even farther than the Jesus Seminar book I had read in Alabama. As I later discovered, Spong wanted to get rid of all of the supernatural elements in the Bible, arguing they were nothing more than a superstitious culture's way of explaining what we now made sense of in other ways. While the class was not overly conservative, they were at least moderate, so it was no surprise they were not happy with Spong's theology. When Steve sat in on my class one week when he was visiting, he referred to Spong as the "Spong of Satan," which should give an idea of how people were reacting.

The class simply stopped reading the book after only a couple of chapters. I thought, though, that, since we had spent the money on the book, we should keep reading it. I also believed we shouldn't stop reading just because we disagreed with the author, as there might still be something we could learn from the book. There was something Spong was going to teach me, if no one else, as he helped change my entire outlook on Jesus and helped me take one more step back in my faith development. After spending the first half of the book arguing that none of the supernatural events—the virgin birth, all of the miracles, and the resurrection—actually happened, Spong then spends a chapter arguing for the divinity of Jesus. To any traditional Christian, whether Evangelical or Mainline, conservative or progressive, such an argument appears absurd from the outset, but what Spong argues is that Jesus met everyone he encountered with unconditional love, and such an approach cannot be explained by any human means. He writes, "Beneath the God claims made for this Jesus was a person who lived a message announcing that there was no status defined by religion, by tribe, by culture, by cult, by ritual, or by illness that could separate any person from the love of God. If love is a part of what God is or who God is, then it can surely be said of this Jesus that he lived the meaning of God. According to the Gospels, he lived it with a consistent intensity. It was as if his source of love lay beyond every human boundary. It was inexhaustible. It was life giving."[4] He later concludes, "The story of his life was drawn in the Gospels as if its purpose was to proclaim that nothing one could do and nothing one could be could separate any person from the love of God. When these disciples forsook him, he loved his forsakers. When one of them was said to have denied him, and another to have betrayed him, he loved the denier and the betrayer. When his enemies abused him, he loved his abusers. When they killed him, he loved his killers. What more can one do to live out the meaning of the God who is love?"[5]

This approach changed the way I looked at Jesus, moving him from someone whose focus was on supernatural events, moving him away from the resurrection to the life he lived and the way he dealt with every person he met. Instead of seeing Jesus as this distant figure who had come as a sacrifice for the sins of humanity, he became a divine person who loved everyone he met on a day-to-day basis, which was much more meaningful. Many people can die for other people; we hear stories about such behavior on a regular basis, but it is impossible for us to live for others on a daily basis, but that is what Jesus did and that is what he was calling those who followed him to do. Not only was I glad I finished reading the book, but I began sharing Spong's ideas

4. Spong, *Why Christianity*, 125.
5. Ibid., 128.

whenever I could, including in sermons I've preached over the past ten years, whenever they fit.

I had not completely removed all the extremes from my life. Near the end of my first year in Macon, I built on my concern about my possessions, as I had continued to get rid of my books. I now went even farther with two steps. First, I thought I needed to spend more time with other people, as I could often spend weeks not seeing anyone outside of church or work, spending all of that time in my apartment reading or spending time on the internet. I thought a roommate would be a good idea to help me have another area of community in my life. I had always gotten along well with roommates, but I had always known them before. I also knew that, when I found a roommate, I would be able to get rid of half of what I owned, which I did. I simply answered an ad in the paper, though, which was probably not the best approach. I ended up living with someone I eventually called "Psycho Pat." When he had a few days off from work in a row, he would spend all night staying up with friends playing Dungeons and Dragons; I once walked in to find him on the couch, a woman's head in his lap, and a porn film on the television; he would have brief relationships with heavier women, he said, because they were more willing to have sex; and, near the end of my six weeks living with him, he began saying that people were trying to break into the apartment, but he scared them off by shooting at them, using a gun I did not even know he had. Luckily, a couple in my church needed someone to house sit for six months, and I was glad to help out. I decided to find community elsewhere, focusing even more on the church. I actually joined the congregation, the first one I had become a member of since I was a teenager. Mark had convinced me that joining the church was worthwhile, as it would enable me to become more involved and invested in the life of the congregation, and he was right. After I joined, I was made a deacon, a position I had never had in any church, being too young when I was in college, then out of the church ever since. I was then made chair of the worship committee, which required me to sit on the church board. I was able to see church politics much more closely. To some people, that would be a condemnation into the depths of hell, but I enjoyed getting to know people better and see how the church actually functioned. It also showed me that Mark and the leaders of the congregation had faith in me, and they believed I could help with the work of the church. Their trust helped me become more confident in my own developing beliefs.

The second way I tried to lessen my possessions was to simply begin giving things away. I donated bookcases, dressers, and other pieces of furniture to the local Goodwill and began functioning with fewer possessions. I ate dinner on the floor or on my desk, as I had gotten rid of my table; I kept only one reading chair, giving my couch to my sister; and I used a bookcase to store my clothes, as I had gotten rid of my chest of drawers. My goal was to ultimately own only as much as I could carry in my car, which, given how often I moved, made a good deal of sense to me. However, such an approach certainly did not work well with my idea of having more community, as no one could come over and spend time at my apartment, given that there was nowhere for them to sit, and most adults were not fond of sharing a meal on the floor. The one moment that helped me begin to curtail such behavior was when DJ asked me a question about a book he and I had both studied in a class in college. He was going to be teaching John Fowles's *The Magus*, and he had a question about the epigraphs, which were in French, as he wanted to know if I had a translation for those. We had studied Fowles's novel in Dr. Dibble's class, so I was sure I would not have gotten rid of that book, even though I was now down to fewer than 200 books, having gotten rid of over 1400 in the past three years. However, when I looked at my shelves, the book was not there. I even looked at the bookstore where I typically sold my books, but I could not find it on their shelves, either. When I realized that I had gotten rid of a book that was so important to me, having notes in it from Dr. Dibble's class, I realized I was going too far. I decided to take a more moderate approach from then on, only buying books I planned to read and keeping those numbers at a more manageable level. Such an event helped move me to a moderation I desperately needed.

However, even though my spiritual life was going well, my personal life was not going well. I had moved from teaching English to running the library, as I had originally planned to leave the school after one year. That year had gone so poorly I felt I didn't want to teach anymore, never wanted to teach again, actually, so I had applied to library positions. When I had an offer from a university in Alabama, the school where I was teaching offered me their library position, which allowed me to continue living in Macon and attending church there, as I did not want to leave that community, if I could avoid it. The work in the library was not going well, though, partly because I was simply bored with the work, but also because I still had to deal with the students I did not much like. Being high school students, they tried to push boundaries, leading me to have to deal with the same discipline issues I dealt with in the classroom, becoming a police officer, not someone who could help them find great books for research or reading for pleasure. At the same time, I had begun dating a young woman I had met at the church, as Mandi had been hired to sing in our choir. We had been dating for several months, but, in February of my last year in Macon, our relationship had begun to fall apart. When it ultimately did end, it did not end well, as we continued to see each other on a regular basis, given our connection at church. I also was not able to spend as much time with friends who could have helped me deal with the situation. Most of my friends in Macon came from church, and they were friends that she and I both spent time with, so those outings were now problematic. Steve had moved to Savannah, so I saw him less often, leaving me with a job I did not enjoy, a relationship that had fallen apart, and a lack of friends to help me through the situation. I was ready to leave and find a new job and new situation, my response to almost any difficult time.

I had not planned to apply to teaching positions, but I was encouraged to do so through a conversation Mandi and I had at Steak 'n Shake before we broke up. We were talking about my writing, as I was often frustrated by the slim results I received in publication, so much so I regularly considered stopping. This dinner was one of those times, as I kept talking about how I probably just needed to give it up. In a non sequitur, Mandi simply looked at me and said, "You're wasting your life in the library; you need to get back to teaching." I was certainly intrigued by her comment, so we talked about that for the rest of the dinner, forgetting about the writing. She pushed me to apply for college teaching positions, but I tried to explain just how bad the job market was, how I had gone on the market a few years before, applying to over one hundred schools only to receive one phone interview as a result of my work.

However, I talked to other friends, and they all suggested it was at least worth a try, and they certainly agreed that I was a good teacher, though they also pointed out I was not wasting my life in the library, as I did good work there. I applied to both private high schools and colleges and universities, just to see what would happen. Most of the high schools were more interested in me as a librarian and asked me to consider that role, but I was anxious to get back into the classroom, as high school library work left me bored much of the time. I only applied to a few college and university positions, as I wanted a place where I thought I had a real chance at a job and a place where I could focus on teaching, not on research, which was never much of an interest for me. I used the job openings from the Coalition on Christian Colleges and Universities (CCCU), as Milligan was a member, and Dr. Dibble had told me about them when I was finishing up my doctorate a few years before. I ended up with an interview at Lee University in Cleveland, Tennessee, that March.

10

Facing the Past

I DIDN'T KNOW MUCH about Lee when I applied, though Milligan had played them in sports when I was a student there. I had worked for the women's volleyball coach my freshman year, so I worked enough tournaments to at least become familiar with other similar colleges and universities. When Jean, the department chair, called me to talk about an interview and asked, "So, what do you know about Lee?" my first response was, "It's about the same size as Milligan." She chuckled, saying, "Not anymore." When I was at Milligan, we had roughly 700 students, small enough for me to recognize every face when I walked across campus by the time I was a junior; Lee had around 1500 students at the same time, which made us almost identical in the world of higher education. However, Lee had changed drastically in the decade since I had graduated from Milligan, increasing to almost 3500 students by the time they interviewed me in 2001, having increased dramatically, gaining close to 200 students from one year to the next. Milligan, however, had never desired to grow and still had not exceeded 1000 students. The two schools also had different backgrounds, as Lee had more recently been a Bible college whose main goal was to produce ministers, missionaries, or other church workers, while Milligan had a longer tradition of a liberal arts education, having instituted their Humanities program in the 1960s. Lee had been moving that direction, but only seriously since the 1980s, which gave them a different feel. Also, the denominations are quite different, as Lee is affiliated with the Church of God (not the Church of God in Anderson,

IN, which is similar to the Independent Christian Church), a charismatic, Pentecostal denomination that had grown rapidly during the twentieth century. Both schools are Evangelical and conservative, but the liberal arts tradition at Milligan had given it more of a moderate slant, while Lee had not moved as far in that direction as Milligan had.

I learned much of this information by reading over Lee's website before my interview, and I also found an admissions video there that let me learn even more about the culture. In that video, one student talked about how much she appreciated professors beginning class with a prayer or a devotion. This practice was one I was definitely not familiar with. When I was at Milligan, our Bible professors might begin with a prayer, though even that was not a daily practice, but no other professors would imagine opening class this way. However, I thought I should try to give myself the best chance for the job, so I asked Jean if I should start my sample teaching class with a devotion or prayer, and she said that students always appreciated professors doing so, but it was not required. I was reminded of a phone interview I had in Mississippi, and I wanted to make sure that I was not behaving the same way I did then. I had applied to local private high schools to try to get a job while I worked on my dissertation, and a Christian high school called me about an interview. One of the main questions the principal asked me was whether or not I was a Christian. I was not, having left my faith behind, but, because I wanted a job, I told him I was. He was not satisfied with that answer and kept pushing, insisting he only wanted people there who truly believed, while, throughout the entire interview, I assured him that I did. When I told Geoff and Sharon about this response later, they were aghast at my behavior, and well they should have been. I later called and left a message, saying I was not interested in the position, though I did not tell him why.

I did not want to make the same mistake this time, as I wanted to find a place where I truly fit. I had taught Sunday school for more than a year, so I was certainly comfortable doing devotions and prayers, but I wasn't sure how I felt about doing them in an academic setting. I thought I should at least give it a chance, though, and I found a way to truly connect it to what I would be teaching. Jean had called to tell me I would be guest lecturing in an American Literature II class, where the students would be introduced to William Faulkner and preparing to read *As I Lay Dying*. I was supposed to give some biographical background on

Faulkner and introduce them to the main ideas of the novel. Despite the fact that I had studied in Oxford, Mississippi, Faulkner's hometown, I really did not like his work, nor had I read the novel. I spent that week doing research on Faulkner and reading the novel, while trying to find a way to connect the reading to the Bible. The novel is about a family, the Bundrens, who are taking their dead wife and mother's bones to Jefferson to bury them, supposedly because of a promise the father, Anse, made. I drew from the end of the book of Genesis, where Joseph makes his children promise to take his bones up out of Egypt and back to Israel whenever the Israelites leave that country.

The class seemed to go well, and the interview seemed to be working in my favor, as well. Only one incident happened that caused me to worry about taking the job. During the lunch with the entire department—not quite twenty faculty members—one professor asked a question about course content. He had once shown a video of an eighteenth century drama on the first day of class and had several students walk out because of a tavern scene. He then asked me how I would handle such a situation. I have a tendency to over prepare for almost any situation, and I had certainly done a significant amount of work for this interview, even going so far as to make a list of books I would teach in typical classes, just in case I was asked. However, I had not prepared for this question, as it simply never happened at Milligan when I was a student. We would have never thought about walking out of a class because something in a video or novel offended us. However, I answered by talking about context and setting up work before we talk about it, which seemed to satisfy him and the others. I realized after I was hired that he asked such a question at every interview, and, unless someone completely botched the answer, no one else really much cared about it. After the lunch, though, another faculty member came up to me to try to set my mind at ease, saying, "I've taught here fifteen years, and I've never had any problem teaching what I wanted." This comment did comfort me, so I had a bit of a conversation with her about it, adding, "At Milligan, they taught John Fowles's *The Magus*, and there was no problem there." She paused, then said, "I'm not sure I'd teach that." Instead of comforting me, she actually caused me to have even more worry about what I would or would not be able to teach. However, I had taken enough jobs throughout the years that I knew I could always leave if the situation did not work out, and I would get the opportunity to teach college, for at least a year or two. When the job offer came, I took it, moving to Cleveland in the summer of 2001.

If I was worried about what the students at Lee would be like, I was not worried about finding a church, as I had done so successfully in two other small Southern towns. However, I was soon to learn that Cleveland was not like other Southern towns when it came to religion. Describing Cleveland to people who do not live here, even people who live in Chattanooga, thirty minutes down the interstate, is difficult. Because Cleveland is the headquarters for the Church of God, not just the city where a Church of God college is located, it has a very different feel to it, which affects every aspect of daily life. It is not surprising to go to the bank or the grocery store and hear people talking in distinctively religious terminology, perhaps even praying for one another in very public places. No matter which restaurant one is eating at, there will be people praying before their meals, and they will probably be in the majority, not the minority. This atmosphere affects churches that are not affiliated with the Church of God denomination, as well. The other major denomination in Cleveland, not surprisingly, is Southern Baptist. However, even Lee students refer to the style of worship at those churches in Cleveland as "Bapticostal," a combination of traditional hymns and praise choruses, where people stand and clap, though the worship is still more subdued than Pentecostal churches. Mainline and progressive churches also lean more toward moderate stances, as those churches consist of members who have come from the more conservative or more Pentecostal churches, bringing with them worship styles and ideologies one would not find in mainline congregations in more urban areas. It is common, then, to attend a Presbyterian church for a sunrise service and see a clip of *The Passion of the Christ* played, for example, as I once did.

This environment made my search for a church much more challenging than I expected. Given that I had spent the past two years in a Disciples of Christ church, it would make sense that I would look there first, but I was also interested in a more liturgical service, so I was also interested in the Episcopalian tradition. Given my Presbyterian background, I found I was missing the formality of such a service, so I decided to meet with the rector of the Episcopalian church to see if I would like that approach to worship. He and I had an enjoyable lunch, as he took me to Gardner's, a local deli, which is still one of the best lunch places in Cleveland, and we had good conversations about religion. He even gave me a copy of J.B. Phillips's *Your God Is Too Small*. I was encouraged to give their service a try. However, what I found was that the service was too formal, too liturgical for me. It was much more high church than I was used to, much more similar to Catholic services than to, say, a Presbyterian service. While I enjoyed the theology of the service and parts of the formality, the idea of having to use the bulletin to keep up with every aspect of the service and to have the Eucharist (or communion) in such a formal fashion was simply too much of a move for me to make.

I turned then to the Disciples congregation in town, which I had learned a bit about before I even moved. While they did not have a website, they had a generic email address listed on the denominational website, so I sent them an email. The response was odd, as the question came back to me, "Is this the Kevin Brown who attended Central Church of Christ in Johnson City?" The author explained that he had been the youth minister there just over ten years before, and I knew exactly who he was. Scott had been the youth minister while I was in college there; he was the one whom I included in the wrestling match in the hotel room. He and I had not gotten along too well, as I did not believe he was as spiritually focused as he should have been when he was in charge, and he believed I was too extreme in my views, both of which were probably true. However, he had also left the Independent Christian Church and moved to the Disciples, and he was now in his first full-time ministry position in the Disciples denomination. I had a connection who would tell me the truth about the church, which was a great help in looking for a congregation. When I asked him to describe the church, he said that it was "conservative for Disciples, but liberal for Cleveland," a description I found to be as apt as any I could come up with to describe them. When I moved to town, he invited me out to dinner just to catch up. When the server came to take our order, she asked if we wanted anything to drink. Scott looked at me with a look of slight fear and questioning, and I was puzzled for just a couple of seconds. I then said, "Order whatever you want. It won't affect me," so he ordered a beer. He was afraid that drinking with me would get me into some sort of trouble. Such behavior did not comfort me, given that I was worried about how non-Lee people perceived Lee, but I really did not believe I would get into any trouble for sitting at a table with someone drinking a beer. During my interview, the Dean of our college told me that faculty at Lee drank, often had a glass of wine or beer with dinner, but they were encouraged not to do so in front of students, which made sense. Since I don't drink, I knew I wouldn't have a problem with that request.

Scott told me he would not pressure me to come to church at the Disciples church, but that I was welcome to do so. He told me about how helpful they had been to him during his divorce and how they had supported him through that difficult time. He was clearly still in the role as minister, though, as he did not tell me about a variety of problems there, nor did he suggest other churches in the area I might find more to my liking. He did tell me about a local organization I might be interested in working with, but, otherwise, I still got the impression he wanted me to give the congregation a chance. Given that my mainline options in Cleveland were sparse, I agreed to come the next Sunday. The church was small, which I liked, but the congregation was not warm. A few people spoke to me when I came in, but no one took the time to introduce themselves to me or to have me sign the guest book. No one followed up on my visit with a note or email. Even Scott left me alone after my visit, as he said that he would do, leaving it up to the congregation to do so. Even though the service was fine, I decided to explore other churches, even if it meant driving to Chattanooga to do so. I was disappointed not to find a church in Cleveland, as I knew I could be more involved if I were closer to the congregation, but I also needed to find a place that fit with where I was, spiritually.

The next few months were frustrating, though, as I explored a variety of churches in Chattanooga, ranging from Presbyterian to Methodist to another Disciples congregation to a Congregational church. Only two merited repeated visits to help me see whether or not they were the place I should attend. The first was the Disciples congregation in Chattanooga. There were a couple of people who were extremely friendly, one of whom was a retired English teacher, giving us an automatic connection. She sent me a note after my visit, and she invited me to the Sunday school class she taught, where she introduced me to help people get to know me. However, she was the exception, as the church was quite cold otherwise. During my first two visits, neither of their ministers spoke to me. On the third Sunday, when I actually sought the ministers out and met the wife of the Associate Minister, who took me to introduce me to her husband, neither of the ministers seemed to care I was there at all. They were more interested in talking to the people who were already regular members. I knew I did not want to be at a church that did not aim to create a close community, as I had learned how important that was to me, so I looked for another congregation.

When I found the Congregational church, I thought that my search was over. The minister was extremely friendly and welcoming, as were the other members of the church. They had a fellowship time after the service, and they invited me to attend and made me feel like a part of their community. I was invited to a Sunday school class and to a lunch they had at a building they owned in a wooded area. They also were much more progressive than the churches in Cleveland, as they hosted a PFLAG (Parents and Friends of Lesbians and Gays) group at the church and had openly gay and lesbian members. The sermons I heard focused on ideas of social justice, which were worked throughout the worship service. When I went to the Sunday school class, I was happy to see that they were studying a book by the Jesus Seminar, though one I had not read. I visited the congregation several times. However, this congregation showed me what was more important to me than I had known, as it seemed to match up perfectly with what I was looking for, but it still left me feeling quite empty. First, while I was happy to see how open and affirming the congregation was toward gays and lesbians, I was made uncomfortable by the assumption that I was gay. Because I was a single male who was interested in their congregation, people made the assumption that I was homosexual, telling me about the PFLAG group and other such ministries. This assumption relates to my second problem, which was the emphasis on social justice. While I certainly supported such ideals, the church focused so much on those issues that Jesus seemed to get left out of the discussion. The congregation seemed more of a social justice organization than a church that recognized the importance of such issues. Spirituality seemed to take second priority to those issues, so I felt that my spirit was ignored.

Sunday school showed me this problem more than any other. They were studying a book by the Jesus Seminar, and I was eager to have such intellectual discussions as I had had in Macon and Tuscaloosa. However, the conversation on the day I attended was about whether or not Jesus spoke Aramaic or Greek. Since I had not read the chapter, I sat quietly through the discussion, listening to people make valid intellectual arguments on both sides, drawing from what they had read. However, the question that kept coming up in my mind was, "Who cares? What does it matter if Jesus spoke Aramaic or Greek or Latin or Russian?" The focus was entirely academic with no practical or spiritual application. It did not help me answer the question that was the most important to me: "How, then, should I live?" The minister looked at me near the end and said, "Kevin, you've been quiet. Do you have any thoughts?" I shared the thoughts I had and raised the idea that it was irrelevant as to what Jesus spoke if it did not affect our lives. I even drew from other Jesus Seminar books, where they had discussed whether or not Jesus was poor, as we often assume, or middle class, based on Joseph's occupation. That discussion, I argued, mattered, as it talked about how we treat the poor and how Jesus identified with the poor. This conversation, though, had none of that application. No one responded to my question, and they looked disappointed and possibly even slightly indignant that I would call their discussion into question. What I realized was that I needed a combination of the intellectual and the spiritual, a balance between my old fundamentalism that took the Bible seriously and the progressive theology I had learned about in Tuscaloosa and Macon. Too much focus on either extreme left me empty and unfulfilled. Unfortunately, it was and is too easy to find churches and Christians who live only on one of these extremes. I had certainly done so, but I was beginning to understand that there was a life in the middle. I continued my search for a new congregation.

Given that I could not find any church that worked better for my situation, I returned to the Disciples congregation in Cleveland, as Scott and I had had supper yet again. He did not pressure me to attend, but he did invite me to visit again, which I did. People were much friendlier this time around, with two women coming out of the choir very quickly after the service to welcome me. I thought that my first visit might have been an exception, that I might simply have caught people on a bad day. I decided to continue attending there, given my lack of other options, despite my continued doubts that this church was the right one for me. Ironically, Scott announced within the month that he was taking a job at another congregation and would be leaving within a few weeks. His departure actually put me in more of a leadership position than I would have hoped, after just a few weeks, but, given the lack of leadership, especially by younger adults, it was a position I was willing to take on. When I say that Scott put me in a position of leadership, I mean that he literally assigned me such a place without asking me first. He simply told the

Sunday school class he had been teaching that I would be teaching the class, given his move. I was there when he told them this news, but he had not talked about it with me ahead of time. He probably assumed I would not mind, as I had always been a leader in the youth group and college class when he was our youth minister; since I was a teacher, he went further and concluded I could teach the course as well as anyone. The next Sunday, I took over, beginning a book on parables that they had wanted to study. When that Sunday came, I spent the first part of the class talking about the background of parables, giving the Greek background for the word, then asking the question of why Jesus bothered to use parables at all. If he wanted people to hear the good news and change their lives, the question of why he used devices that were designed to throw people off the track rather than simply using straightforward sermons or speeches, such as the sermon on the mount, was rather puzzling. As I was writing comments on the board and talking about these ideas, one young woman in the class looked surprised and commented, "You're actually going to teach us, aren't you?" I quickly got the impression that this church, even this Sunday school class, did not seriously subscribe to the Disciples' emphasis on an intellectual approach to faith. Instead, that influence of the old-fashioned Pentecostalism, which often focused more on emotion and feelings, seemed to be more prominent. When I began to actually try to teach them, they were surprised; a few even came less often than they did in previous months.

I almost had not even joined this particular class, despite the fact that it clearly matched my age group better than any others. It was called The Twenty-somethings, though only four people out of close to ten in the class were under thirty; however, given the average age of the church, which hovered somewhere in the fifties, this class fit anyone who was remotely young or behaved as if they were. What almost prevented my staying in this class was a comment made in my first few weeks there. I was sitting next to a young man, talking about the town, as I was still relatively new, when he made a racist comment about the Hispanics who lived there. As I was still new, I was surprised by such a remark and got out of the conversation as quickly as I could. Growing up and living almost all of my life in the South, I was used to such comments, even in church. When I was in Macon, for example, an older woman in the church made a few racist comments from time to time, yet, as Mark assured me, she actually treated people of all races the same, as he had seen her reach out to all ethnic backgrounds through various ministries. I don't want to fall back on the traditional "That's how they were raised" argument, but, in her case, I believe it fits. In Cleveland, though, this young man was several years younger than me, and I was barely over thirty. I could find no explanation for his comment other than simple racism. He never made such a comment again, and I later found that he had a tendency to talk about all kinds of issues he knew nothing about. However, it still gave me considerable pause when I thought about the class and the church.

When Scott left, the church also took a turn toward the more conservative side, as Scott had pushed for a more progressive theology. One of his early debates with members of the congregation was over the inclusion of an American flag in the sanctuary. Many, if not most, Southern churches have a flag, as well as the Christian flag, located at the front of the sanctuary, and this congregation was no different. However, Scott's argument, which is one I had heard before, was for the clear division of church and state, not because the church should not have a voice in matters of the state, but because the state should have no place in the church. We are Christians first, the argument goes, not Americans, and our allegiance should lie with Jesus over and above our national boundaries. The flag was still there when I began attending, and the only time I saw it leave the sanctuary was when people carried it out to march in with it on a July 4th celebration. Our interim minister helped this slide to a more conservative stance, as he had come out of the Independent Christian Church tradition, and it was unclear to me if he was ordained as a Disciples minister, though I believe he was. He had not attended seminary, though, and was instead trained in organizational management, a subject we heard a great deal about over the next few years, as he worked it into almost every sermon. He was clearly well-educated and definitely a smart person, but his sermons had no practical value for how to live one's life, though they certainly gave a good deal of insight into how churches should or should not be structured. When he did stray from that issue, it was usually to talk about how the morals of America had slipped from what they once were, often subtly attacking gays and lesbians more than anyone else, as he often used a verse from 1 Corinthians, among others, to describe our society: "Do not be deceived: Neither the sexually immoral nor idolaters nor adulterers nor men who have sex with men nor thieves nor the greedy nor drunkards nor slanderers nor swindlers will inherit the kingdom of God."[1] Oddly enough, he never criticized greed as an example of our problems, though he clearly saw how influential capitalism was, even in the church, often quoting one of his favorite maxims: "Get what you can, and can what you get." He had done quite well in the canning business, which certainly did not encourage him to criticize the greed that undergirded our entire economic system. I did not gain a good deal of spiritual edification from his sermons.

I was also struggling in my job at Lee, not with the academic material I needed to teach, as I was enjoying getting to teach college students for the first time, at least on a full-time level. Instead, I was encountering the conservatism I was worried about when I took the job, and which I was not as prepared for as I had expected. The problems began in my first semester in a freshman composition course I was teaching. I had picked a variety of readings for the students, trying to collect readings on subjects that would interest a wide variety of students, both academically, but also spiritually. We spent a couple of days talking about sports, as such readings are often left out of composition courses, and there are usually students who enjoy sports more than anything other than Jesus (and maybe a few for whom sports would take a slight edge, especially when it comes to college football in the South). I was even glad I found a reading that combined sports and faith, as that confluence is seldom discussed in Christian circles, as most Christians assume that athletes who use their fame for a pulpit to proclaim the good news must be a worthwhile endeavor. However, the reading I chose called that approach into question, pointing out at least one flaw in such thinking. I gave them the background on the author, Jack Higgs, who had been one of my professors at East Tennessee State University and who was one of the preeminent scholars on sports and religion, pointing out he had been active in athletics when he was younger and still loved sports. I gave some background to his argument, telling them that he questioned our praying before sporting events, not because God was indifferent to how we spent our time, but because such games were not worth the time for prayer, which should be reserved for more serious matters. I should have felt the grumbling beginning in the room at that point, but I missed it.

Instead, I pressed on to one of my favorite quotes from the opening chapter of his book *God in the Stadium*, where Higgs quotes Jack

1. 1 Corinthians 6:9–10.

Saarela, the former chairman of the Campus Ministry Cooperative at the University of Florida: "I have problems with ministries that parade winners up on a stage—athletes, entertainers. The implication is if you accept Christ, you can be a winner, too. It's not any more honest than Madison Avenue saying if you want to be a winning person, drink a certain beer. To me, Christianity is about a man who died on the cross. He was a loser. He appealed to the losers in society."[2] I pointed out that the athletes who stand up and speak about God are the ones who win, that those who lose never thank God for the outcome of the game; instead, they talk about the reasons they lost that are only connected to the earthly realms. The contradiction seemed perfectly clear to me, so I assumed they would see it, as well, when it was pointed out. I was wrong. They argued with me immediately, pointing out that they had seen athletes thank God for their abilities, even in the midst of losses, though they had no evidence to back up such assertions. Anyone who has taught students in their first year of college could have explained to me that any freshman college students behave in much the same way. They take what they believe to be true and defend it vigorously without any real thought, whether the subject be religion or sports or clothing or music. It is in the nature of being eighteen years old and on one's own for the first time in one's life. However, because I went in to Lee with the expectation that they would be closed-minded, I could only interpret this event as evidence of that closed-mindedness.

However, there were other situations that bothered me on deeper levels. In that same class, students were required to write a research paper, and I decided to structure all of their papers around an argument. I allowed them to write on any topic, though I took away such subjects as abortion and homosexuality, issues I had not let any of the non-Christian students I had taught when I was an adjunct professor at the community college write on, either. Those topics just led to screeds and jeremiads. I made the poor assumption that, simply by avoiding a few controversial issues, I would have no problem with their topics. Again, I was wrong. One student, in particular, chose a topic that led me to question my decision to take the job. She wanted to argue that Catholics are not Christians, as she did not believe that a great deal of evidence would be needed to convince the reader of this fact. From a purely academic standpoint, she did a poor job, as she looked at Catholic

2. Higgs, *God*, 14.

theology that was woefully out of date and did not put it into any sort of context. Instead, she picked quotes that would support the conclusion she had already arrived at and used those to support her supposed argument. Again, many first-year college students use the same approach, so her academic issues are a separate concern here. What bothered me was that when she gave her speech, which they were required to do, she tamed her argument considerably, arguing that Catholics focused much more on a works-based approach to salvation than Protestants, who focus on grace. The fact that she made that adjustment let me know she knew her topic was controversial and would have offended several members of the class. She also knew there might be Catholics in the classroom, and she was not overly confrontational, so she did not want to have to clearly say that Catholics were not Christians, as she would have to answer questions at the end of her speech. She knew she could not defend such a position, yet she continued to believe that the people sharing the classroom with her, attending chapel services with her, who were Catholic, were not going to heaven. That type of approach to religion was one I could not abide, but I did not feel it was my job to argue theology with her, though I could point out all of the academic errors she was making in her paper.

I had to take such an approach to several subjects that I wanted to speak more freely on. Students often wanted to write on evolution and creationism, no matter how clearly I tried to dissuade them from doing so. These papers were always awful, mainly because they were poorly argued and even more poorly researched. I never had a student actually read Darwin or one of the more modern proponents of evolution, such as Richard Dawkins, despite my clearly telling them to do so. I assured them they could not argue against something they did not understand, and they could not understand evolution by reading Christian authors who were clearly biased against it and using only them in their argument. It was this clear disdain for the other side of an argument that bothered me so greatly, a clearly anti-intellectual approach to their faith. Also, they were easily offended, especially by language they considered inappropriate in the readings and by any mention of, sometimes any allusion to, sex. In that first semester, in a different composition course, I had assigned a reading with the word "fuck" in it. I thought the reading was a useful one for the course, and I had not read the article recently; I had forgotten all about the curse word. I saw it again when I re-read the article for the course, but I did not think anything about it. I had read works with curse words in them when I was a student at Milligan, and I never heard of a student complaining about such language; I believed the students at Lee would be the same. Instead, a student from the Bahamas came into my office to complain about the word. Rather than having an intelligent discussion about the use of such language, I took her article, marked out the word, then handed it back to her. I never thought more than one person involved in such exchanges might be closed-minded on a particular subject, so I never addressed the issue in class, as I should have.

I hit the problem with sex much more often, though, as I simply never noticed it was there unless it was explicit. I was so used to reading contemporary fiction, with all of the sex that shows up there, I simply read right past it. However, even I knew there could be a problem with a short story I was teaching in my second semester. Margaret Atwood has a short story called "Rape Fantasies," which was left out of the American publication of *Dancing Girls*, but, oddly enough, is included in several anthologies that professors use for composition courses. I had found the story in such an anthology when I taught at the community college in West Tennessee. I'll readily admit that the title alone would make most people avoid the story altogether, but I thought it set up a wonderful discussion about a topic we often avoid, especially in the church. The narrator's co-workers talk about supposed "rape fantasies" they have, but, as the narrator rightly points out, they are sex fantasies, not rape fantasies, as her co-workers envision handsome men sneaking into their hotel room to have sex with them. They do not focus on the awful repercussions of actual rape. The narrator begins to tell some of her own, and they are absurd, as, in one, where she is unable to get the plastic lemon out of her purse, as she has been told to carry one for protection. She hands her purse to the supposed rapist, digs through her purse until she finds it, then has to have him take off the cap, as it's too tight, before she squirts him in the eyes with it, as she has read one should do. In all of her fantasies, she and the man end up feeling sorry for each other and often begin a relationship. It's fairly clear that she, too, is deluded about rape, despite her pronouncements earlier about the flaw in her co-workers' thinking. At the end of the story, though, the reader is given a hint that the narrator might actually be talking to a man who is about to rape her. Just as in her fantasies, she believes she can talk her way out of the rape that is about to happen, showing her to be even more mistaken than her co-workers. The story is a wonderful example of narrative voice and what that voice reveals, as well as hides. More importantly, though, it can lead to a wonderful discussion of how we talk about rape in our society and how we don't. That's the type of discussion I was hoping to foster.

A young woman met with me before class and told me that the story made her uncomfortable, not because of the rape, which would have made sense to me, but because she found the story "erotic." As a friend and colleague of mine said when I told him this story, "I cannot think of a less erotic story than that one." There is never any sex in the story, never even a hint of sex in the story, and the language is far from arousing. However, I assured her that she could skip the class discussion that day, and I would not count her missed reading quiz against her. When I arrived in class, a male student, one of her good friends, was also not there. Those students who were there told me how much they enjoyed the story, and we had a great discussion. A few days later, Jean, my department chair, called me into her office. Someone had sent an anonymous email to the president of the university complaining about the story I was teaching. They had a few facts wrong, as they referred to the story as a novel, among other things, but, in general, they were complaining about the content of the story. Jean handled the situation well, as she did not insist that I stop teaching the story. Instead, she simply asked me to consider why I was teaching it and be able to articulate that to my class when I taught it the next semester. She wanted me to set the story up better, explain why I included it in the class to avoid such problems. I understood that any story about rape, even one that was handled so well, could cause problems, so I told Jean I did not plan to teach it the next semester. However, I had learned a valuable lesson about life at Lee: the students had a good deal of power, and they were not afraid to use it. I was not worried about the administration or the faculty, but the students caused me a great deal of concern, so I would have to watch them.

When I encountered another problem that summer, I took a different approach to solving it. I was teaching a course for high school students through a program Lee called Summer Honors. They invited high school students who showed academic promise to campus to give them a taste of what college life is like. The emphasis is admittedly on the social side, but we still tried to show them at least a bit of what we wanted them to do in the classroom in college. My course was designed around the South, so we looked at music, movies, humor, food, and, of course, literature. I had already hit a bit of trouble with the movies, as I showed them clips of Robert Duvall's excellent film *The Apostle*. The movie portrays a Pentecostal minister whose life is a bit out of control. He has trouble controlling his anger, and he ends up having to leave town because of something he does. He travels to a small town, but he cannot resist the call to ministry, so he ends up leading a small church and helping to revitalize them and giving them hope again. One townsperson, in particular, played by Billy Bob Thornton, though, does not like what Duvall's character is doing, so he threatens to bulldoze the church. Duvall not only stands in front of the bulldozer, he puts his Bible on the ground in front of it. Ultimately, Thornton's character cannot roll over the Bible, and he gets saved. At least, that's how I've always interpreted the scene. When I asked the class about it, though, one student said, "I've seen this movie, and no one ever prays the sinner's prayer in it." For those who are unfamiliar, the sinner's prayer is what one is supposed to pray in order to be saved. The person must admit that he or she is a sinner and ask Jesus into his or her heart or life; only then is one born again. The student was right, as no one does state the sinner's prayer in exactly those terms, but it's clear that characters, such as Thornton's, change their behavior, which is the definition of repentance, and come to Jesus. However, because the characters do not follow the letter of the law, they are not saved. The sarcastic part of me wanted to point out that no one in the Bible ever prays the sinner's prayer, either, but, honestly, I simply did not think of that at that time. If I would have been better prepared, had known the culture better, I would have expected such a comment and could have guided the discussion to a more fruitful question of what one needs to do or say in order to receive salvation. Instead, we had run out of time, and I let the opportunity pass.

However, the real trouble came near the end of their two weeks on our campus. I had assigned a short story by Tony Earley, "Charlotte," which I think exemplifies the distinction between the new South and the old South better than any story I've read. Earley uses professional basketball and wrestling, along with a bar in Charlotte, to highlight how the South is changing and becoming more urban, less rural. I was looking forward to our discussion of that story. One student, though, the younger sister of one of our English majors who was actually quite wild, had a problem with the story. The main character and his girlfriend were clearly having sex, as she takes one of his chest hairs off of her bare chest. The sex is never described beyond that, but it is clearly taking place, and they are clearly not married. Some readers might even wonder if they're in love. The student objected to the story. Having seen what could happen, given my previous experience, I simply gave in to the student. I found another short story by Earley, told the class that they could choose which one they wanted to discuss. Those who were bothered by "Charlotte" could read the other one. I then split the two-hour class time into two one-hour blocks and met with each group individually. Both classes had good discussions, and I avoided trouble. However, I was so frustrated with what had happened and how I felt I needed to handle it, I wrote one of the few short stories I've ever written. In it, a professor is trying to teach Flannery O'Connor, a clearly Christian author, to a college class, but they misinterpret the story and contend that O'Connor is arguing for Satanism. At the end, the professor is so angry, he yells, "It's Flannery fucking O'Connor!" He is fired for his use of profanity in the classroom.

I was that frustrated with the situation I found myself in, as I felt the students would confront every one of my choices, even those I thought would cause no trouble at all. I had made the decision by that summer to leave at the end of the next year. Since I had signed my contract for the following year, and since there was no chance of finding a job by that point, I planned to work out the next year. I would teach my classes to the best of my ability, and I would remain involved with the English majors I had met through our English honor society, but my thoughts were focused on the job search. The problems I was having might have been alleviated if I had not taught all freshman classes that first year. In my second year, I taught sophomore-level literature surveys, as well as one upper-level English class each semester. In those, it was clear I could have more complex discussions with students. For example, in a class discussion on Dante's *Inferno* in one of the sophomore-level surveys, the idea of suicide came up. We debated whether or not people who committed suicide could go to heaven, as Evangelical Christians were split on the subject, though the emphasis was often toward their not going to heaven, based largely on old Catholic theology. There were students, though, who strongly argued for a wider view of grace, enabling people who had committed suicide to still find salvation. They used the Bible to support their argument and made a compelling case. Others argued on the opposite side, though, when I pointed out that their beliefs were based on Catholic theology, not the Bible, they were not open to that criticism. What frustrated me was not the fact that they would not change their minds, as that was not my goal; instead, it was the fact that they would not engage with a view that differed from theirs, that they simply insisted upon their beliefs even when presented with ideas that challenged those. However, I saw such instances of real debate on a regular basis in upper-division classes, showing quite clearly that our freshman students did improve in their thinking, though that improvement was slow, as is all education. I simply was unwilling to see it because I already had preconceived notions of what the students were like.

I also had another problem with my job. I wanted to write, as well as teach, though I never took the writing part of my life as seriously as I should have. However, I attributed that lack of enthusiasm to a problem with the demands that my job put upon me. I insisted I did not have enough time to write, nor did I have the mental energy after teaching freshmen and grading all of their essays. I argued that the last thing I wanted to do when I came home was to sit down in front of a computer or a sheet of paper and try to write. I had enough to do with words and ideas at my job. The same issue also came up with reading, as I certainly did not have as much time or energy to read as a college professor as I did as a librarian, an irony I pointed out to anyone who would listen. In addition to those problems, I also felt haunted by the parable of the talents.[3] I felt that I had been given several of them: teaching, writing, preaching, and librarianship. However, the life of a college professor does not lend itself to such a wide variety of interests, so I always felt like I was letting my talents go to waste, burying them in the ground, as the parable presents it. I used both of these concerns as my reason for leaving.

I should point out that the first problem, the one of time, simply has no basis in reality. In one year, I watched 150 movies while working at Lee. Cutting even half of those out would have given me ample time to write, despite my protestations I did not have the mental energy. I simply was unwilling to set my priorities and have any sort of self-discipline, a problem that was continuing to bother me. I could have read and written much more than I did, but I simply made the choice not to. As for

---

3. Matthew 25:14–30.

the talents, when I told one class I was leaving Lee and gave them that as one of my reasons for doing so, one of the students simply shook his head. He then vocally disagreed with me, arguing that one needed to be focused on one goal in order to succeed, and he used Michael Jordan as his example. When Jordan was focused on basketball, he was as successful as anyone who has played the game; however, when he began to dabble in baseball, he lost that focus and was unable to regain it even when he rejoined the Bulls in the middle of the season, as he was unable to carry them to the championship that year. I disagreed, but I certainly took note of his point. Because of these concerns, I decided to go back into library work again, as I could attend seminary part-time to become better trained at preaching, while still having time to read and write as I would like. I even believed I could teach part-time after I finished seminary work, should I feel so inclined. I took a job at an independent pre-Kindergarten to twelfth-grade school in Tacoma, Washington, about as far away from Tennessee as I could move. I had not intended to go that far, but it met all my criteria, as it was close to a seminary, and I was curious about life outside of the South. I attributed many of the problems I had with the supposedly closed-minded students to the South and the level of religious intolerance I found there. I thought a more progressive place, such as Washington state, might be more to my liking.

However, life became rather complicated before I left. After I had resigned and was working out my time, I was asked to help out on a school trip in May. I had gone on a trip with Donna, one of my colleagues, the year before to Boston, and she conducted another trip that toured the South. The history professor who co-taught the classes with her was willing to teach, but she was unable to go on the trip because of a surgery she needed to have. They had asked other professors, but no one was willing or able to go, and they needed another body along. My trip would be paid for, but I would not be paid, as I was not teaching any courses. Still, it was a trip through parts of the South I had not seen, such as Charleston, South Carolina; Montgomery, Alabama; and New Orleans, Lousiana, so I agreed to do it. I had heard through some students that there was a student in one of my classes who had a crush on me. Given that I was leaving, I had no hesitation about trying to find out who it was, as I had broken up with a girlfriend back in December, so I was certainly looking to date, even if I were moving. I then heard that one of the students planning to go on the Southern trip was that student.

I went into the World Literature course, the one where the person with the crush was, and asked about who was planning on going on the Southern trip. Three young women raised their hands, so I had the crush narrowed down fairly quickly. On the trip, I spent some time with those three, as they were the three I knew the best. As the trip went along, though, I found myself spending more and more time with Courtney. I only learned later she arranged parts of those times, but many of them actually were simple coincidence. For example, I would often sit nearer the back of the bus to watch movies (there were TVs and a VCR on the bus), as it was easier to see. Since I knew the three English majors, I went to their area, but only the seat beside Courtney was open. If it would have been beside one of the other two young women, I would have sat beside one of them. As we got to know each other better, it was clear she was the crush, and I found I enjoyed talking to her. She confessed her crush to me on the last night of the trip, but I knew that, as long as I was employed by Lee, I should not say anything, which is what I told her, clearly communicating how I felt without saying it. I saw her the day after we were back, and I asked her out on a date, which she accepted. Four weeks before I was to leave for Tacoma, I had a date with one of my now former students who would be in Cleveland for another year. We spent a good deal of time together during those weeks, but we agreed simply to enjoy our time together and not worry about what would happen when I left. Our parting was rougher than both of us expected, but we agreed to keep in touch, while also agreeing we could date other people. I then left Cleveland, moving to a part of the country I knew almost nothing about, leaving behind someone I had just begun dating, knowing all along that this move might not be the best one I had ever made. Cleveland had clearly not been the place of growth that both Tuscaloosa and Macon were. I could only hope Tacoma was better than I expected.

11

A Firm Foundation of Questions

ANYONE WHO KNEW ME when I was at Lee before I moved to Tacoma and also knew me after my time in Tacoma recognized that a profound shift happened in the year I was gone. I have talked with numerous people as we tried to discover what happened that helped create a shift in the way I live that is as important as my years in college when I began to truly think about my faith for the first time or the years just after college when I decided to leave the church, then changed and decided to come back. The change that occurred in and just after my time in Tacoma, though, did not have obvious roots in my spiritual development, but the change was driven by spiritual lessons I had been hearing all along, but only now took note of.

My struggle to find a religious community in Cleveland had nothing to do with a lack of choices, though many of those choices were nearly identical to each other, different only in name; my struggle in Tacoma came from the opposite problem, as there's a reason that area of the country is referred to as "the unchurched Northwest." Despite the fact that Tacoma is more than four times the size of Cleveland, the number of churches in each town seemed roughly equal; Cleveland might have had more. The joke that is only partly a joke in Southern towns is that there's a church on every corner; in Tacoma, those spots were reserved for coffee shops, living up to the stereotype, as many of them appeared to be former one-hour photo booths converted to drive-through locations, much like Vegas and wedding chapels. I had difficulty finding a place to worship, but for slightly different reasons. It was not difficult to find more progressive theology; however, the absence of the more extreme versions of conservatism actually made those churches less progressive, as if people needed the other extreme to react against. The real problem, though, came from a lack of hospitality, as I felt every church I visited was equally cold. Ministers seemed indifferent to my presence, and no one made an effort to help me feel welcome. There was no one like Denise from Tuscaloosa who felt called to sit beside visitors and help them through the service, no one like Sarah from Macon to guide me to the guest book, or no one like Mark to want to meet for lunch to answer any questions I might have about the church. After exploring a variety of churches, then, I ended up at the Disciples congregation I first visited, mainly out of habit. There was nothing particular about it that made it appeal to me, but nothing, also, that bothered me. I ultimately did meet with the ministers, but it was at my urging, not theirs. They were very helpful when we had lunch, talking about Sunday school classes that might interest me and ways I could get involved in the church, but their interest seemed to simply be a response to mine, as they were not proactive in helping me become a part of the community, just reactive.

My job was also not what I had hoped it would be. As the high school librarian, I could spend entire days with little to do in the library. In my first few months, I improved the collection by weeding out a variety of old books that should not have been there, rearranged the library to make it more conducive to studying, and attempted to meet with the department chairs to see what needs they had when it came to the library. However, on most days, I was finished with any significant work by nine in the morning, so I had to find ways to fill the time, even creating a blog for much of my time in Tacoma, just to have something to do. One advantage of this free time and of my role as librarian is that I was able to meet a wide variety of people from across the campus. One of those people was our chaplain, Fred. The school had a religious background, having once been connected to the Episcopalian church, but now it was clearly secular. There was a chapel on campus with a full-time chaplain, but his role was to encourage religious acceptance and diversity, not proclaim a particular doctrine. He taught a world religions course, as well as yoga in the chapel. He was a Quaker and focused on their idea of the divine spark within every human being. Oddly enough, though, he could be one of the angriest people I had ever met when it came to political discussions. During my year there, the U.S. invaded

Iraq, and Fred did not agree with this policy at all. Whenever discussions would drift toward the political in our lunch room, he would grow quite angry, not at any of us, even if we disagreed with him, but toward President Bush and members of his administration. He certainly was not a particularly positive role model for the Quaker idea of interpersonal peace, though he clearly felt strongly about peace between nations. He gave me one of the best opportunities of the year, though, as he knew I was interested in world religions; he and I had talked about various issues from time to time, such as when I would see him sitting on a bench reading the *Bhagavad-Gita*, one of the Hindu sacred books, and we would talk about it and other Eastern religions, especially Buddhism. When he took a group of students to visit a Buddhist monastery, he invited me to go along with them. I found a way to miss a day of work, not that I believed my absence would be felt, and went with them. I finally had a chance to practice meditation, which I actually enjoyed more than I thought I would. My mind is not particularly quiet, but the few minutes we spent in meditation had a rather powerful impact on me. More importantly, though, I had an opportunity to question one of the monks, as we all sat and drank tea together.

The students were rather shy about asking questions when given the chance, so I filled in the gaps of conversation with my questions, having waited several years for such an opportunity. The main question I had was about what I perceived to be a contradiction in Buddhist teachings. I understood the Buddhist idea that there were no dualities, that words like *good* and *bad* were only labels that we use to talk about actions when they are only used to continue the supposed divide that does not exist. When I say I understood this idea, I should point out that I mean I understood it in an intellectual sense, not that I comprehended it to my core, as one does with a religious belief that is part of who one is. However, in reading through Buddhist and Taoist religious texts, I noticed there were many discussions of what a wise man should do and what a foolish man does. If there are no dualities, I wondered, how could one make a distinction between a wise man and a foolish man? I presented her with this question, and she nodded as I asked it, clearly having heard it before. She responded simply, "That is the problem with language. We cannot communicate without it, but it also limits what we can talk about." She seemed absolutely fine with the supposed contradiction, simply attributing it to the limits of language. Her approach was the antithesis of Western Christianity's method of solving supposed contradictions, especially in the conservative Christianity I had taken part in a decade before. We would have twisted all sorts of logic to make whatever seemed to be a contradiction match up to what we argued, no matter how absurd we had to make ourselves sound, much like the man I heard about who carried a card in his wallet to prove that Jesus was in the tomb for three twenty-four-hour-periods, as the Bible must be literally true when it says that Jesus was in the tomb for three days. However, her acceptance of this contradiction made perfect sense to me, though it did not satisfy my intellectual problems with the doctrine. I had not seen such an idea applied directly to the Bible, but it also made sense to me once I began applying it. The Bible was not a science or history textbook or even a handbook to life in the sense that my Evangelical friends talked about it; instead, it was a record of a group of people's experiences with the divine, a way for them to explain what it was like to encounter God. Unfortunately, language limits our ability to talk about such subjects, so we are left with a book riddled with seeming contradictions when language is what causes the problem. I often liken such a problem to talking about being in love with someone. I ask people to tell me about why they love their spouse or significant other or someone important in their lives; the answers are terribly mundane, focusing on someone's sense of humor or kindness, which, they have to admit, millions of people on earth share. I want them to see that such an emotion goes beyond language, that any attempt to explain such a feeling becomes dull and sometimes contradictory, as we love them for something that also annoys us.

Unfortunately, I was not in a religious community that encouraged such discussions, so I was left without much chance to discuss such ideas, at least with the people I was meeting in Tacoma. I never felt like I was a part of the congregation where I was worshipping, though the problem came from both sides of the situation. My lack of commitment was clearly a problem, as I was only partially present in Tacoma, almost from the time I arrived. Since Courtney and I had started dating, even though we were not exclusive and were not sure what the future looked like for us, part of me wanted to be back in Tennessee. That desire was reinforced by my distance from Steve and DJ and my family, as my parents were beginning to get older. Even though I participated in the life of the church by playing in the handbell choir, serving as a reader in the worship service, and attending, and ultimately teaching, Sunday school, I was never invested in the congregation. I did not join the church, as I knew by October that I would not be staying in Washington more than a year. I had lived in such a way before; almost every time I decided to leave a job or I was nearing completion of a degree, I began to disengage, even if I did so in ways only I could perceive. What I have found in life is that one cannot live in two places at one time, with one proverbial foot out the door, as we only have enough energy to invest in one place, and even that is a struggle. In one of my favorite movies, *High Fidelity*, John Cusack's character is trying to convince his ex-girlfriend to get back together with him. After her father dies, he comes to the realization of why she left, of why their relationship did not work out: "I can see now I never really committed to Laura. I always had one foot out the door, and that prevented me from doing a lot of things, like thinking about my future and . . . I guess it made more sense to commit to nothing, keep my options open. And that's suicide. By tiny, tiny increments."[1] My frequent moves had been much the same, and here I was doing it one more time, leaving me without a community where I could use my gifts and where I could find the support I needed.

However, the church also did not help to make me a part of that community, as I was treated like a visitor even after I had been attending for months. Part of the problem was that the members of the church wore name tags, partly to help visitors know their names, but also partly to clearly distinguish members from guests. While this practice sounds helpful, as members could then be more welcoming to visitors, it actually created a two-tier class system, separating those who were officially members from people like me who came week after week, but who never joined the church. Because of this system, no matter what I did in the church, as long as I never joined, I would never be seen as part of the official membership. After I served as reader in a worship service, someone asked a woman I sat near if I were her son or nephew visiting from out of town, as if the church would simply ask a guest to participate in worship in that manner. I had also already participated in a hymn with the handbell choir during one of our worship services, causing me to question her logic even more. The worst example of this practice, though, came when Courtney came to visit me during her Fall Break. I had been attending for several months by this point, and I was

---

1. *High Fidelity*, 2000.

certainly known by the people who sat around me and should have been recognizable to almost everyone because of my participation in worship. However, when Courtney and I walked into the narthex outside of the sanctuary, we were greeted in a warmer manner than I was accustomed to. One woman insisted we sign the guest book, which I did not even know existed before then, as no one had ever asked me to sign it. There were pew pads that people passed where everyone could sign in at the beginning of worship, so I had always assumed those took the place of a guest book. I was clearly mistaken, as this woman wanted to make sure that we felt welcomed and that the church had our address on file. Courtney's visit showed how clearly I was seen as an outsider, as several people were much more welcoming on that Sunday.

What I realized was that I was now part of a much more sought-after demographic. While it's true that churches want young people in their pews, what they really want are young families. Even though Courtney and I did not have any children with us, the people at the church could assume that we were possible parents, as we were the right age to either have young children or be thinking about having young children. I had moved from being a young, single male who attended church—certainly someone most churches would want to have attend—to part of a couple who could provide for the church's future for decades to come, once we produced children. I realize such thinking sounds mercenary to those outside of the church, and when I have told this story in the past, I usually make it sound even more so, referring to Courtney and me as "possible breeders," as if we were cattle. Churches themselves often use terminology that de-humanizes people, calling families "giving units," seeing them only in terms of how much money they can bring to the coffers. Nothing about this approach is consistent with Jesus' teaching, as he welcomed all people, regardless of their age or giving ability, but the business side of churches sometimes wins out. People see their churches beginning to decline in membership, as younger Christians look for churches with substantial youth programs that smaller churches are simply unable to provide, and older members begin to die off. However, this approach is one of the worst mistakes smaller churches can make, as their job is not to try to provide what the larger churches can, not to compete with them, but simply to be the communities that God is calling them to be. If there is real spiritual growth, the churches will remain alive, as there are always people looking for those types of communities.

Thus far, I have not portrayed my time in Tacoma as having any benefits at all, which calls into question my decision to move that far away from home. However, there were substantial, practical benefits that went beyond my chances to meet a variety of new people and experience a culture very different from my own. I did have an opportunity to do what I had planned to do, to read and write more than I could as a college professor or high school teacher, and even to watch more movies than I had done in the previous year, which was a pleasant side benefit I had not planned on. Apart from my not being able to attend seminary or teach part-time, the move was having the effects I hoped it would. However, I found I missed teaching much more than I expected. I found myself craving time in the classroom that I was no longer allowed to have. Whenever classes came to the library for any type of instruction, I was in a much better mood that day, looking forward to going to my job, as opposed to the days when I knew I would be finished with any work, usually that I had to create, by nine or ten in the morning. The type of teaching, though, was not what I enjoyed, as library instruction is much more lecture-based, where I stand in front of them and walk them through how to use a database or our library catalog. Those rare occasions where a student needed substantial help to find resources and I felt like I was actually teaching simply reminded me of what I was missing, what I once had and gave up. I had missed teaching before, but never to this degree. Also, I found I missed being seen as a teacher. When I was in Macon, I had moved from being an English teacher to my job as a librarian; all of my peers saw me as someone who could do both jobs, someone who was a teacher who worked as a librarian or vice versa. However, in Tacoma, no one there had ever seen me be an English teacher, though it was clear from my background that I had been one. They treated me like a librarian, not like a fellow teacher. We never talked about teaching techniques or even the literature they were teaching, despite my efforts to engage them in such conversations. Instead, I was seen more like staff than part of the teaching faculty, something almost all high school or college librarians understand and struggle with themselves. I was missing teaching and simply being a teacher, and I knew I wanted to go back to English, at least one more time.

However, since I had the year in Tacoma where I did not feel challenged by my job, and I had more free time than I was used to or might have at any time in the future, I decided to take advantage of it. Here is where Mark's comment about discipline finally became helpful, though it took me almost three years to actually put it to use. He had told me I had discipline simply because I would get up on Sunday mornings and go to church when I did not particularly want to, so I now had to make the decision to do something, even when I did not want to. This definition of discipline sounds simple, but it's exactly what discipline is. Sy Safransky, editor of *The Sun*, a journal out of Chapel Hill, North Carolina, once quoted his friend Robert as saying, "Self-discipline is remembering what you really want."[2] It was time for me to learn this lesson.

First, I decided I needed to drop the weight I had gained after I had left Indiana. I had climbed back to 200 pounds when I was in Cleveland, though I had dropped about fifteen of those before moving to Tacoma. That put me forty pounds heavier than when I moved from Mississippi to Indiana, and I was tired of carrying them around. I began to make changes in my diet, taking my lunch to school every day, even when the Head of the Upper School had our chairs' lunches provided for us. I started running after school every day, starting with only a few miles, but ultimately building up to long runs approaching the double digits, a distance I was not even sure I could run when I lived in Macon. By the time I left Tacoma at the end of the year, I had lost just over twenty-five pounds. More importantly, though, I finally began to apply discipline to my writing, moving it from becoming a hobby to a passion. I decided to work on three projects I had talked about for years, but had never done anything about. That summer, I wrote a screenplay I had put off because I did not have the time when I simply lacked the discipline to write it. The screenplay was not great, but it was the first major project I had worked on since I wrote my dissertation more than seven years before. What was most important about writing the screenplay, though, is that it gave me the confidence I needed to begin the two other projects, the ones that helped me take the next step in both my religious and intellectual development.

The first was a project I had thought about even longer than the screenplay, as I came up with the idea when I was teaching in Indiana seven years before. The junior English class I taught centered on British literature, and I taught the class chronologically, beginning with *Beowulf*. I had not read the work since my freshman year of college, and we read a prose translation there, so I had missed the poetic aspects of the work.

---

2. Safransky, "Sy Safransky's Notebook," para. 3.

In teaching it in Indiana, we used a translation by Frederick Rebsamen, who tried to keep the aspects of Old English poetry that the author of the work used, including kennings (hyphenated metaphors, such as *son-king, friend-warriors,* or *battle-wise*) and the caesura (a pause in the middle of the line). Even though I was not well-trained in reading poetry and did not much enjoy it, I loved Rebsamen's work with the poem. I then thought, "What story is more epic than the life of Jesus?" I thought I could write an epic poem using the Old English techniques to retell the life of Jesus in a new manner. I had long been fascinated with retellings of the Christ story, ranging from *The Last Temptation of Christ*, which I read while I lived in Macon, to *Jesus of Montreal*, a French film that portrays an actor who creates a passion play, but whose life then begins mirroring the life of Christ. I recognize the irony of my enjoying Kazantzakis's portrayal of Jesus in *The Last Temptation*, given that I had signed a petition against the movie version roughly fifteen years before, but now his image of Jesus' defending Mary Magdalene as the woman caught in adultery from John 8 remains one of the best images of Jesus I have ever seen. The fact that I was now able to use my creative work as a way to process my thoughts on the life of Jesus, incorporating the new ideas I had been exploring for the past few years, helped me to merge my creative and critical worlds with my religious questions and faith, taking a step forward I needed to take. I would spend every evening reading through a passage of one of the gospels, then try to put it down in a more poetic form, using kennings and caesuras to add to the heft of the story of Jesus' life. Again, the poem is not particularly good, lacking any solid comparisons or even interesting visions of Jesus, and I have never tried to publish any portion of it or even revise it. However, the discipline I used to work through such a project showed me I could do serious long-term writing if I decided it was worthwhile and that writing could matter to me beyond simply being creative work I enjoyed doing.

Both of those developments led me to the last project I worked on while in Tacoma, moving me to combine my religious interests, my reading interests, and my critical interests. Since I was obsessed with retellings of Jesus' life, I decided to do critical work on novels that attempted to reshape the story and present it to a modern audience. I read over a dozen such novels, focusing on five that seemed the most interesting: Kazantzakis's *The Last Temptation of Christ*, Norman Mailer's *The Gospel According to the Son*; José Saramago's *The Gospel According* to Jesus Christ, Anthony Burgess's *Man of Nazareth*, and Nino Ricci's *Testament*. My main focus was on why the authors presented the gospel characters the way they did in their novels, especially looking at ancient church writings to see their influence. For example, one question that helped me begin this project centered around Mary Magdalene. Almost all of the novels I read presented her as a former prostitute, as many Christians today believe her to have been; however, there is no evidence in the gospels that she was a prostitute. I was curious as to how both the authors and contemporary Christians make that connection. In my research, I discovered that Pope Gregory announced her to be a prostitute in 591 and that this belief was church doctrine until the middle of the twentieth century; I wanted to explore why novelists and Christians continued to portray and believe something that was easily disproven. The exploration broadened out to novelists' portrayals of Judas, especially his motivation for his betrayal of Jesus, to Pilate's life before and after his washing his hands of Jesus' death sentence, even the explanation of the absence of Joseph from Jesus' life. As Anthony Burgess wrote, "The more I read Matthew, Mark and Luke the more I became dissatisfied with their telling of the sacred story. They remain fine propagandists but mediocre novelists. 'The devil entered Judas,' says John. How hopelessly inadequate."[3] I wanted to use the early church documents to fill in the gaps, to show where so many of our ideas about the characters from the gospels come from when the gospels are notoriously empty of background and motivation. I spent most of my year there working on this project and left with a completed rough draft that neared 200 pages, roughly as long as my dissertation. However, this work was better written, and, more importantly, it mattered to me. Here was information I found fascinating, that I could take into church and use in Sunday school classes or sermons. I was able to combine my spiritual interest in the life of Jesus with literature that had had a personal effect on me, but that would also work well in a college classroom, where I was planning to return. I believed I could publish this book, but, whether or not I did, I had accomplished a project I never believed I could finish. I left Tacoma having learned that discipline could affect my entire being, not just one aspect of it.

In leaving, I hoped to return to Lee, to go back to a job that was better than I gave it credit for, to return to where Courtney lived and

---

3. Burgess, *You've Had*, 304.

where I would be closer to friends and family. I talked to Jean about returning, and she was very enthusiastic, as I had left on good terms. However, I would need to go through the hiring process again (though without the interview), as they had three open positions, and it would not have been fair to the other applicants to simply give me the position. Since I was going to have to compete for the job at Lee, though, I knew I could not count on it, so I also told Jean I would apply other places, just to make sure I found a job for the following year, and I even used her as a reference, which was odd. I looked at both Christian and non-Christian colleges, but, with the job market as bad as it was and with a clear lack of publications on my part, I knew Christian colleges offered the best opportunity for a full-time, tenure-track position. I was right, as the only interview I received was at Trevecca Nazarene University, just two and half hours away from Cleveland, Tennessee. The Nazarene denomination is similar to the Church of God, as they both have Pentecostal roots, and they're both on the conservative side of the Christian spectrum, but, given that I thought I had been and could be successful at Lee, I thought the same way about Trevecca. The interview went well, as I answered questions honestly and did a solid presentation, so I was fairly certain they would offer me the job; however, I was also fairly certain I did not want it because I had a couple of concerns on my end from the interview. First, I filled out an information sheet, and one of the questions was about my marital status. Since "Divorced" was one of the options, I marked it, wanting to be honest and not having anything to hide about that situation. During the morning of my interview, though, three different administrators asked me about it. In the first session, when I responded, as I usually did, "I was young, and I made a mistake," the administrator did not seem to be satisfied with this answer. He clearly was trying to establish if my divorce met the criteria the Bible lists for a legitimate divorce, especially as found in Matthew where Jesus says, "Moses permitted divorce only as a concession to your hard hearts, but it was not what God had originally intended. And I tell you this, whoever divorces his wife and marries someone else commits adultery—unless his wife has been unfaithful."[4] What I found particularly interesting is that, once I had given him a bit more information, mainly that the divorce was my fault and I was simply not mature enough to handle it, he commented, "We have a significant number of faculty who are divorced,

4. Matthew 19:8–9.

about half of the science department, I believe." I'm not sure if he was saying that to comfort me, that I would be accepted there, or if he were simply dismissing the issue altogether. I had hoped the second, but when the second and third administrators also asked me about it, I became concerned that how I lived my life would be a major concern there. I knew my behavior would not cause any trouble, as I did not participate in the vices most Christian schools are concerned with, such as smoking or drinking, but their intense focus on my life made me wonder what would happen if I said something that went against their beliefs.

Further causing me concern along those lines was a part of the contract that required me to attend chapel services and their week-long revival that happened once a semester. I was told that faculty were encouraged to go forward and pray with students at the altar during that revival, especially. While I was then and am now regular in my church attendance, I have never been particularly good at chapel attendance while working at Lee, as the worship style is not at all what I prefer. I was worried about a required attendance at Trevecca, as well. At Lee, when I was first hired, the understanding was that we were encouraged to attend, but it was clearly not required. I knew numerous faculty who had received tenure and who were well-respected who seldom, if ever, attended chapel. Trevecca seemed to have stricter requirements on my religious life, and I knew I could not live with those restrictions on my religious thought and freedoms. Even though they told me they were planning to offer me the job, I turned it down, as Lee contacted me the day before and told me I would be re-hired there. Though I had my concerns about returning to the conservative Evangelical world, especially after my experience at Trevecca, I believed Lee would give me the opportunity to be who I was, while I respected who they were. DJ actually told me I should view myself as a missionary, going into a foreign culture. While that metaphor works on one level, in that it was my job to learn and respect the local culture, it did not work on a more important one. I did not view it as my job to go to Lee and convert those students, to help them see the world as I see it. Instead, my job was to teach them English, while living a life that reflected what I believed to be true Christianity, which coincided with theirs on the important aspects and the majority of the nonessentials.

When I was officially rehired at Lee, I returned to Cleveland to visit Courtney over my Spring Break. While I was there, I had a brief conversation that was one of two events that helped me make the most significant change since I returned to the church, the two events that helped make me who I am today. I had already made a decision about how I would be different when I returned to Lee and Cleveland, partly based on a conversation I had with a colleague in Tacoma. I was hired at the same time as Brian, a French teacher from Georgia. He was clearly glad not to be living in the South anymore, as he was bothered by the religious and social conservatism there. I understood his frustrations, especially as the outspoken nature of the most conservative elements often gave Christianity a bad name, such as when people burned books or demanded they be removed from libraries. He and I had seen one such story in the news shortly before I left, and he asked me why I would want to go back to a place where such events happened with disturbing regularity. I assured him that such things happened everywhere, such as the Arizona church that burned J.R.R. Tolkien's books, among others, but I also told him I agreed with his frustrations. I assured him, though, that, when I returned, I would speak up in such situations and make it clear that not everyone from the South agreed with such actions. I also thought I should speak up because not all Christians agree with such actions.

When I was planning on returning to Lee, I told myself I would be the best professor and the best church leader I could be. Those were the two goals that would drive my actions, as they would take precedence over writing and reading and watching movies and any other behaviors I had previously thought more important than those two areas. I also thought of them as separate goals, a division that would have to change for me to truly succeed. That's where the conversation comes in that helped change my view of my job and my life. While I was visiting over that Spring Break, I spent some time around the department seeing people whom I had been friends with when I was working there before. One morning, though, I was wandering from office to office, unable to find anyone I had gotten to know even remotely well, while I was waiting for a department lunch I was going to attend. I needed to stay there for the next hour or so, as leaving and coming back did not make any sense, but I was not able to find anyone to talk to. I ended up outside of Sabord's office when he saw me and invited me in. Sabord had taught at Lee for almost forty years by that point and would pass that milestone by the time he retired. He had grown up in the Church of God denomination, even spending time as a child preacher, and had seen its development, along with Lee's.

While I was at Lee the first time, I had not spent much time talking with him, as we were clearly separated by age and generation, but I also thought we were divided by religious outlook. However, what I came to learn about Sabord was how open-minded he was on religious questions, as he was always able to consider other viewpoints, even if he ultimately disagreed with them. He had earned the respect of everyone in the department, no matter where they fell on the progressive-conservative divide. When he invited me in, we began talking about Lee and his early time at the university, as he, too, had worked at Lee for a brief period of time, then left, and come back, so he was encouraging me by telling me about his time. He wanted me to see that Lee was a place where one could get a second chance, where my deciding to leave would not be held against me, and I could succeed, if I worked hard at doing so. In the midst of his story, there was one sentence that he simply dropped in, but that had a profound effect on me. In talking about why he worked at Lee when it was much smaller, more of a Bible college, when the pay was not good and he could have gotten a job elsewhere, he said, "We always viewed working here as Christian service." My idea of coming back to Lee and Cleveland to be the best professor and the best church leader I could be kept the two areas of my life separate, with my job being one aspect, while church was another. Sabord did not view the two as separate, even though he was also heavily involved in his church. For him, though, his job was ministry, combining the two parts of his life that clearly defined who he was, removing the false separation I continued to use in talking about my life.

At the end of my first year back, that idea was driven home and finally sunk in to help change my overall view of life. Lee had received a grant from the Lily Foundation to pursue the idea of calling, and one aspect of that program was a Faith Integration retreat for faculty members. A group of faculty would meet for a retreat, then meet a couple of times during the following school year, to talk about readings and how we might better integrate our faith into our teaching. To be honest, the sessions did not directly affect my teaching, as I did not walk away from any of the sessions with ideas of how my classes would be affected by our discussion. However, one of the readings changed me, which ultimately changed my classes and everything else about my life. One of our first readings was a book by Parker Palmer called *Let Your Life Speak*. While some Evangelicals think Palmer is too wishy-washy in his faith, many Christian professors enjoy his writings, as he draws on his Quaker background to talk about his teaching. Again, the book was not helpful in how I might change my courses, but he did have one short section that helped me see myself in a different way. In talking about himself as a teacher, he writes, "By looking anew at my community work through the lens of education, I saw that as an organizer I had never stopped being a teacher—I was simply teaching in a classroom without walls. In fact, I could have done no other: teaching, I was coming to understand, is my native way of being in the world. Make me a cleric or a CEO, a poet or a politico, and teaching is what I will do. Teaching is at the heart of my vocation and will manifest itself in any role I play."[5] Once I read that, I realized it was true for me, as well; it explained the struggles I had had for the past decade, as I was trying to figure out who I was and what I should be doing with my life. I moved back and forth between teaching and library work, as neither one satisfied me, but only because I did not know who I truly was. When I went into library work, I wanted to use it as another means to teach; when I did not have an outlet for the teaching aspect of the work and had to spend my time cataloging or weeding books, I was unhappy in my work. When I became more focused on my personal reading and writing, drifting away from my teaching, I became unhappy again, feeling pulled in two different directions, as I had been unwilling to devote myself fully to my true calling, the teaching. Most importantly, though, what I finally learned was that there was no separation between the sacred and the secular in my life, that everything in my life could be sacred. My teaching was not just another job I was doing; instead, it was a calling, a vocation that provided my life with meaning, that enabled me to help others by using the gifts I had been given. My writing became an outlet for talents I had been given, a way to say what I felt needed to be said in the world instead of something I did for a hobby. My church work, whether teaching Sunday school, serving on a church board, or guest preaching, took the talents I had been given and used them for clear good, but that church work was not separate from my teaching; it was simply another aspect of it.

My life actually became more integrated and whole, enabling me not to feel pulled in different directions, but giving me one clear direction

---

5. Palmer, *Let Your*, 21.

that simply manifested itself in a variety of ways. Instead of my various interests fighting with one another, all of them could work together to give my life purpose and meaning, something I had not found before. When I was a teenager, I kept my life in compartments, with Christian music or politics in one box and my academic work in another. Once that box became problematic in college, I saw no other solution than to get rid of the box. There was no one to show me a way the various boxes of my life would all fit together in one whole, leaving me to find such an approach to life through Buddhism, my conversation with Sabord, and the Palmer reading, leaving me to find another way to be a Christian outside the traditional church, but that brought me back to it, after all.

12

Conclusion

The Questions Always Continue

In literary criticism, scholars often talk about characters who are in a liminal phase or who experience liminality, which is when they are in a period of transition or live between two worlds. For example, in African-American literature, characters who can pass as white and who move between both worlds, white and black, are described as liminal, as the transition between the two worlds offers potential for conflict, but also opportunity for change and growth. Most college students live in such a place, as they leave home and begin to gain independence, but are not yet fully on their own, relying on parents for some support, but on themselves for more and more. By the time I graduated from college, I found myself in a liminal stage, religiously, even before I left the church. This dichotomy is best exemplified by the mail I received one day when I went to the post office. I had several pieces of mail, but the two I still remember from that day were from the American Civil Liberties Union and the American Family Association. Somehow, I was on the mailing list for an organization that most religious conservatives vilified and for one that spent its time fighting against what it saw as the secular liberalism sweeping America. I thought, even then, that it was no wonder I was confused on where I stood, as parts of me clearly still supported each side of the argument these two groups exemplified, but I had not found a way to reconcile myself to those parts of my life, seeing them as contradictory instead of complimentary.

Even though I have been back at Lee for eight years and married to Courtney for almost two, have found a more progressive church where I seem to fit in much better than my first time here, and clearly have some obvious stability in my life, I see myself in a type of liminal stage yet again, living in two subcultures of Christianity, yet using both to strengthen my faith, not as warring factions pulling me one way or the other. Among my more conservative colleagues, friends, and students, I am seen as a raging liberal, putting forth arguments about non-literal readings of the Bible they believe weaken its place as the Word of God, among other heresies. In a class one day, for example, we were talking about words with connotations, especially ones related to gender. I gave them examples, such as *police officer* or *nurse*, asking them which gender they immediately thought of. I asked if they had any other examples, and a student in the back left corner said, "Preacher." The students in my class associate that word with men, as women are not allowed to preach in many of their denominations, so I told him I thought that was a great example. I must have said something that hinted that I thought female ministers were fine, as a student came to ask me about the subject after class, specifically wondering how I reconciled female ministers with passages in I Timothy that forbade women from positions of authority, such as I Timothy 2:11–15, which states, "A woman should learn in quietness and full submission. I do not permit a woman to teach or to assume authority over a man; she must be quiet. For Adam was formed first, then Eve. And Adam was not the one deceived; it was the woman who was deceived and became a sinner. But women will be saved through child bearing—if they continue in faith, love and holiness with propriety." I simply explained that I thought such passages were driven by culture and were, thus, not universal or applicable to our situation today. The student had clearly not heard such an approach before and was clearly bothered by it, and he may have even questioned my faith. While I could have done a better job of explaining my position, such events happen often enough that I know how people on the more conservative end of Christianity see me.

However, in more progressive churches, I am often seen as more conservative, somehow still stuck in my fundamentalist reading of the Bible. Once in a Sunday school class, I wanted to talk about how we read the Bible, so I used the passages on divorce and women that most progressive Christians have problems with, wanting them to talk about how they deal with those passages. Most of the people in class disagreed with the verses, so they simply wanted to toss them out, simply ignore them as if they were not there. They were surprised when I argued that we need to deal with all of the verses in the Bible, being very cautious about what we put forth as no longer literally relevant to our lives today and having clear arguments when we believe such situations to be the case. After just over a decade of being back in the church, I have tried to reconcile these two views, bringing them together to make my faith honest, which makes it much stronger. I do not resent my time in the more conservative branch of Christianity, as I know the fundamentalist approach to the Bible reminds me I need to take Jesus and what he said seriously. When I was in church in Macon, I went out to lunch with a group of friends, which included a couple in their seventies. The man, Charlie, was rather conservative, and he was once complaining about liberals who did not know the Bible. His wife, Joy, said simply, "Kevin is liberal, and he knows it." Charlie could do nothing but mutter his agreement. Because I grew up in the church and played Bible Bowl, in addition to attending both a church and a college in a conservative Christian denomination, I know the Bible quite well and can use it to strengthen my life and the lives of those around me. However, I can also see how culture shapes the Bible, how a strictly literal reading of certain passages weakens the Bible instead of strengthens it. I can see it not as a history or science book, as those who would argue that everything in it happened exactly as they are written do, but as an account of those who saw the divine in the world and attempted to record it with imperfect language, never fully able to express the power of those events, but always striving to do so.

When I talk to people on both sides of the religious divide, I try to hold them to the ideals they profess. In my classes, for example, when students tell me they take the Bible literally, I ask them if they've sold their possessions, given to the poor, and now follow Jesus, drawing on both Matthew 19:21 and Luke 12:33. They give me a variety of reasons for why Jesus doesn't really mean that we should *literally* sell our possessions, that he's just trying to make a point. I ask them what the difference between those verses and Mark 12:31—which tells us to love our neighbors as ourselves—is, why one is literal and the other is not, as they need to know how they make that distinction. I can also deal with controversial subjects now, as I'm not trying to convert students to my way of seeing the world, but trying to help them understand their own, see where their contradictions lie. I teach part of a book by Kevin Roose called *The Unlikely Disciple*, where Roose recounts his experience of attending a Christian college to better understand the Christian world he is not a part of. In the book, Roose talks about the homophobia of a few of the students, so that subject always comes up in class. We don't debate whether or not homosexuality is a sin; instead, we talk about how God loves everyone and how we are called to love everyone, regardless of whether or not we agree with them. We talk about how homosexuality has come to be perceived as a sin that is worse than other sins, including other sexual sins, and what we can do about that. Progressive Christians might argue I'm not pushing the students far enough, but my job is not to change my students' views on homosexuality; my job is teach them to see how they think and let them decide the subjects for themselves.

I have come to embrace this middle ground, this liminal phase, dwelling in the mysteries I do not understand, which bothers people on both sides of the debates we have created. When people ask me where I ended up, theologically, they often want to know about hot button issues, such as abortion, same-sex marriage, or stem cell research, as if these define how I live my life. Certainly such issues are impacted by my faith, shaped by it, but they are not the core of it. Even when they want to know my views on a particular passage of scripture, they are often disappointed, as my view of the Bible has changed to a much more metaphorical reading. I talk about the stories of the Bible in a way that is more similar to the way I talk about the literature I teach than anything else, not because it is not true, but because the authors of the Bible seem more concerned with spiritual truth than literal truth. Then, when people in mainstream churches debate the literalness of the virgin birth, while Evangelicals insist upon it, I mainly shrug my shoulders and think about something else. I do not doubt that God could have sent Jesus into this world through such a dramatic entrance, though I may question why he would do so; there are too many wonders of this world we do not understand for me to doubt such an event. Instead, the point of the story is that God not only was among us, but is among us, in ways we do not see, ways we ignore every day of our lives. The resurrection works the same way, as mainliners might argue that there was no physical resurrection, no resuscitation, as they call it, while Evangelicals quote

Paul who said that if there is no resurrection, all is in vain.[1] The Bible has enough resurrection stories to at least make me believe such events occur more than we can fathom, that our faith in medicine blinds us to miracles that surround us. However, if there was nothing more than disciples' belief that caused them to create such an ending to Jesus' story, then I am not bothered. Instead, I know that the story of the resurrection reminds us that rebirth happens all the time, that second chances are found in novels and movies because they are also found in life, that hope is not merely a word on a greeting card or political poster, but a way to live one's life.

While others insist on correct answers, I muddle through the mystery that is the divine and that intersection with our world. In the same way honest scientists admit the universe is too large and too complex for us to fully understand, though that fact does not prevent them from exploring as much as they can, I know that God and our interactions with whatever form God may take are beyond my comprehension; after all, a God we can understand has no real meaning or importance for our lives. But I also know there are mysteries of the heart worth exploring: How love works and why it doesn't; Who we are and how we know or don't; How we should live our lives. These seem to me to be the key to the divine in this world, as they comment on our relationships with one another and ourselves, as seen through the lens of faith. If I am lucky enough to have another four decades on this earth, I have found my new way: I will spend my time with those questions, not the ones about where I might spend the four decades after that.

---

1. 1 Corinthians 15:12–19.

Bibliography

Borg, Marcus. "From Galilean Jew to the Face of God: The Pre-Easter and Post-Easter Jesus." In *Jesus at 2000*, edited by Marcus Borg. 7–20. Boulder, CO: Westview, 1998.
———. "The Historical Study of Jesus and Christian Origins." In *Jesus at 2000*, edited by Marcus Borg. 121–47. Boulder, CO: Westview, 1998.
Bradstreet, Anne. "To My Dear Children." In *The Norton Anthology of American Literature*, edited by Nina Baym. vol. A. 6th Ed. 272–75. New York: W.W. Norton, 2003.
Burgess, Anthony. *You've Had Your Time: The Second Part of the Confessions*. New York: G. Weidenfeld, 1991.
Campbell, Thomas. *Declaration and Address*. In *The Quest for Christian Unity, Peace, and Purity in Thomas Campbell's Declaration and Address: Text and Studies*, edited by Thomas H. Olbricht and Hans Rollmann. 3–58. Lanham, MD: Scarecrow, 2000.
Genzlinger, Neil. "The Problem With Memoirs," *New York Times*, 30 January 2011. No pages. Online: http://www.nytimes.com/2011/01/30/books/review/Genzlinger-t.html?_r=1&ref=review.
Golding, William. "Thinking as a Hobby." No pages. Online: http://daphne.palomar.edu/christine/e100/thinkingessay.htm.
Gubernick, Lisa, and Robert La Franco. "Rocking With God." *Forbes* 144.1 (2 January 1995). No pages. Online: http://o-ehis.ebscohost.com.library.acaweb.org/cds/detail?vid=14&hid=2&sid=7416db55-d2af-4896-ab10-d77e03d78f5b%40sessionmgr12&bdata=JnNpdGU9ZWRzLWxpdmU%3d#db=buh&AN=9412307523.
Higgs, Jack. *God in the Stadium*. Lexington: The University Press of Kentucky, 1995.
High Fidelity. Directed by Stephen Frears. 2000. Los Angeles, CA: Working Title Pictures, 2000. DVD.
Kirby, Scott. *Dating: Guidelines From the Bible*. Grand Rapids, MI: Baker Book House, 1979.
Lewis, C.S. *Mere Christianity*. New York: Collier, 1960.
Mister Mister. "Kyrie." *Welcome to the Real World*, Warner-Tamerlane Publishing, 1985, cassette tape.
Orange County. Directed by Jake Kasdan. 2002. Los Angeles, CA: Paramount Pictures, 2003. DVD.
Palmer, Parker. *Let Your Life Speak: Listening for the Voice of Vocation*. San Francisco: Jossey-Bass, 2000.
Safransky, Sy. "Sy Safransky's Notebook." *The Sun* 320 (August 2002). No pages. Online: http://www.thesunmagazine.org/issues/320/sy_safranskys_notebook.

Spong, John Shelby. *Why Christianity Must Change or Die: A Bishop Speaks to Believers in Exile*. New York: HarperOne, 1999.
St. Clair, Barry, and Bill Jones. *Dating: Picking (and Being) a Winner*. San Bernardino, CA: Here's Life, 1987.
The Student Bible. Grand Rapids, MI: Zondervan, 1986.
Taylor, Steve. "It's Harder to Believe Than Not To," *I Predict 1990*, Myrrh Records, 1987, cassette tape.
Trott, Jon. "Bob Larson's Ministry Under Scrutiny." *Cornerstone* 21.100 (1993). No pages. Online: http://www.ondoctrine.com/1lars003.htm.
U2. "Ultraviolet (Light My Way)." *Achtung Baby*, Island Records, 1991, compact disc.
van Biema, David. "Who Are Those Guys?" *Time*, 1 August 1999. No pages. Online: http://www.time.com/time/magazine/article/0,9171,28859,00.html.

www.ingramcontent.com/pod-product-compliance
Lightning Source LLC
Chambersburg PA
CBHW060604230426
43670CB00011B/1961